Inking
FLORALS

A step-by-step guide
to creating dynamic
modern florals in ink
and watercolor

Isa Down

First published in 2020 by Walter Foster Publishing, an imprint of The Quarto Group.
26391 Crown Valley Parkway, Suite 220, Mission Viejo, CA 92691, USA.
T (949) 380-7510 **F** (949) 380-7575 **www.QuartoKnows.com**

ISBN: 978-1-63322-836-8

Digital edition published in 2020
eISBN: 978-1-63322-837-5

Printed in China
10 9 8 7 6 5 4 3

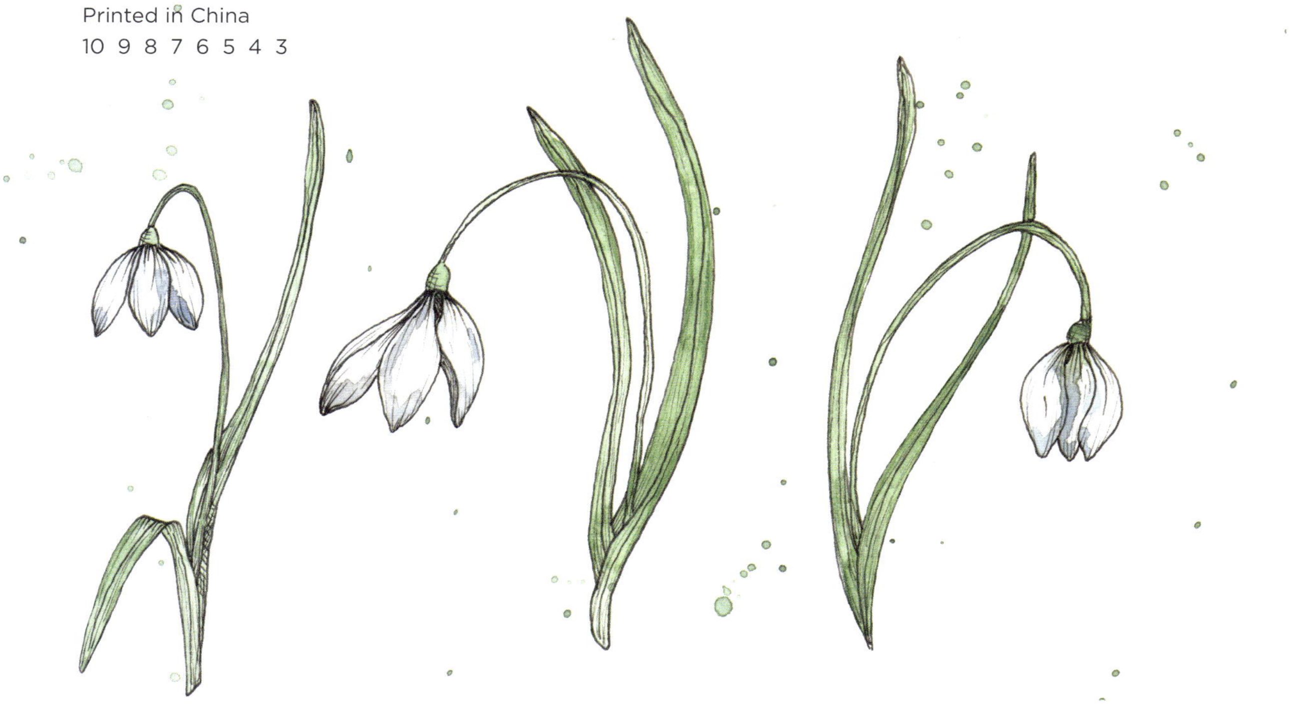

Table of Contents

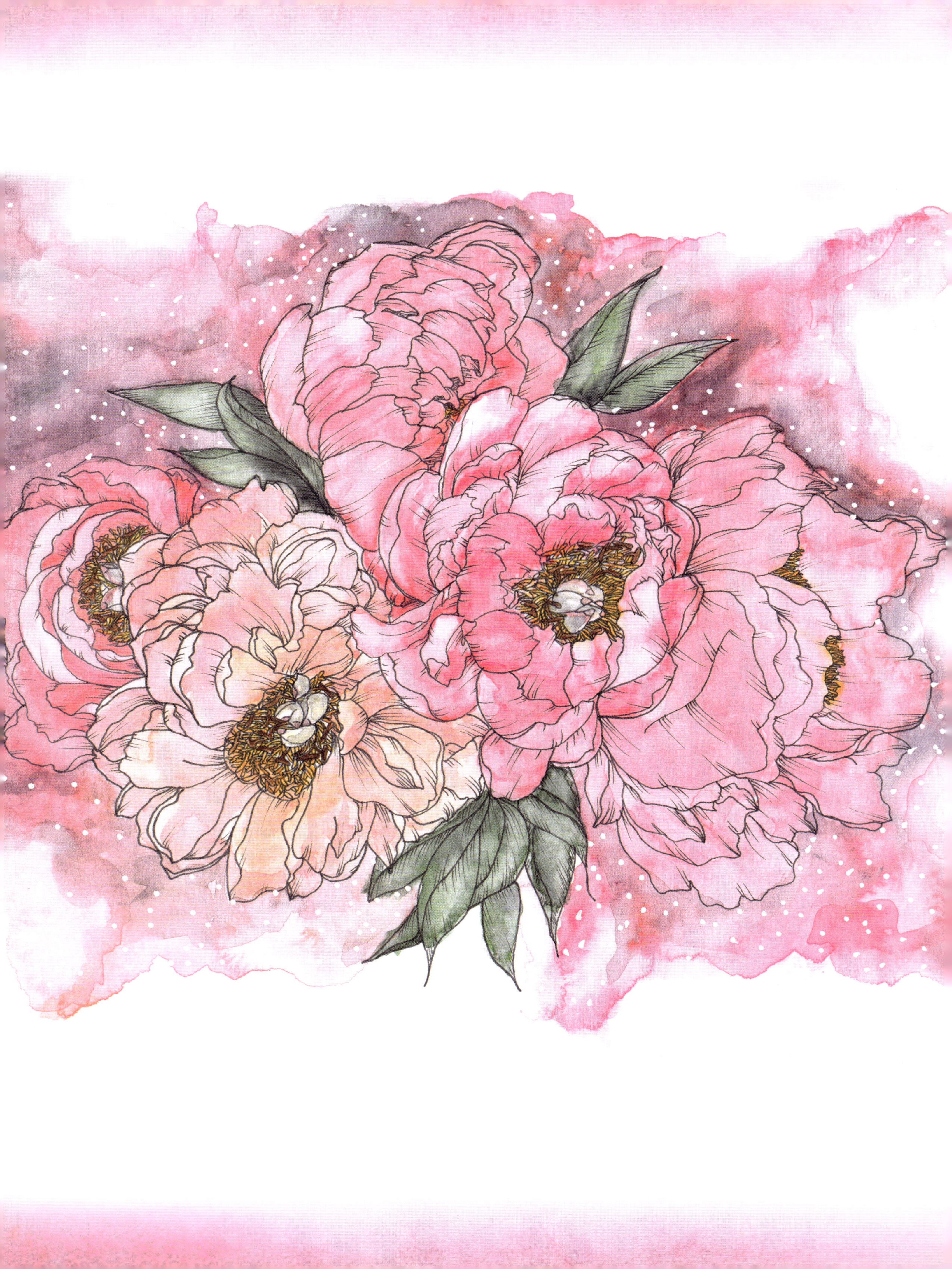

Introduction

Let me tell you my story.

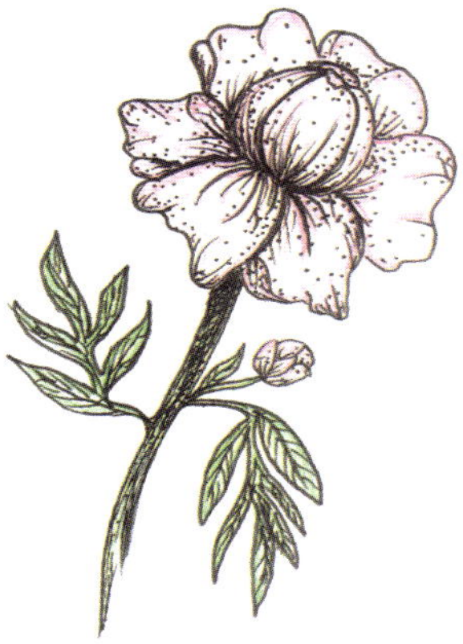

In the spring of 2017, feeling restless, I sat down and drew a not-so-great peony. I remember looking at an artist's truly magnificent rendition and trying to sort out how she made her lines move so easily, giving the illusion of folds and twists. My hand shook and my lines were uncertain.

I was so proud and full of joy when I sat back and took in my finished piece, massaging away the cramp in my hand from clenching my pen too tightly. And so I kept drawing. Because that joy I felt, the empowerment from creating something that even slightly resembled what I was attempting, fueled my creative fire.

Everything I have learned since then has been self-taught. I've fumbled through turning mistakes into intentional additions and whimsical curves in petals. In fact, when I first started drawing, I forced myself to draw in ink without first making a pencil sketch. I wanted to train my eye and hand to work together, without overthinking the imperfections. Since then, I have sat down (almost) every day with pen and paper in hand, agreed to teach courses, created commissions that were far beyond my knowledge base, and kept experimenting until I found what worked best for me.

And I did this because I felt strongly that, no matter what, I would be able to figure it out. (Knowing too that I wasn't going to submit a project I wasn't pleased with and that I didn't understand the process behind.) I pushed myself endlessly and learned so much in the process. Allowing myself to fill the space of the artist's role, step into that title and know that I could fill it over time, and grow into the space gave me everything I needed to work past my fears and embrace growth. I learned that there is room for me.

And there is room for you too, my friend.

Actually, there is endless and expansive room, if you believe strongly enough that you are capable. You will continuously learn and expand, no matter what level of "success" you reach, and I encourage you to jump right in today. I see you there, holding this book, wanting to learn more and do more and be more! Take my hand and let's jump together, my friend.

Listen closely. Lean your tired head in and hear these words: You are enough. There is room for you. You are stardust and rainstorms and branches hanging low with the weight of a thousand blossoms.

Finding Inspiration

Inspiration can be found anywhere—if you are paying attention! Recently, I returned to Vancouver Island, where I lived for several years. I had not been back in many years, and the last time I was there, I was not a floral artist. This time, I was absolutely floored by the plethora of stunning flowers blooming everywhere. I barely noticed these flowers when I lived there and hadn't a clue that rhododendron grows so abundantly there, or that there are magnolia trees. So, what had changed? There were no more flowers now than before. What had changed was my ability to observe—and observation is at the heart of inspiration.

Here are a few things you can do to find inspiration in your creative journey and build your powers of observation so that you really see the flowers all around you.

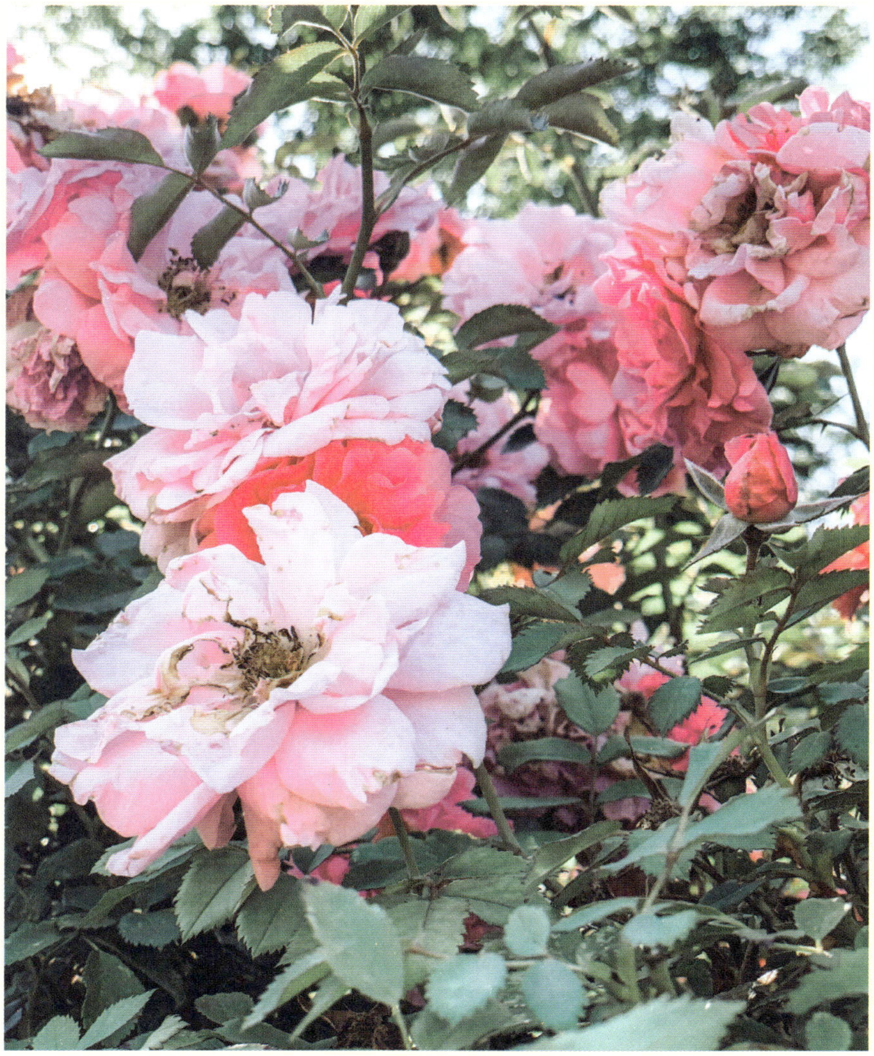

Go on Walks

If nature inspires you, one of the best ways to engage with it is by walking outside. Whether you're in a forest or meadow or simply walking along the street, keep an eye out for colors and shapes that inspire you. By intentionally looking for these things, you will increase your ability to observe, and it will become second nature to you over time. You may surprise yourself with how much inspiration you see in the world around you.

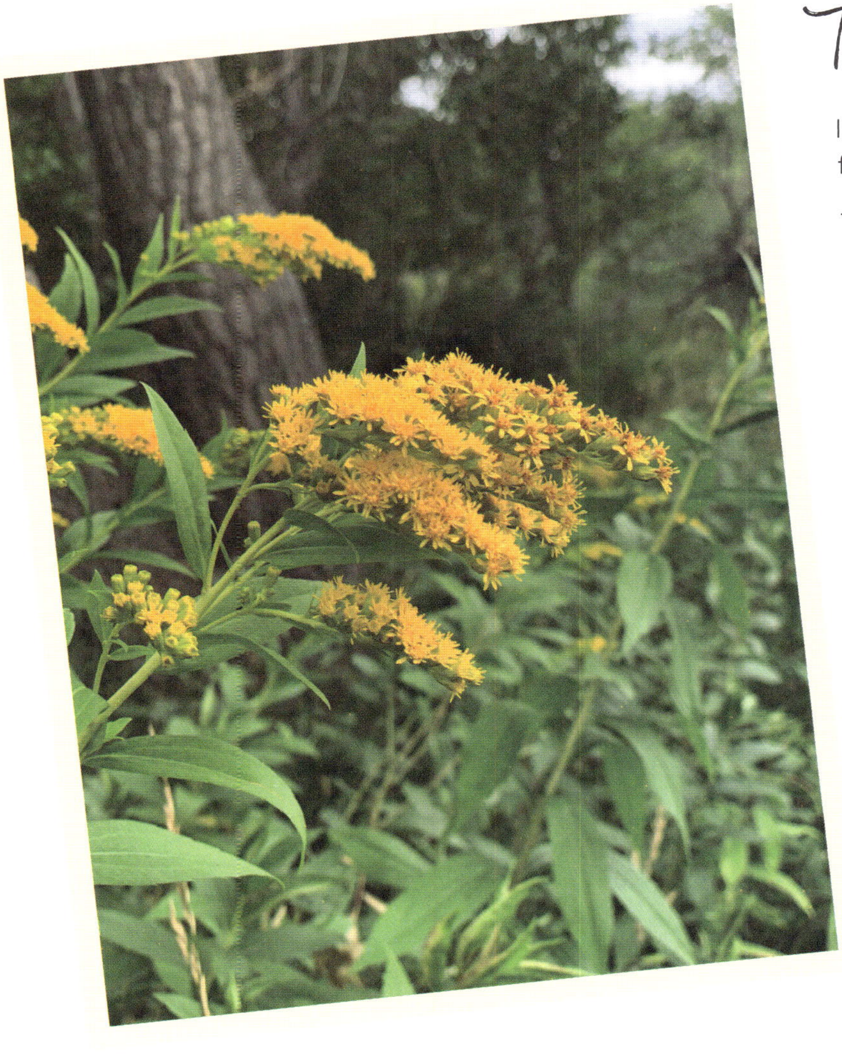

Take Photos

I highly encourage you to create your own floral reference photos. There is a hidden joy in photographing the inspiration you find in your everyday life and manifesting this into a beautiful piece of art. Taking reference photos requires considering angles and lighting, as well as ensuring that you capture a plant's essence and components. It is amazing what you learn about a plant by doing this, and it will serve you well in the future. The better you understand the flower you are drawing, the more easily you can create any angle or aspect of that plant in your own drawing. This allows you to create endless pieces, patterns, digital files, and stationery from one set of reference photos or from your imagination.

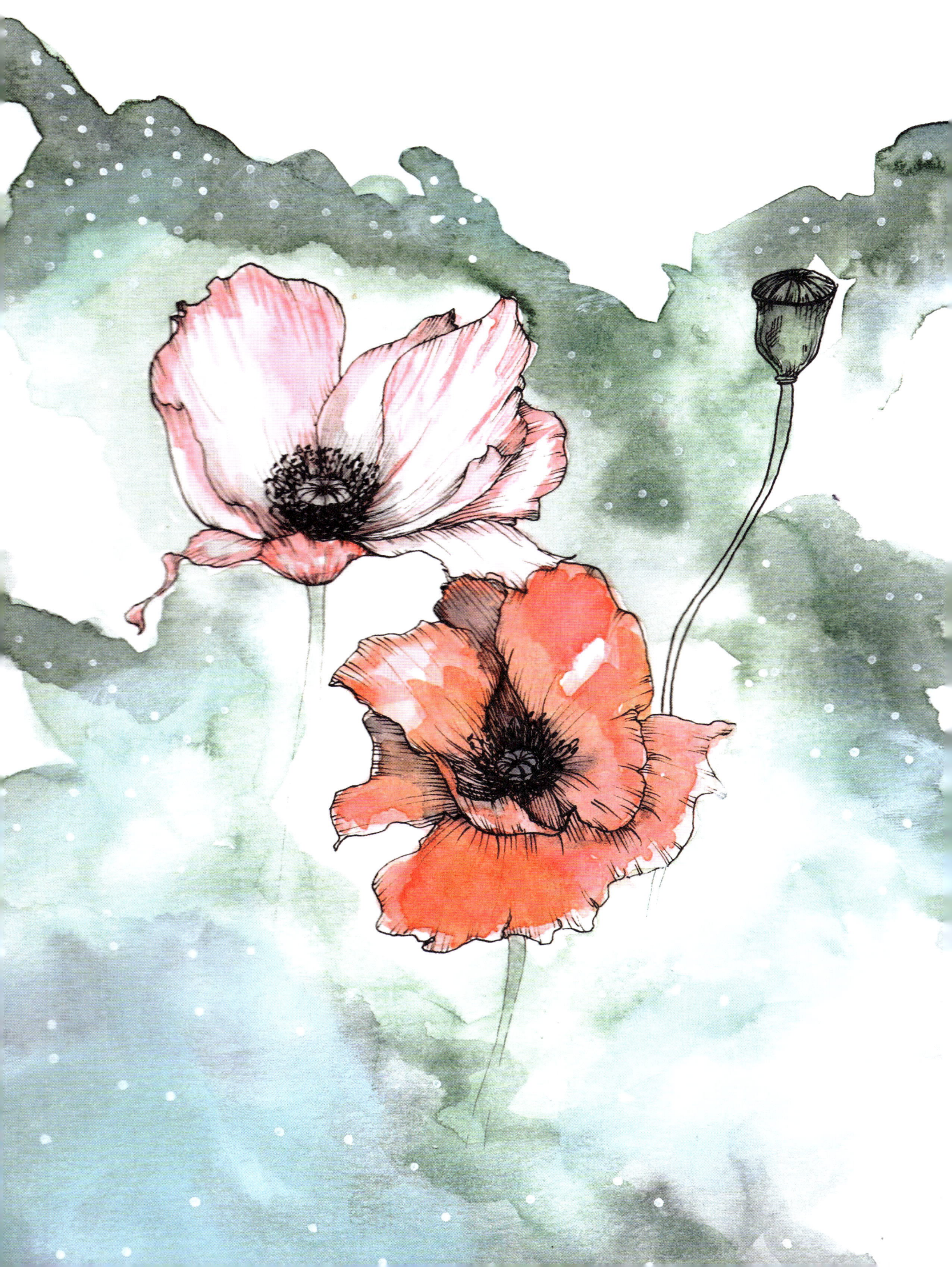

The Blank Page

The blank page can terrify any artist, seasoned or new. I have a few methods for getting past this "blank-page syndrome." I do much of my creating in my mind before I s t down to the page, and I think as much about layout and colors before I pick up a paintbrush as I do when I actually sit down to create my art. The page is never truly blank when I already have the idea fleshed out in my head!

On days that I feel truly blocked, I set a timer for 5 or 10 minutes and allow my pen or brush to create whatever comes out, without forethought—and without judgment. Create nonstop until the timer goes off, like a stream-of-consciousness piece. When the timer goes off, you'll either be done, or you'll have found inspiration and can continue creating.

Just Do It

The best advice I can give is very simple: just start! While there is a benefit to thinking through aspects of creating, do not let this become a barrier to actually creating. Sit down, pick up your brush or pencil, and begin!

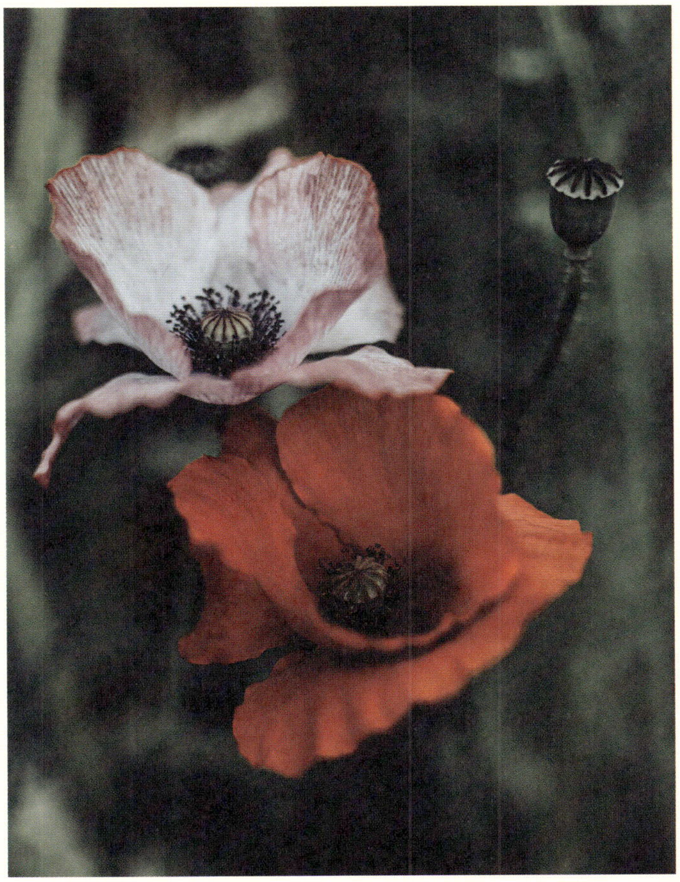

Tools & Materials

Choosing art materials is a very personal decision. We all have our own sense of what feels right in terms of ink flow or how the brush holds water. I encourage you, both in your earliest days of creative discovery and as you continue in your artistic career, to explore different materials. The more comfortable you get with your chosen media and materials, the more predictable your work can become. And while that may be the desired outcome, it's also fun to see what you can create with foreign materials. You never know; you may surprise yourself. There is a difference between having a specific artistic style and becoming predictable, and it's a lot of fun to experiment and keep your creative mind fresh.

Among new artists in particular, there's also a sense that in order to feel legitimate, they need a specific set of prestigious materials. Sure, the high-end materials are super dreamy, and the quality can be stunning. But that doesn't mean you can't create some truly phenomenal work using cheap brushes and a small set of paint colors.

That said, there are a few specific materials that you will need to complete the step-by-step projects in this book. Over the next few pages, I will provide the details that I look for in my personal art supplies to give you direction as you head out to your local art-supply store to explore.

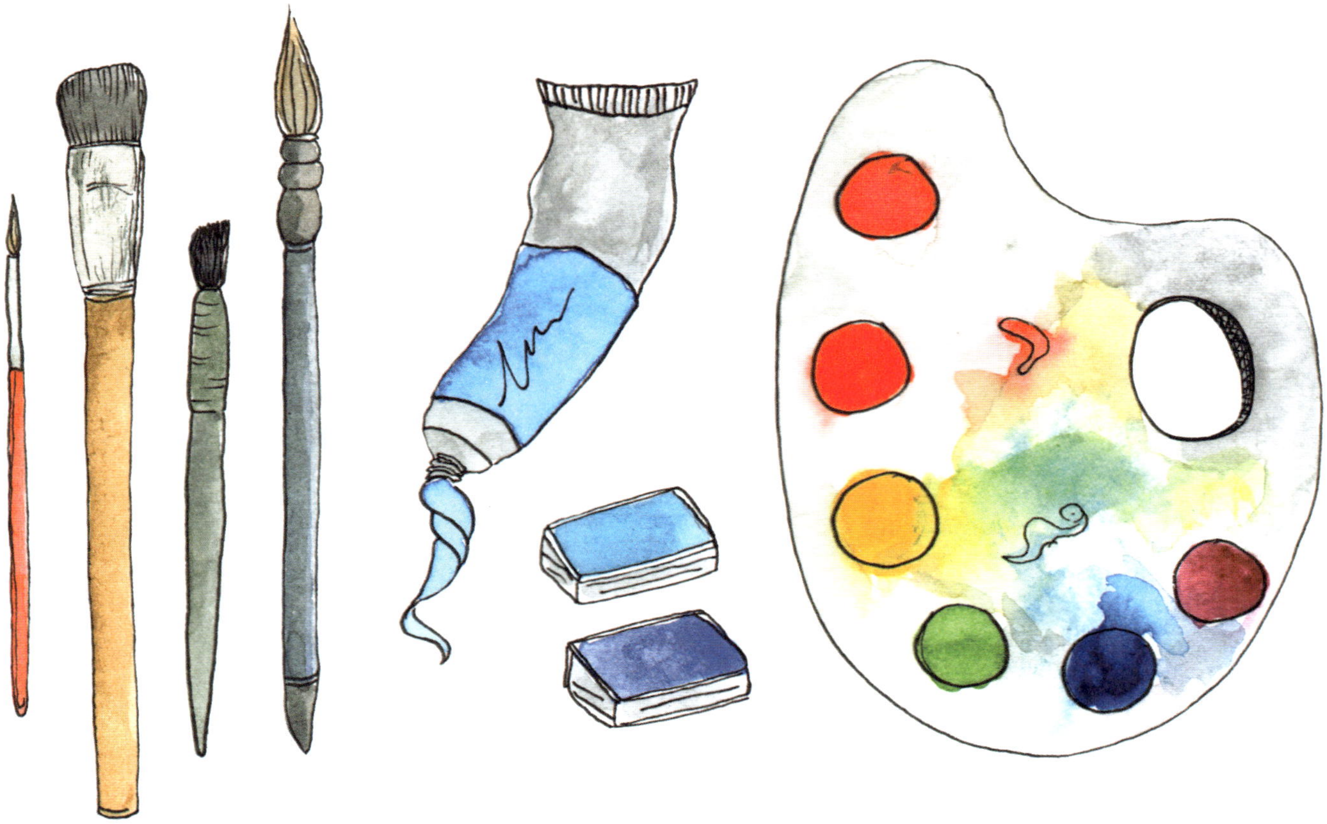

Paper

Let's start with the most fundamental tool: paper. While I do incorporate watercolor in-o my artwork, I rarely use watercolor paper. I find that it absorbs too much of the ink from my fineliner pens, making them bleed or skip over the texture of the paper.

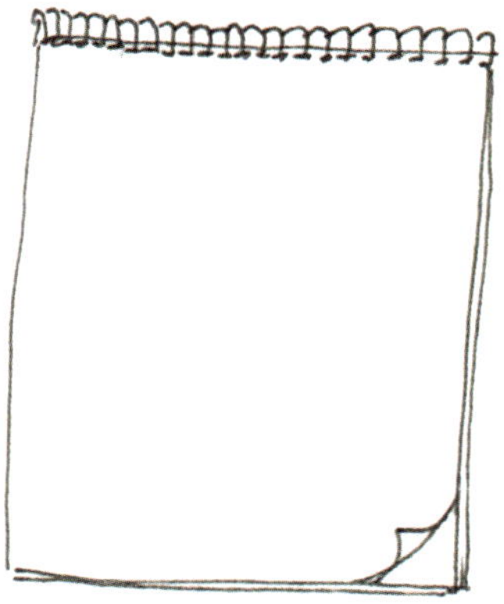

Instead, I use Bristol paper. It's smooth enough for ink and sturdy enough for watercolor, as well as sufficiently thick for original art pieces and durable for scanning and storing. For a painting with multiple layers of watercolor. I choose watercolor paper, as it will not buckle with added water, unlike Bristol paper.

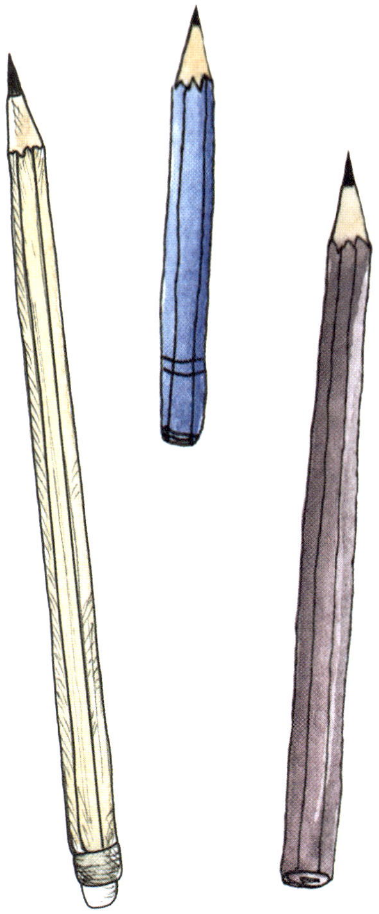

Pencil & Eraser

Some artists prefer sketching with harder graphite pencils, as these create lighter (more subtle) lines on the page that are easier to cover with watercolor. Other artists prefer softer graphite that won't leave grooves or indents in the paper.

Experiment to discover which you prefer, though I recommend using a light touch with either type of pencil. When working in the style that I do, the pencil type is less important, as I draw over the pencil with ink and erase my pencil marks before applying watercolor. I use mechanical #2 pencils. Just make sure you have a good eraser to go along with the pencil you choose.

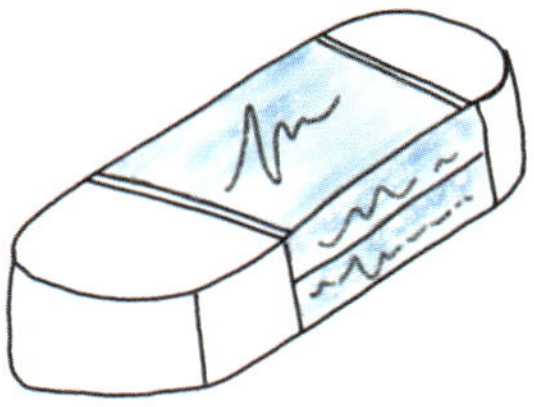

Ink Pen

From fineliner to dip pens, there are so many options for ink; however, I recommend a fineliner pen with archival ink. Whether you choose a one-time-use pen or a refillable one, you want archival ink, as it will not bleed when you apply watercolor over it, as long as you wait until the ink has dried. Archival ink also won't bleed through the page, which is particularly useful for drawings created in a sketchbook.

Once you've chosen your ink pen, consider the size of the nib. I veer toward the very thin—0.2 mm (005) or smaller, with the occasional 0.25 mm (01) thrown in. The thickness of your pen nib dictates the quality and mood of your drawing.

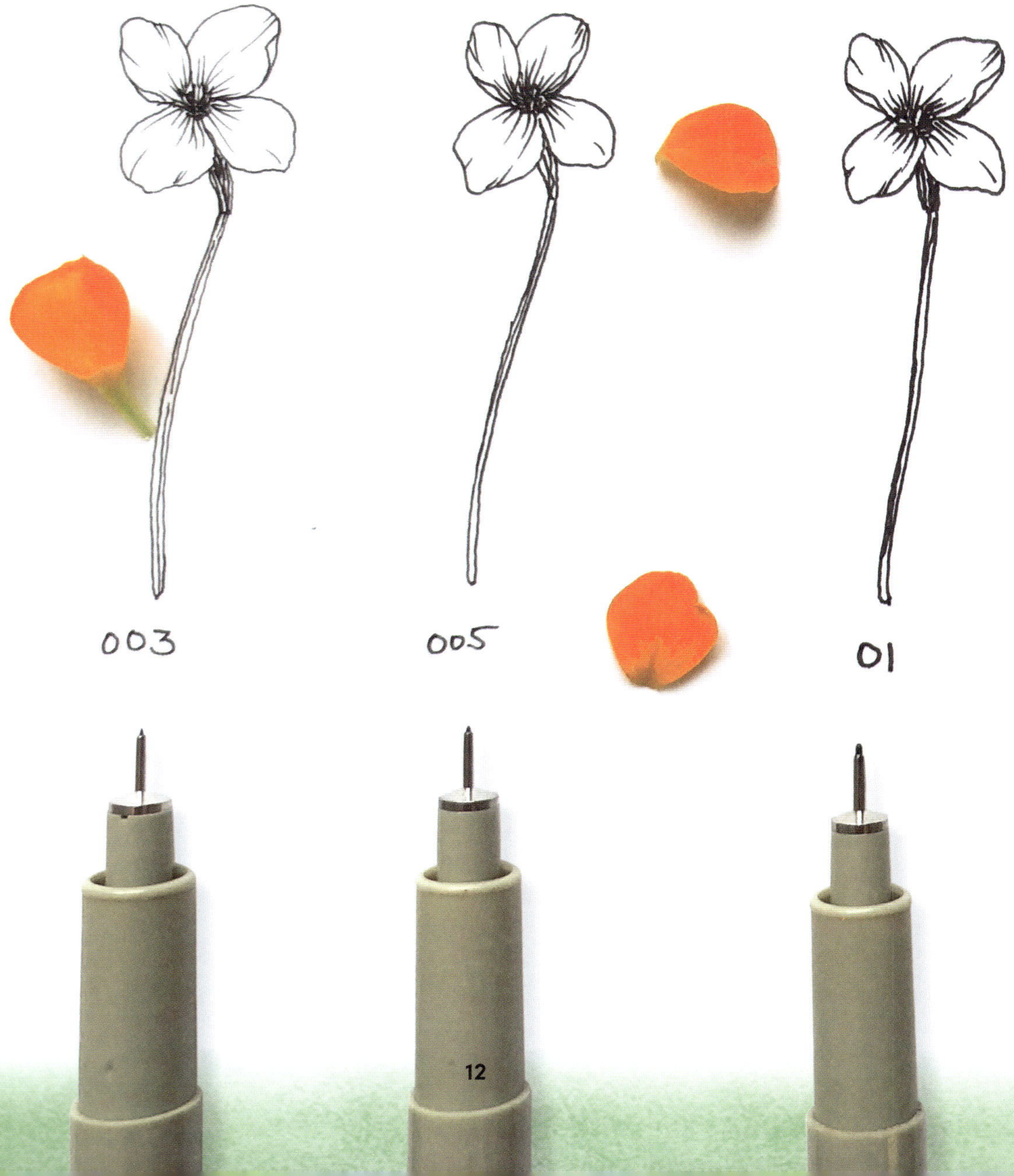

If you want a lighter, more detailed drawing, choose smaller nibs. If you prefer bolder lines with less minutiae, go larger. There is no wrong answer—do what's right for you!

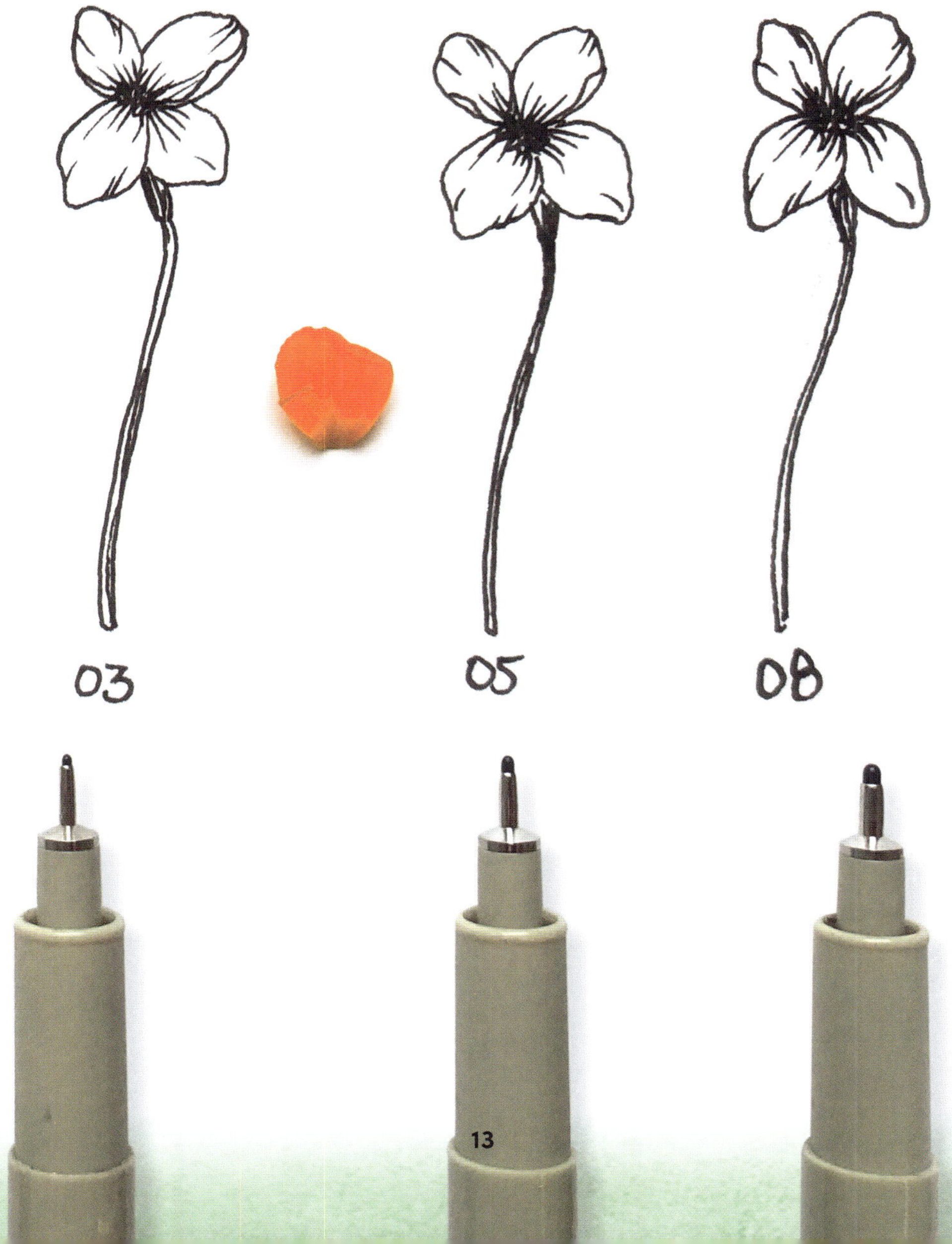

Watercolor Paints

The beauty of watercolor is how easily you can mix the colors. You do not need a 100-color palette to create a diverse array of hues, making this a very affordable medium for the novice artist.

I started my watercolor journey with a six-color set (red, yellow, blue, brown, black, and white), and it was more than enough to not only allow me to feel out the flow of the watercolors, but also to learn about color mixing. Because of how limited my palette was in the beginning, my color mixing remains incredibly intuitive to this day. This allows me to create the color that I feel is right, rather than one that is scientifically or strategically correct, which works well with my style. If I were to go into scientific botanical illustration, I would become much more exacting in my color mixing.

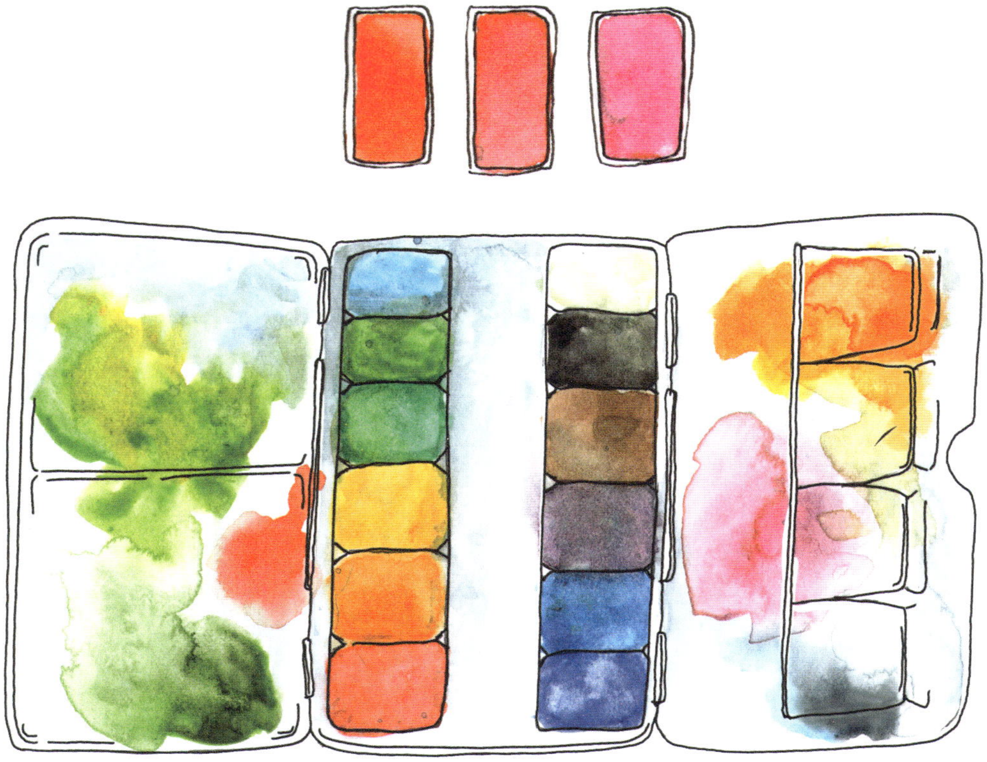

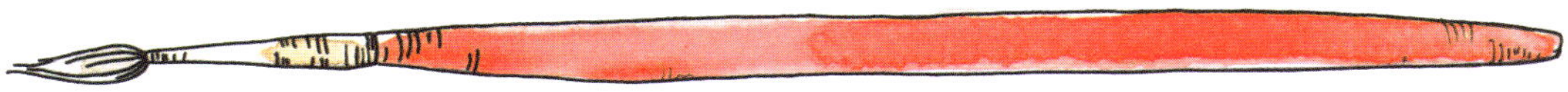

Brushes

Shhh! Don't tell other artists this, but I say any ol' brush will do. I have a few very nice paintbrushes that hold water and paint like a dream and apply so smoothly to the page. But nine times out of ten, I reach for the synthetic brushes I got as part of a $5 set. They let me spatter my paint better and I can create different textural effects without worrying about how much it will cost to replace the brushes.

It's always nice to have a variety of qualities and brush sizes. I prefer brushes that come to a narrow tip at the end, allowing me to create fine lines with even the largest of brushes, and I primarily use round brushes. You will want at least a size 8 or 10 for watercolor washes and spattering, as well as a size 1, 2, or 3 brush for fine details.

The smaller the number, the smaller the brush.

Techniques

Here are some tips and tricks I've learned over the years.

Reference Images

Unless you know a flower inside and out, you may find yourself wanting to look at a reference image while you draw. My favorite method is to take photos of the flowers and leaves I see while I am out and about. This way, I can take the photo at the exact angle I want so that I can draw the flower at home, just as I saw it in nature. If possible, I take several photos of the reference plant—the whole plant, a smaller section of it, and a close-up of the flower itself.

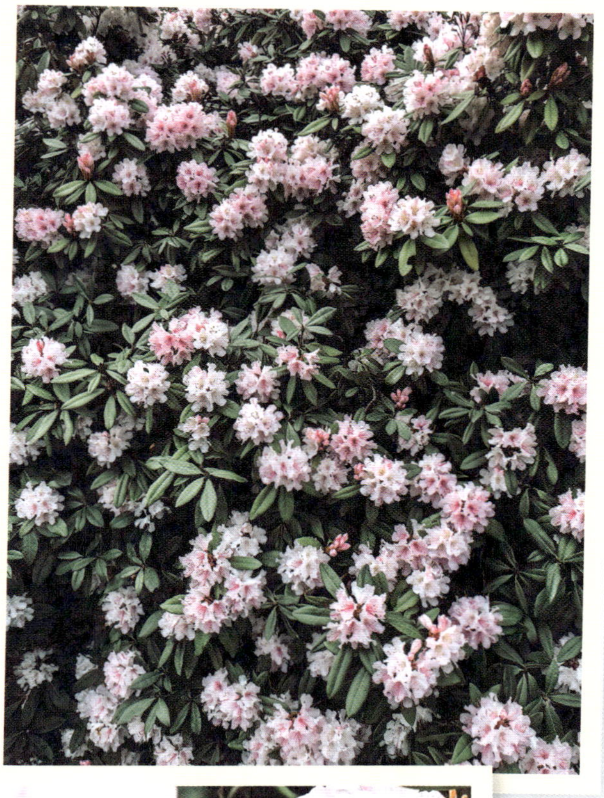

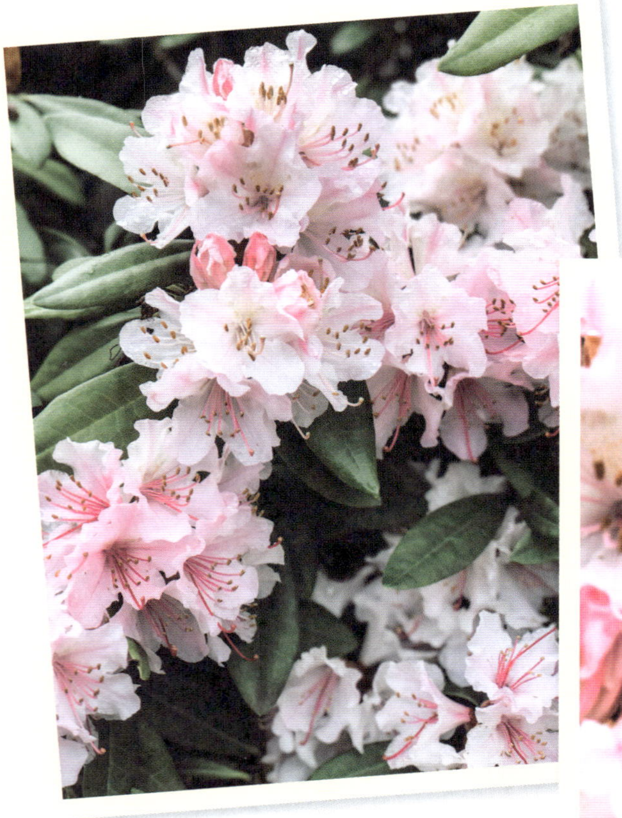

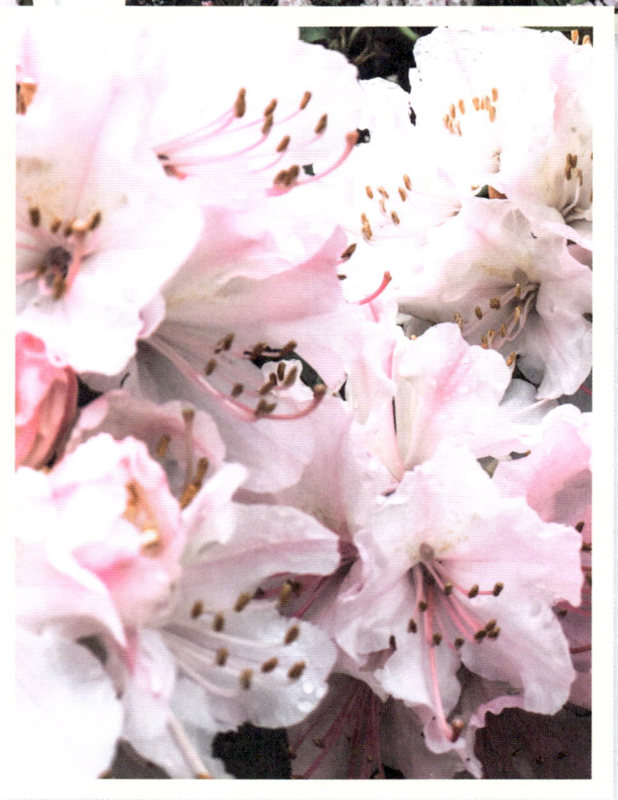

If you aren't able to take your own reference photos, there are free photo-sharing sites with images that are freely usable without copyright attached. You can also use image searches, but keep in mind that most of these photographs are copyrighted by their creators. To avoid accidentally infringing on copyright, I take the following steps:

I look for the specific angle or folds that I want in a particular petal, flower, or leaf and take 5 to 10 reference images that help me create my final piece. That means 5 to 10 reference images for a single flower. I have been known to take each petal from a separate image, as well as the angle, leaves, and so on. This way, I not only create my own original piece using several photographs, but I have also learned enough about that flower that I can usually draw it from memory in the future.

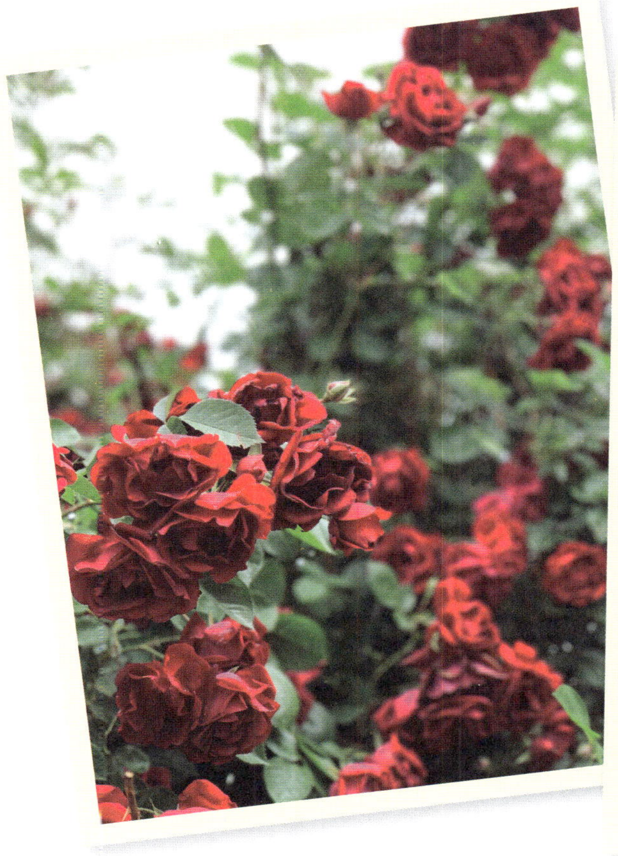

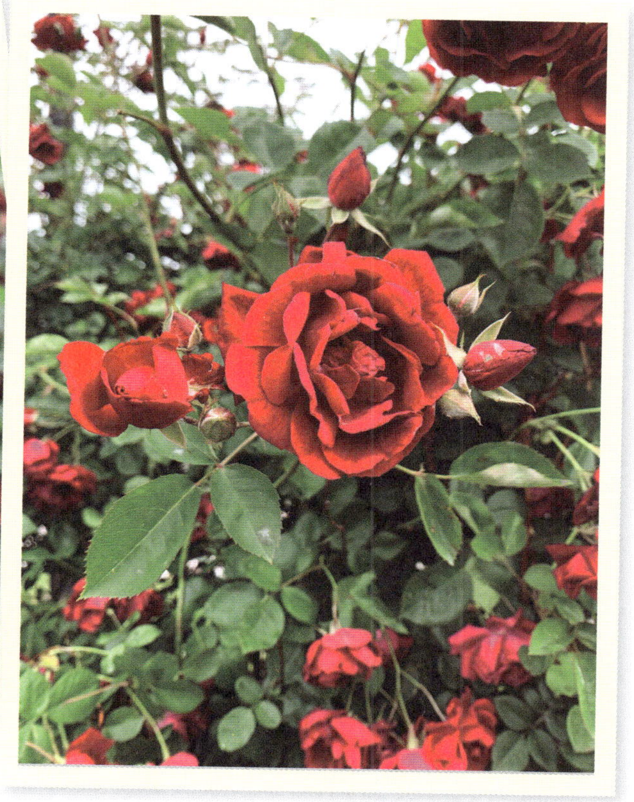

Shading with Ink

GRIP When using ink, the most important aspect of shading is your grip on the drawing tool. If your grip is too tight, your lines will appear forced and inorganic, and you will have very little control over the shape you create. Likewise, a very loose grip gives you insufficient control over the shape you create, leading to lines that are floppy and lacking in structure.

I encourage you to practice on a piece of scrap paper, without the pressure of shading a drawing that's important to you. Practice finding the perfect balance of your grip on the pen; you want precise control over the pen while maintaining a looseness to your wrist to allow for organic movements and slight variations in the pen lines.

FLICK TECHNIQUE This is my go-to method for shading using ink fineliner pens. Resting your pen tip at the point you wish your shading line to be the thickest (usually at the base of the petal, or where the shadows will be the darkest), start drawing your shade line in the direction that your petal or leaf curves, and flick your wrist as you lift your pen off the page, following through with the movement of your pen. This creates a beautiful line that tapers at its end.

If you want to create the illusion of more depth and shadow, add more lines closer together. To allow for more light, create thinner lines that are sparser and farther apart.

MARK-MAKING Try techniques such as crosshatching (intersecting sets of parallel lines; use this to add texture) or stippling (lots and lots of dots). Keep in mind that with stippling, the same principle applies for shadows versus light. The more dots you have and the closer together they are, the greater the shadow effect. The sparser and farther apart, the more light you create. To create different effects on the page, vary your marks and their direction (straight or curved).

As you shade, consider the orientation of the subject, whether a leaf is turned toward you or away, and how the petals fold into each other. Similarly, where is the light source for your object? This dictates the density of the lines and creates the idea of shadow and light. These variances will potentially change the direction of your shading within a single leaf, a petal, or another subject.

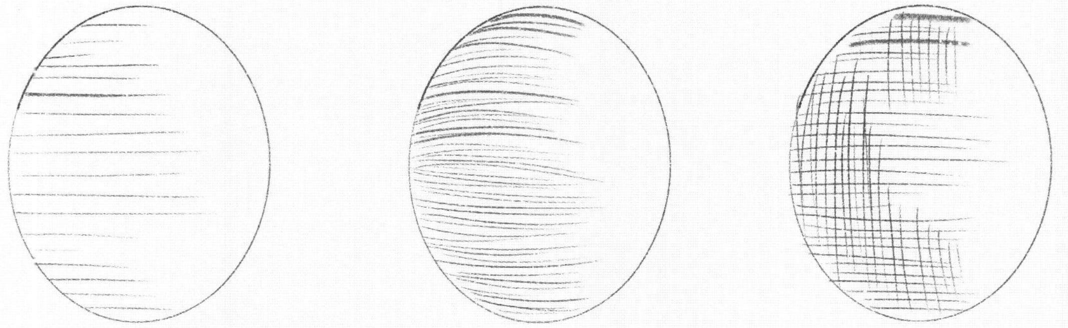

Shading Tips

- Remember your light source and, consequently, where the shadows fall.
- The base/center of your flower will most likely feature darker shadows.
- Make sure you're adding shadow lines into the dips and valley of your petals, in the direction that they fold. This adds movement and makes your final piece look more dynamic.
- Vary the length of your flick lines so that they are not all one length—again to create a more dynamic and fluid final piece.

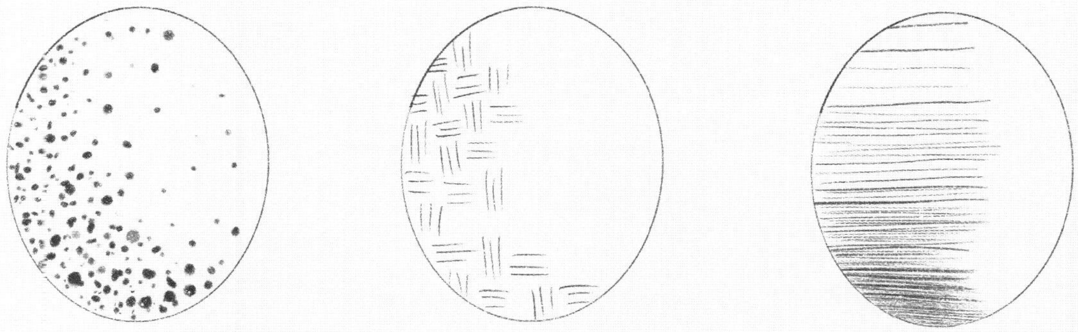

Watercolor Techniques

I use three simple techniques to create my modern watercolor florals.

Wet-into-Wet

I paint wet-into-wet to create the watercolor washes that form the foundation of many of my pieces. To work wet-into-wet, start by applying clear water where you want the watercolor pigment to go. Then saturate your brush with watercolor, dabbing it onto the water on the page. The water will draw the pigment out of the brush and flow beautifully.

Working wet-into-wet gives you less control over your paint, but the result is flowing and beautiful.

Wet-on-Dry

This technique allows me to control exactly where and how the watercolor lies on the page. To work wet-on-dry, saturate a brush with water and pigment, and apply brushstrokes to your dry paper.

Spattering

This is the most fun technique. Saturate your watercolor brush with watercolor and pigment (more than you would use if working wet-into-wet or wet-on-dry), hold the brush 5 to 8 inches above the page, and tap near the base of the bristles while moving your brush in a circular motion above the page. Any spatters that land directly on the surface of the flower can be blended with a clean wet brush. This can take some practice, but once you figure it out, it's so much fun!

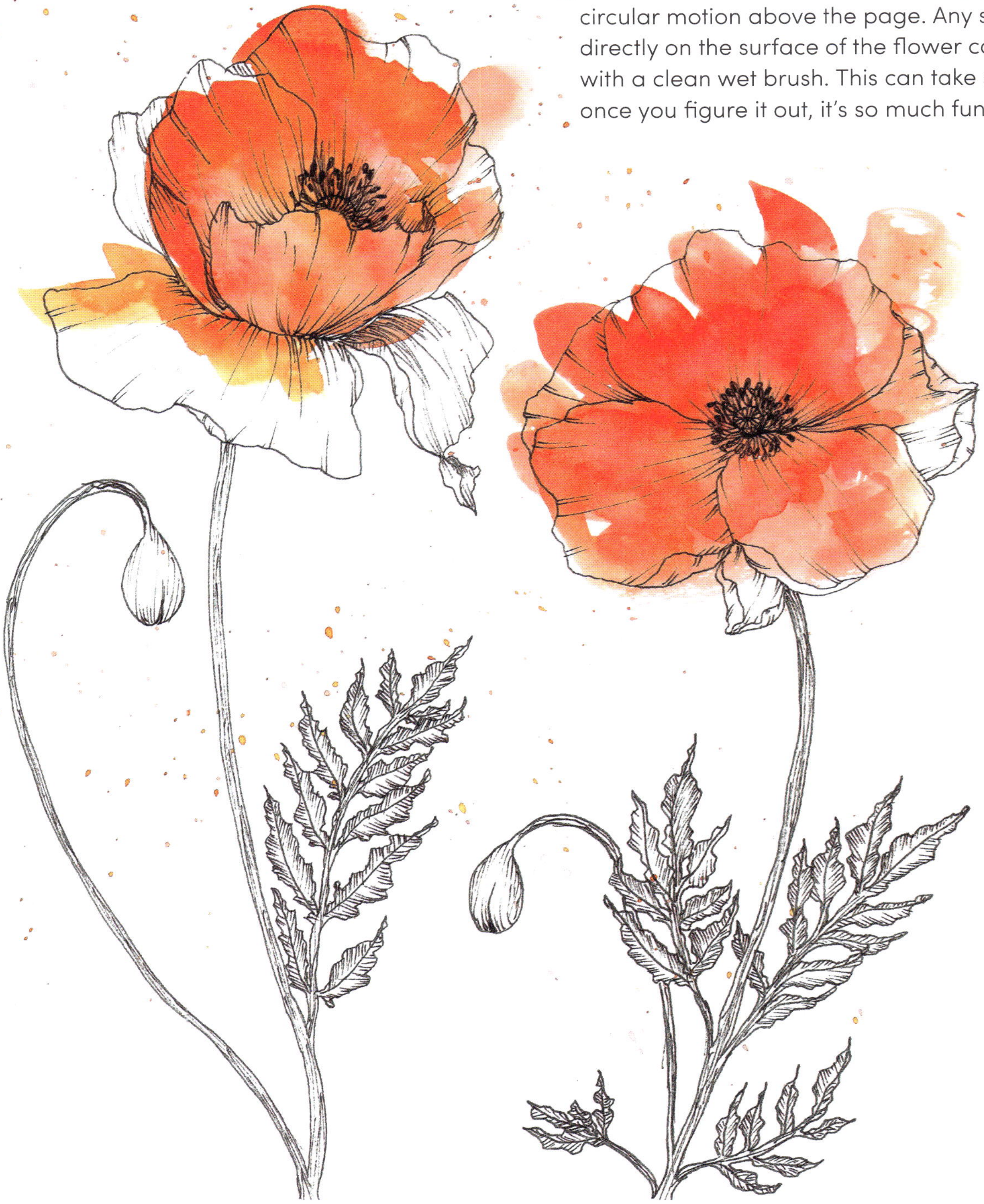

Correcting Mistakes

There are a few ways to correct mistakes when working with watercolor. If you notice an error while your paint is still wet, use a clean paintbrush that is damp but not saturated. Dab this onto the error, cleaning off your brush on a clean paper towel or cloth between each dab. You can also use a clean Q-tip or the corner of a piece of paper towel to remove the mistake.

If you notice the error after the paint is dry, wet it with clean water, and once the water seeps into the paint, follow the steps above. This second technique may not work as well as the first one, but you should still get pretty good results.

If you need to paint around the area of your mistake, let the corrected area dry. If it is even a little bit wet, adding paint near the mistake may pull water into the pigment again.

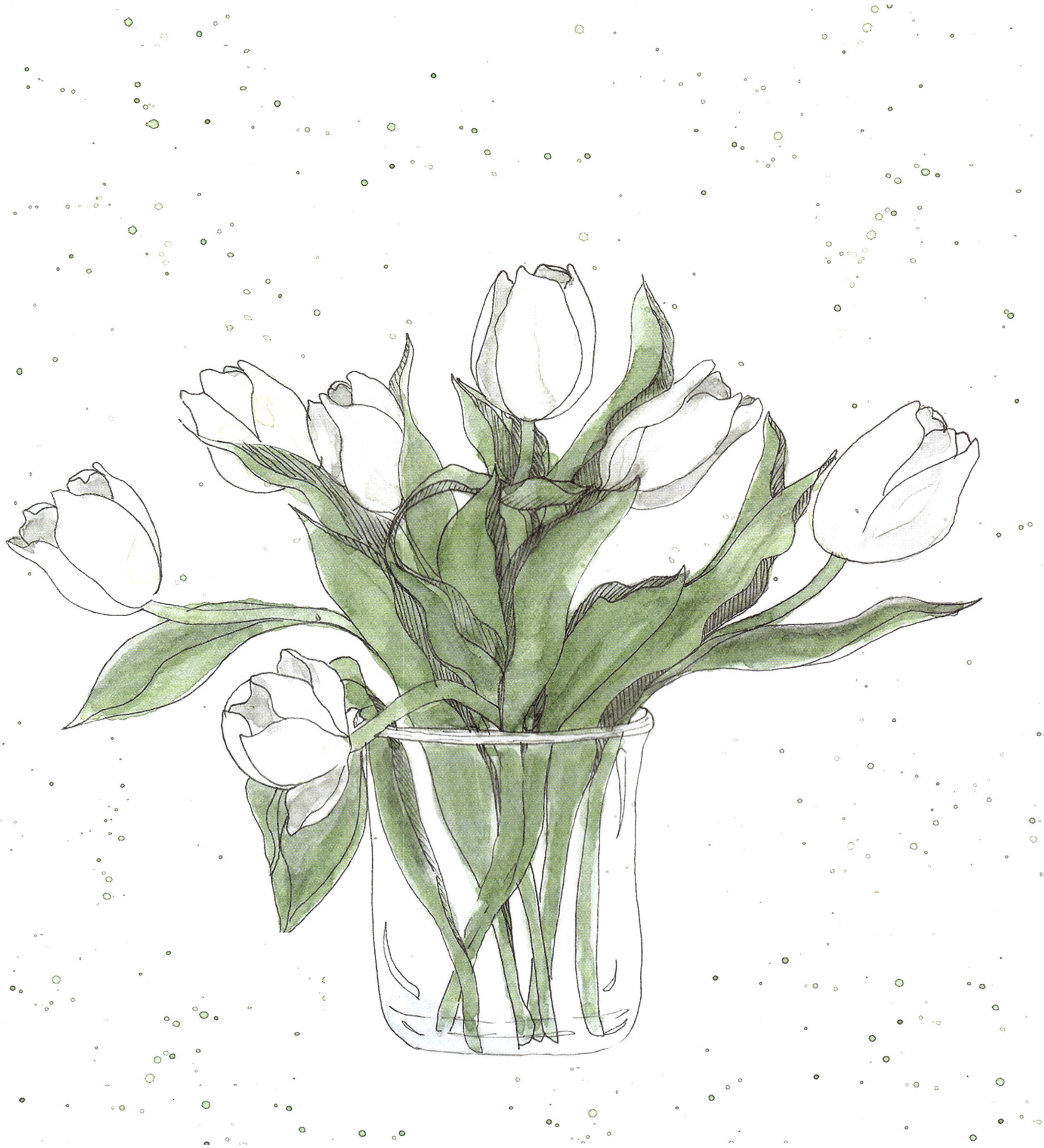

What to Draw First? Ink vs. Watercolor

I vary between applying watercolor before and after I have completed my ink drawing. I choose my technique based on my current mood, but there are a few things to consider as you decide which technique will work best for you.

Applying Watercolor First

I love to use this technique when I have a general idea of the layout of the flower I want to create, but still want an element of surprise and variability in my end product. Using the wet-into-wet technique and applying a modern watercolor wash to the page first will give you a color-filled canvas so that you can play with the leaf and petal placement, as well as emphasize the ink lines.

Applying Ink First

When I want to achieve a more specific layout, I usually ink the floral first. This gives me more control over the end product and allows me to make edits to my floral before applying the watercolor, as I am able to change my pencil sketch before applying ink.

There's no right or wrong way to create your modern watercolor and ink floral. Experiment and find what works best for you. If you follow me on Instagram or have taken any of my Skillshare classes, you will see that I often put watercolor down first. In this book, however, I apply watercolor after the line work is complete.

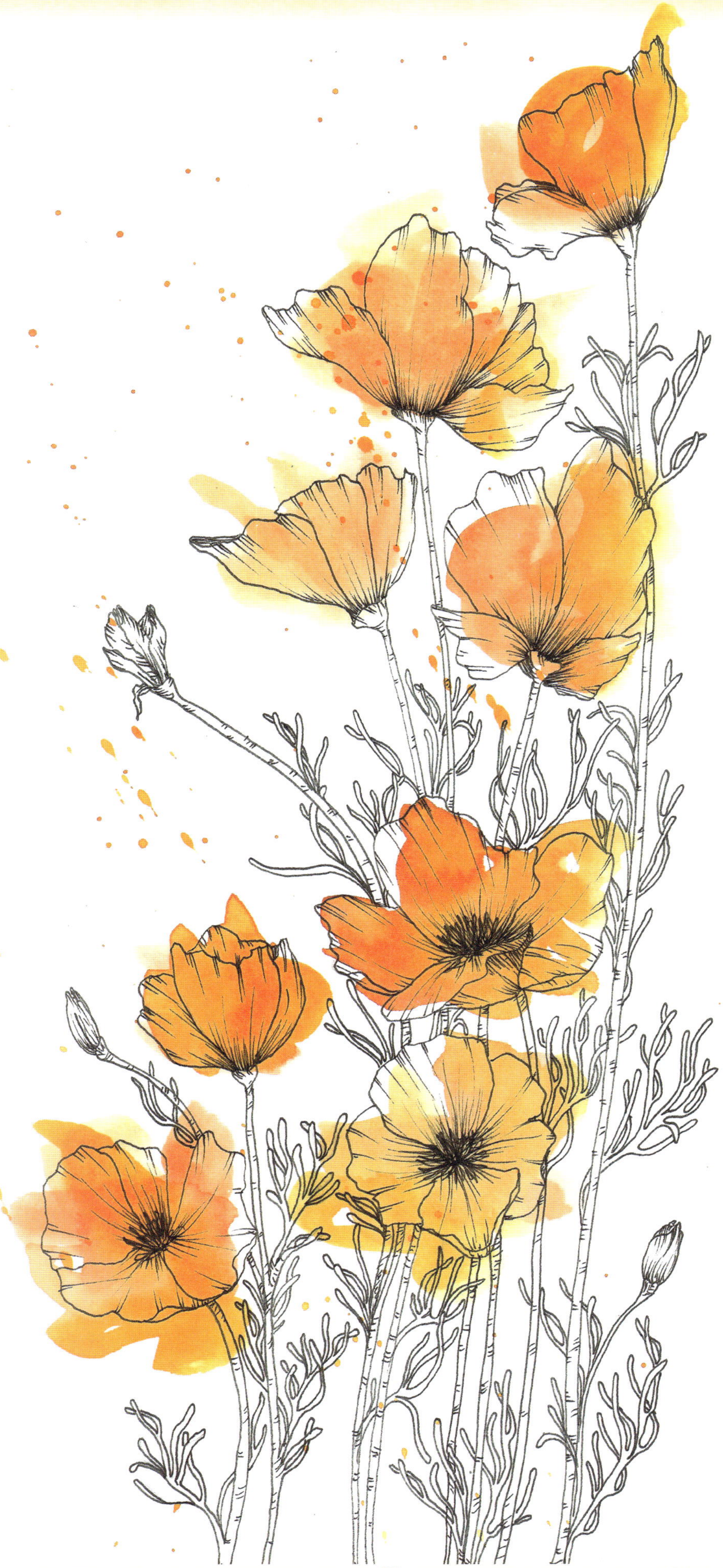

Let's Talk About Color

You don't need to know the complex principles of color theory to create a beautiful piece of art. However, you should have a basic understanding of the general application of color theory and the relationships between colors.

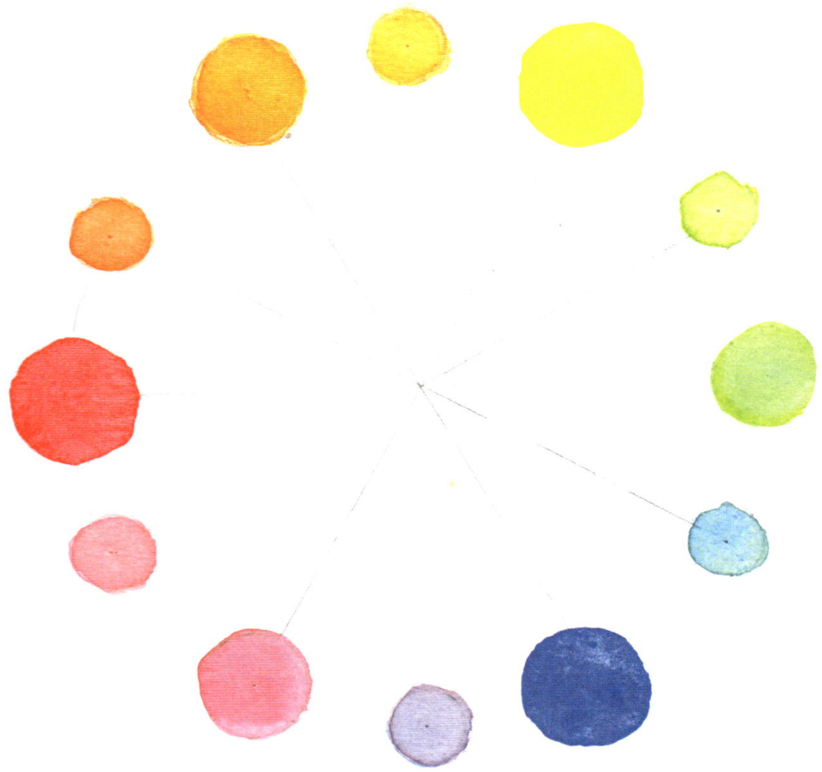

To begin, there are three primary colors: red, yellow, and blue. In theory, you can create any color by mixing these three colors. How amazing is that!

Next are the three secondary colors: green, orange, and purple. These can be created by mixing two of the primary colors (for example, yellow and red make orange, blue and red make purple, and so on).

There are also six tertiary colors: yellow-orange, red-orange, red-violet, blue-violet, blue-green, and yellow-green.

Color Mixing Chart

Here you can see the progression of mixing two distinct colors, allowing for a wide variety of colors to be used.

You may also hear artists use a few other terms, including:

HUE essentially means the same as the word "color." For instance, the hue of chartreuse is green.

SATURATION refers to the purity of a color. You can reduce saturation by adding gray or a color from the opposite side of the color wheel (page 26). Desaturating a color will give you varying shades of gray.

VALUE means how light or dark a color is, on a scale of black and white. So, to lighten (or increase the value) of a color, add white or yellow. To darken (or decrease the value), add blue or black. With watercolor, lighten by adding more water to your pigment/brush, thus increasing the space (white) in the pigment.

COLOR TEMPERATURE Generally speaking, warm tones complement each other, cool tones complement each other, and warm and cool tones contrast with each other. Warm colors are typically associated with welcoming, light, and active scenes, and cool colors indicate calm, distant, and soothing scenes. Color temperature theory can get pretty complex, so if you want to learn more, I suggest taking some time and doing your research!

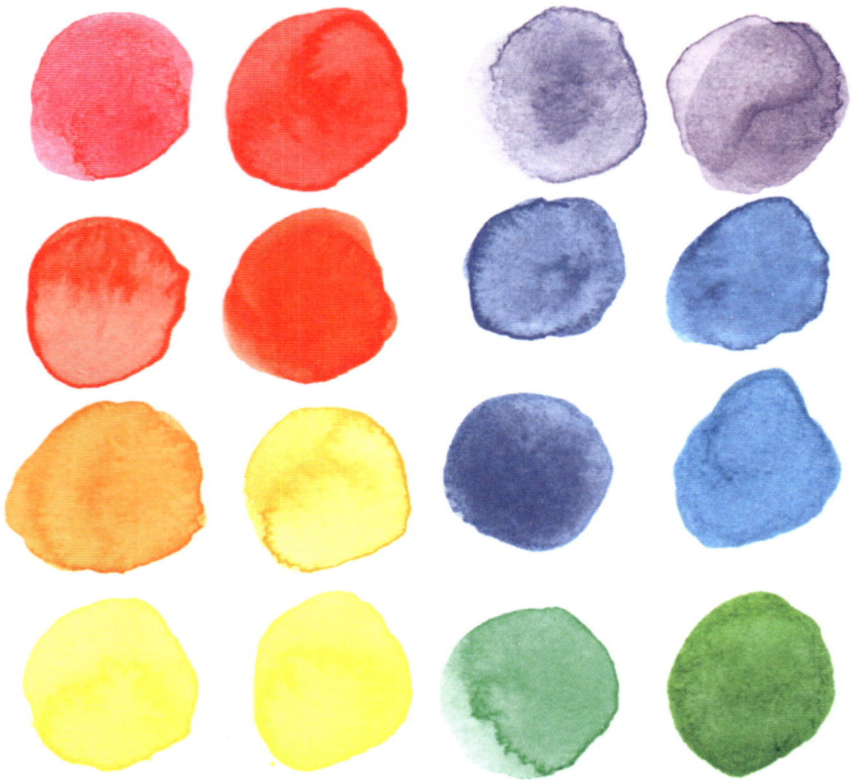

Though the differences can be subtle, the quality of color impacts the entire mood of a piece. From a stormy overcast day (cool tones), to a sunny, brightly lit wheat field (warm tones), how you use color will determine the mood your artwork conveys.

Basic Flower Structure

While it isn't necessary to understand the intricate biology of plant structure and function to draw florals, it is a good idea to understand the basic framework of a flower. As you learn to draw flowers, you may find that you go from carefully drawing very specifically and painstakingly from reference photos to creating your own flowers from memory and imagination. This second stage of floral drawing is incredibly fun—once you understand basic plant structure and come to familiarize yourself with specific plants over time, you'll be able to create the angles of a flower without needing to search for the perfect reference flower first. And this—learning the very simple, basic structure of flowers—is the first step to get you there.

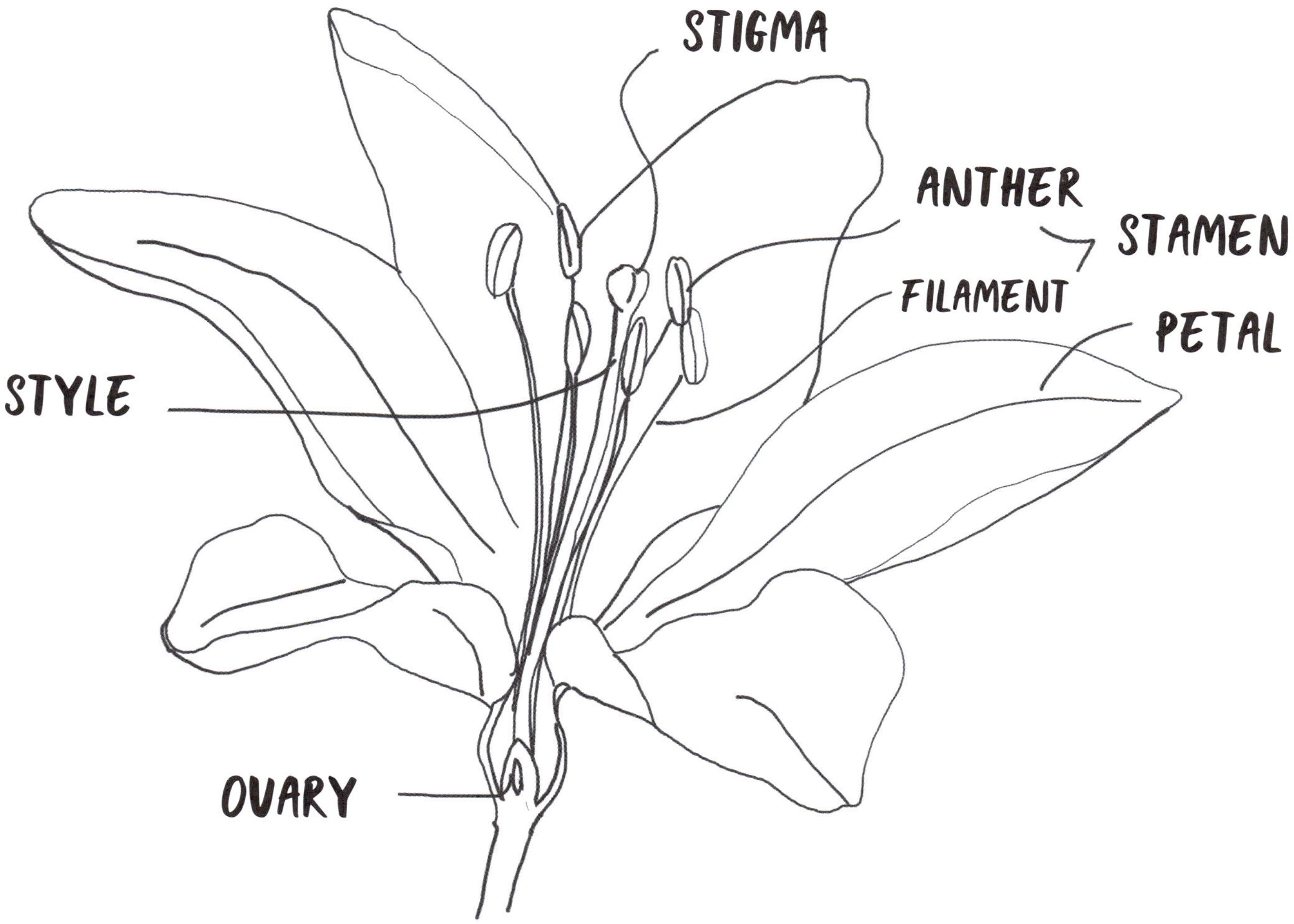

Petal: The part of the flower that attracts pollinators

Pistil: The female part of the flower (located in the center), which contains the:

- **Stigma:** The sticky part at the top of the pistil where the pollen germinates
- **Style:** The long, tubular structure that holds up the stigma
- **Ovary:** Where the ovules (the part of the ovary that becomes the seed) are produced

Stamen: The male, pollen-producing part of the flower. This surrounds the stigma and contains:

- **Anther:** Oval-shaped structure at the top of the stamen that produces the pollen
- **Filament:** The long, threadlike structure that holds up the anther

Now that you have this knowledge in your toolbox, I encourage you to get out into nature and have a look for yourself. Pick some wildflowers, deconstruct them, and see if you can label them. By understanding the separate parts of a flower, you'll be able to structure it however you imagine on paper.

Step-by-Step Florals: The Basic Formula

You can follow this basic formula for each of the floral projects in this book. While I will go into details on different aspects of the individual flowers, it's helpful to read this section first.

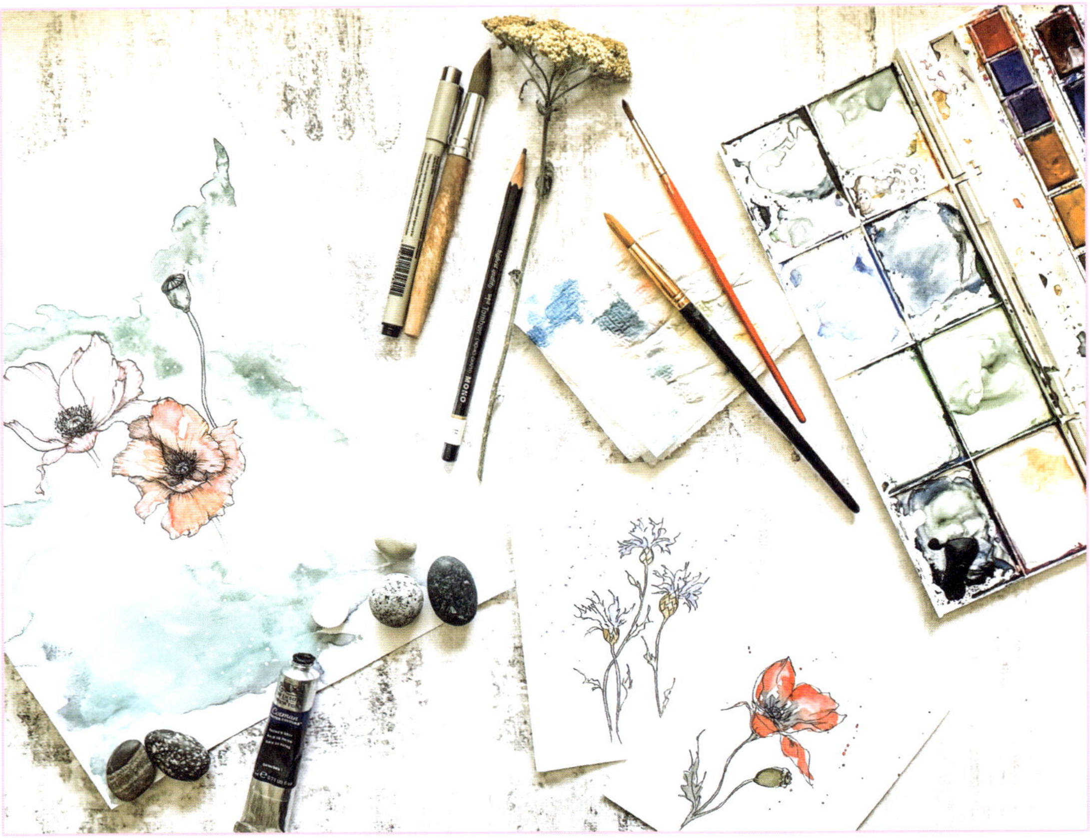

Step 1

Study the shape of the flower—both the overall shape of the bloom itself, as well as the smaller components of the plant. Look for a general shape, such as a circle, an oblong, or a triangle. How do the shapes interact with each other? What shapes make up the center of the flower?

How many flowers are there? Is there just one central bloom, like a rose, or several separate flowers, like in a foxglove? How many petals are there on each bloom, and how many leaves are there? What do the branches look like?

Step 2

With a pencil, lightly sketch the outline of your image, beginning with the middle of the flower and working your way out. This is not the time to add small details, but rather to give the overall shape and movement. If I add any shading during this stage, it is simply to differentiate between petals with intricate folds, as with a frilly peony.

Step 3

Next, using a fineliner pen, trace over the pencil lines. This is your opportunity to make any final changes to your layout. Once the ink is dry, erase the pencil lines so that you can clearly visualize the flower.

If you have not already drawn the center of the flower, add it now using ink. Then add shading lines using a combination of techniques, and let the ink dry.

Step 4

Now it's time to add watercolor! This step can be both exciting and terrifying. Consider what technique and style you are going for, and then have fun and work with confidence. In this book, I have detailed two techniques that you can use to add color to your pieces: wet-on-dry and wet-into-wet (see page 20). You don't need to let your paint dry before moving on to the (optional) next step.

Step 5

I love this step the most, which has become a hallmark of my style. While my florals dry, I use the primary color of my painting to spatter the page with pigment. If any of the spatters land inside the flower, I recommend blending before the piece dries to avoid distracting from your gorgeous watercolor wash and fine ink lines.

Snowdrop

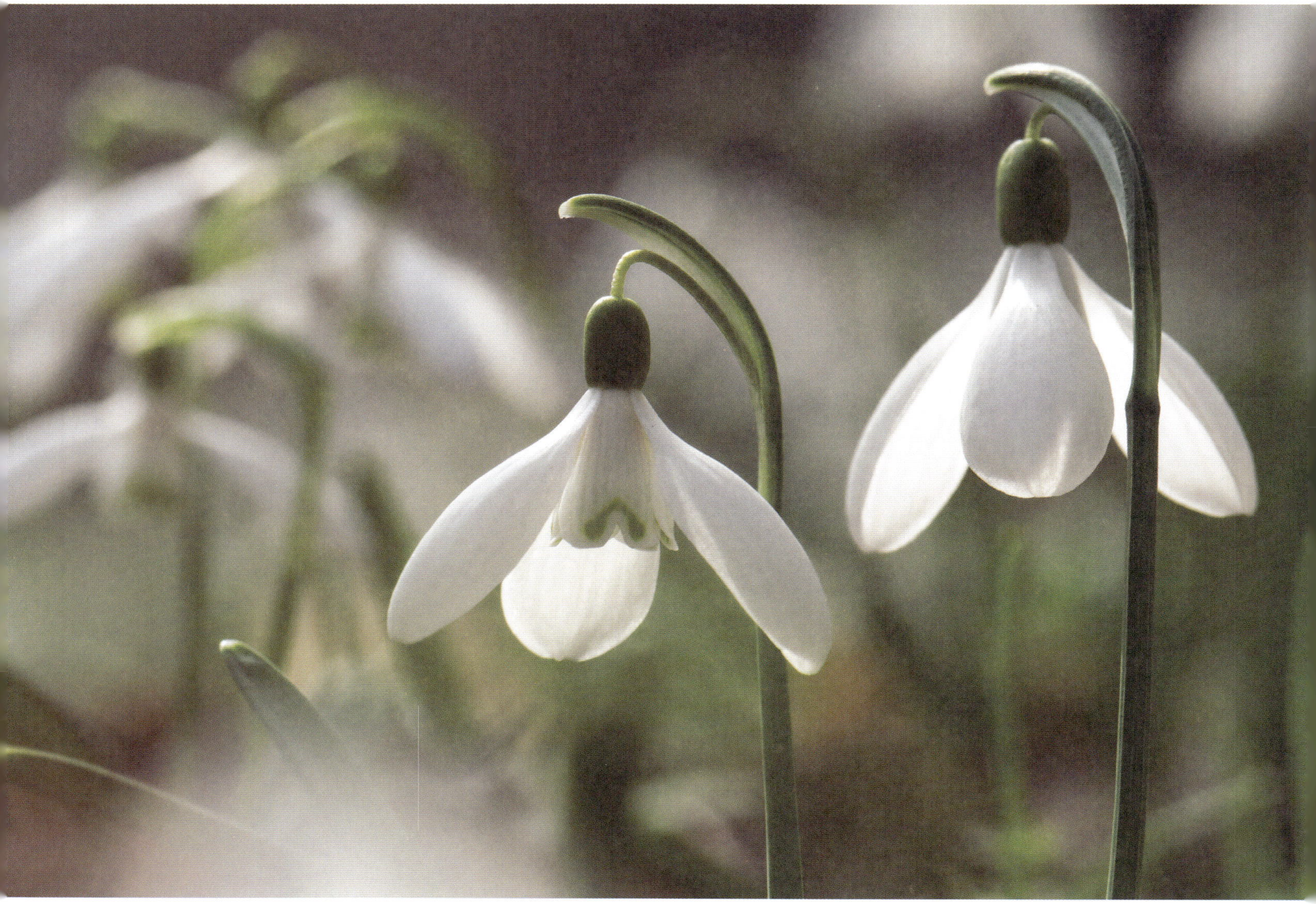

Now let's dive into our inking and watercolor painting projects!

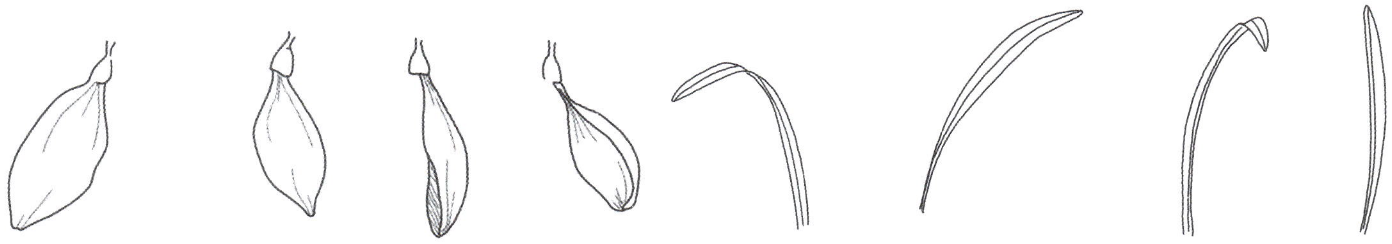

Step 1

To begin, let's review the basic shapes of the petals and leaves that you will use to create a snowdrop. I did a web search for "snowdrops" and used a variety of reference images to create the different angles shown here.

Practice outlining your petals and leaves from different angles. You can trace over these images using tracing paper, or draw freehand.

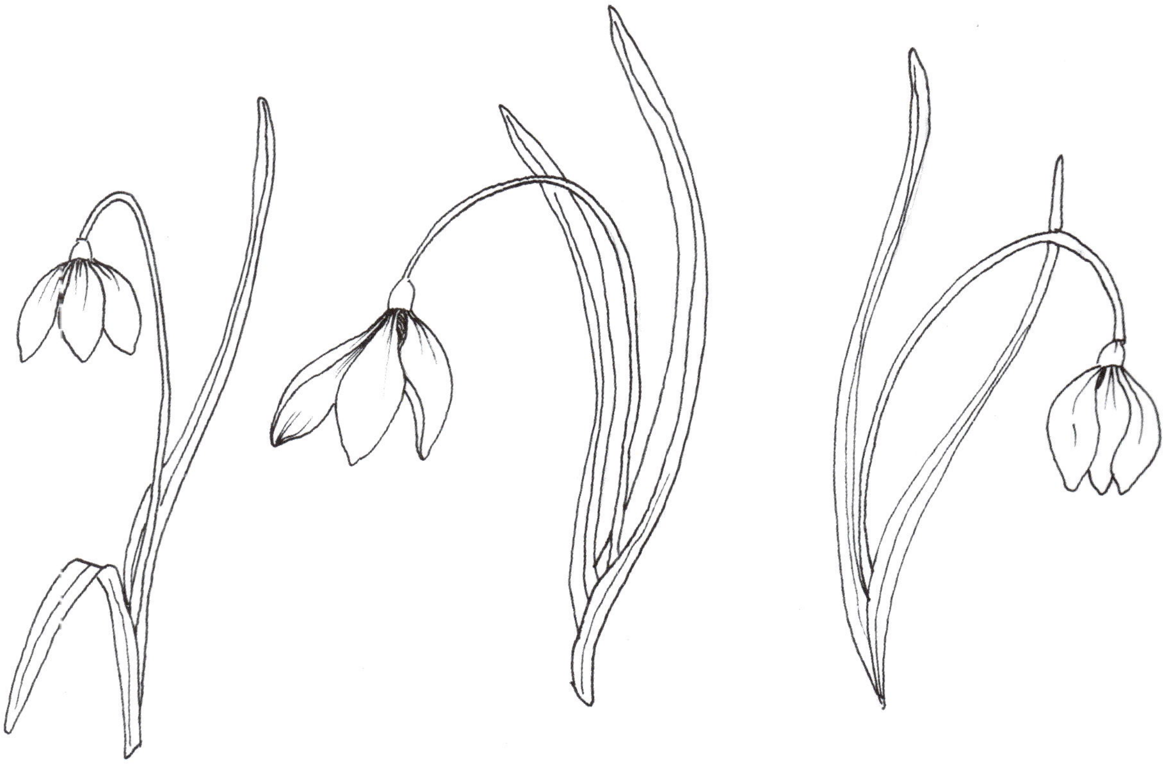

Step 2

Now that you have a basic understanding of the angles and shapes of the petals and leaves of a snowdrop, you can combine them in a pencil sketch. I decided to try three different approaches to the snowdrop, using the angles we practiced in step 1. Next, with fineliner ink, go over your pencil lines and make any final, subtle adjustments. Once the ink is dry, erase the pencil lines.

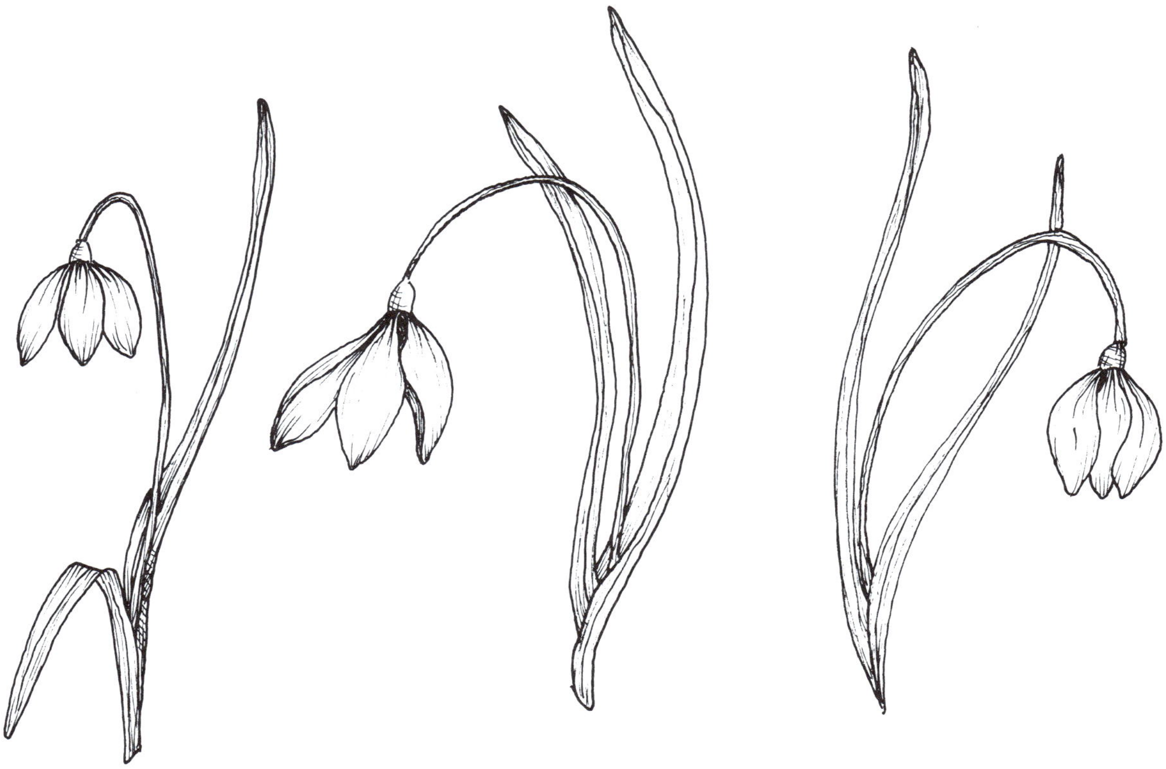

Step 3

Once you have the snowdrop outlined, begin shading. Use the flick technique (page 18) to add subtle curved lines to the petals, as well as straight lines to add shadows to the parts of the petals that lie completely in the shade.

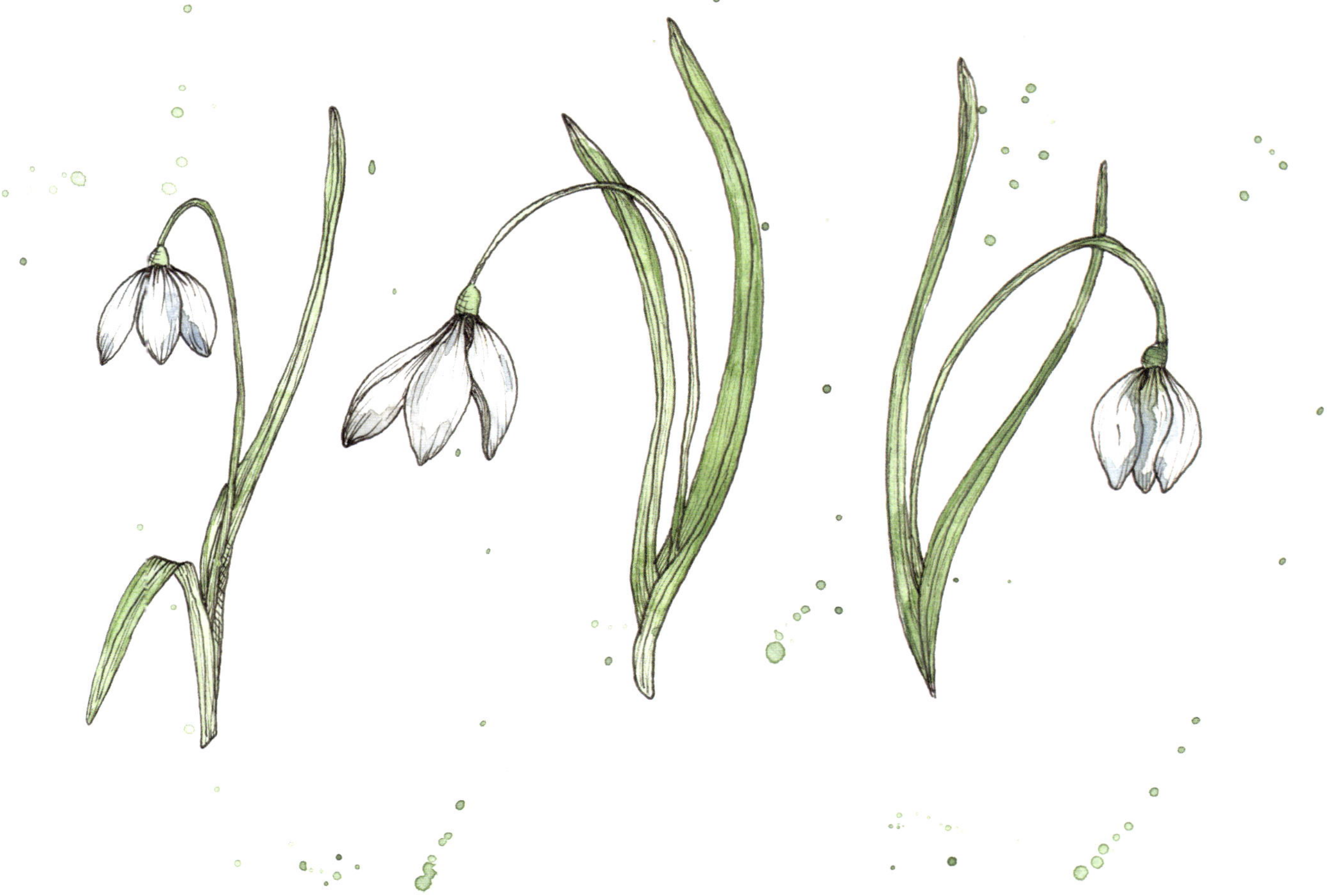

Step 4

Next, add watercolor. I mixed two greens with a subtle hint of yellow to get the color that I wanted. Using the wet-on-dry technique (page 20), apply green inside the lines.

Next, add shadows to the flower. Snowdrops are white, but you want to give them a dynamic feel. Create a gray shadow using orange and blue. Add more blue pigment to create a cooler tone for the snowdrop. Add blue-gray shadows to the petals as well.

Optional: While the paint is still a bit wet on the flowers, drench a round brush in water and green pigment—the main color of this floral painting. Tap the brush gently about 10 inches above the page and let the spatter land whimsically. Dab away or blend in any spots that land on your flower.

Cosmos

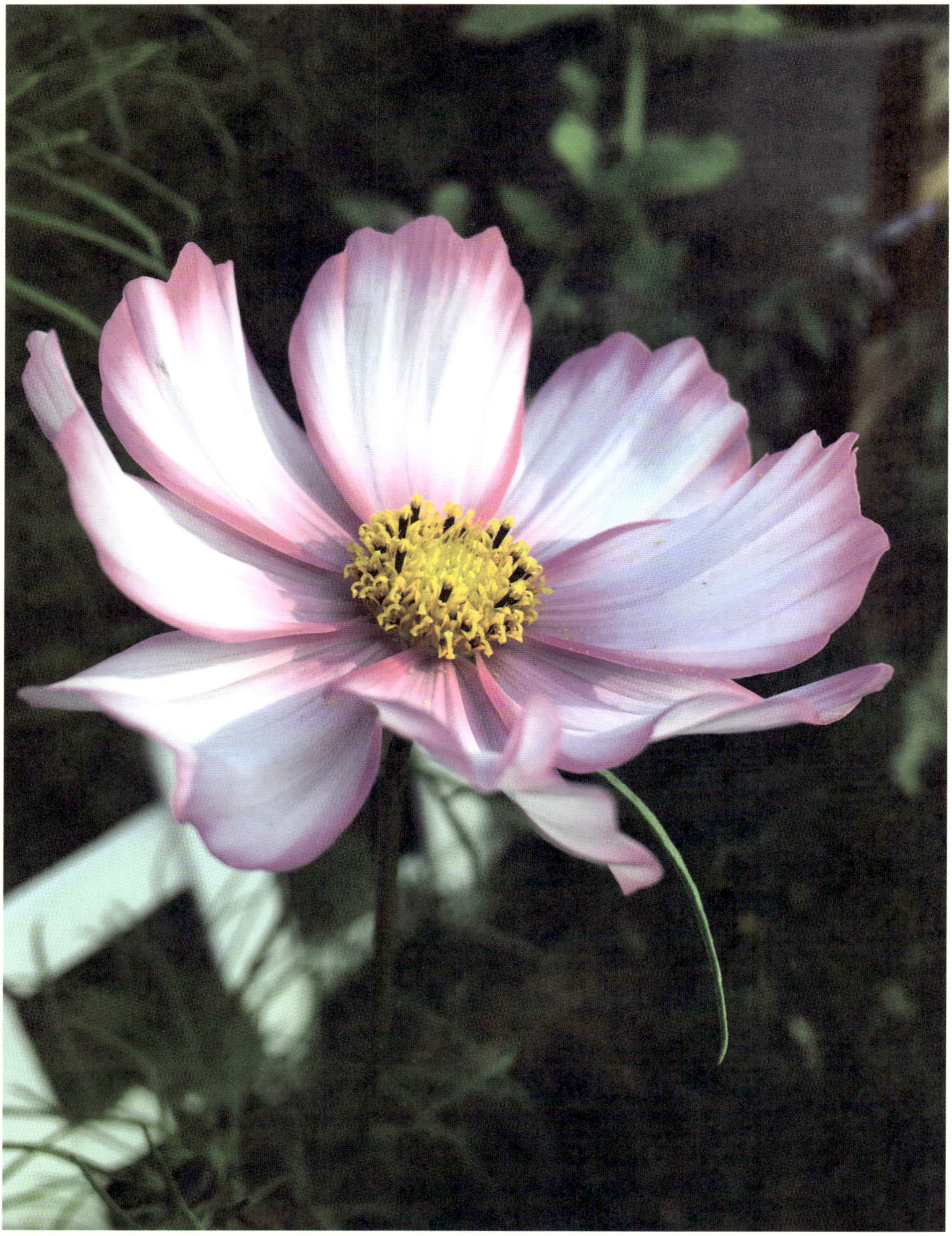

For this project, I used a reference photo that
I took of a cosmos from my own garden.

Step 1

Observing your reference photo, practice outlining the petals and leaves from different angles. You can trace over these images using tracing paper, but I recommend practicing freehand so that you learn how to create these shapes and build your muscle memory to draw clean lines.

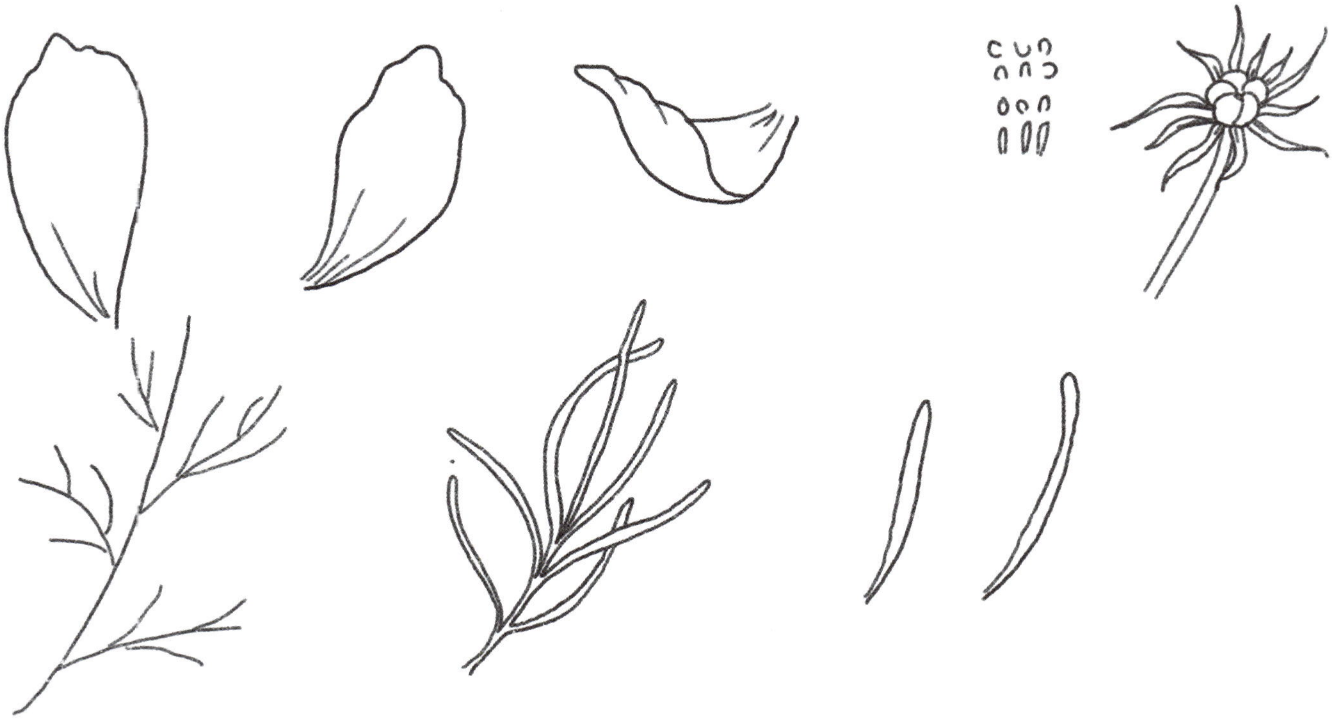

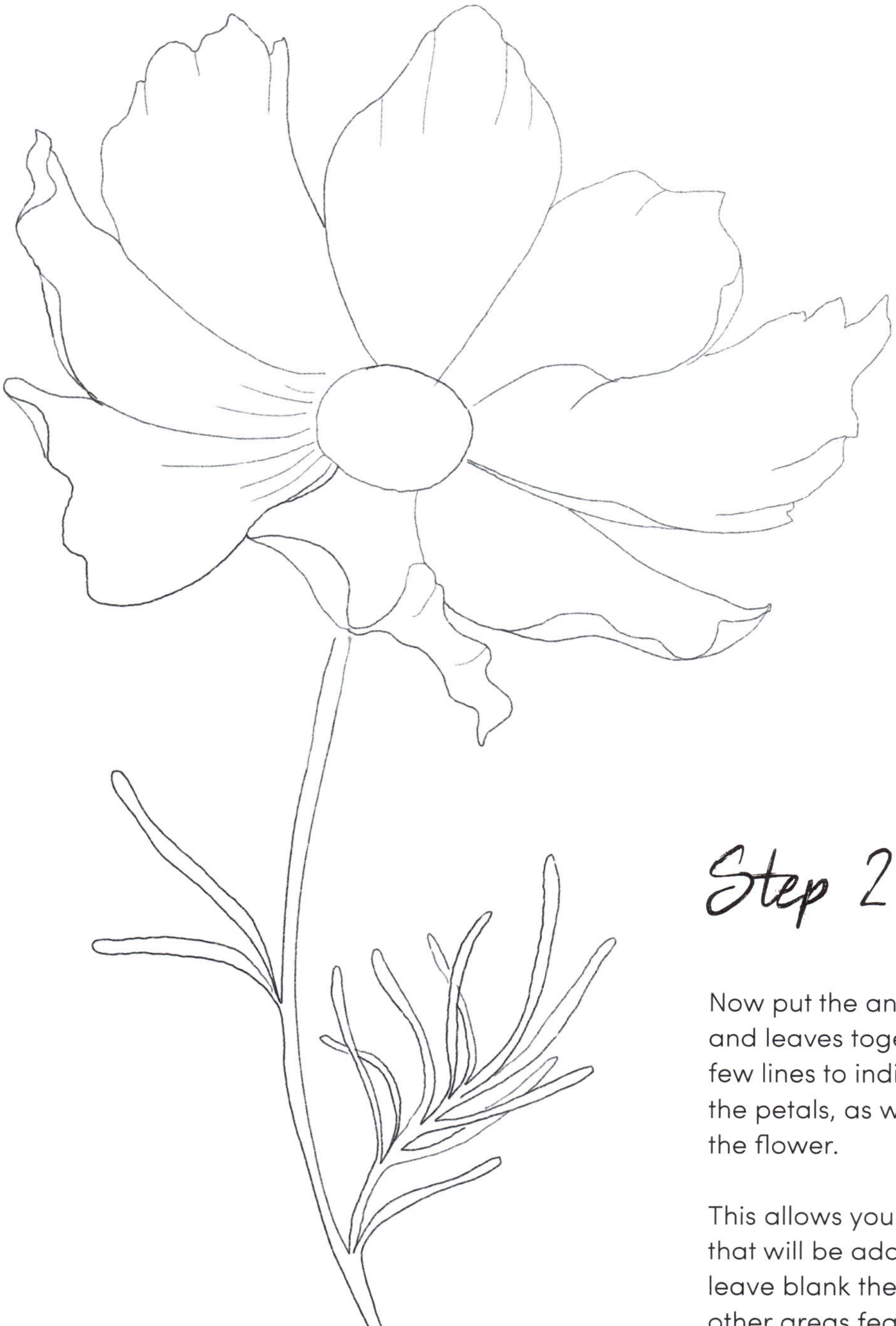

Step 2

Now put the angles and shapes of the petals and leaves together in a pencil sketch. Draw a few lines to indicate the angle of the curve of the petals, as well as a circle for the center of the flower.

This allows you to leave space for the details that will be added at a later stage. You can leave blank the center of the flower and any other areas featuring minute details during the pencil-sketch stage, as they often smudge and details get lost when you add ink.

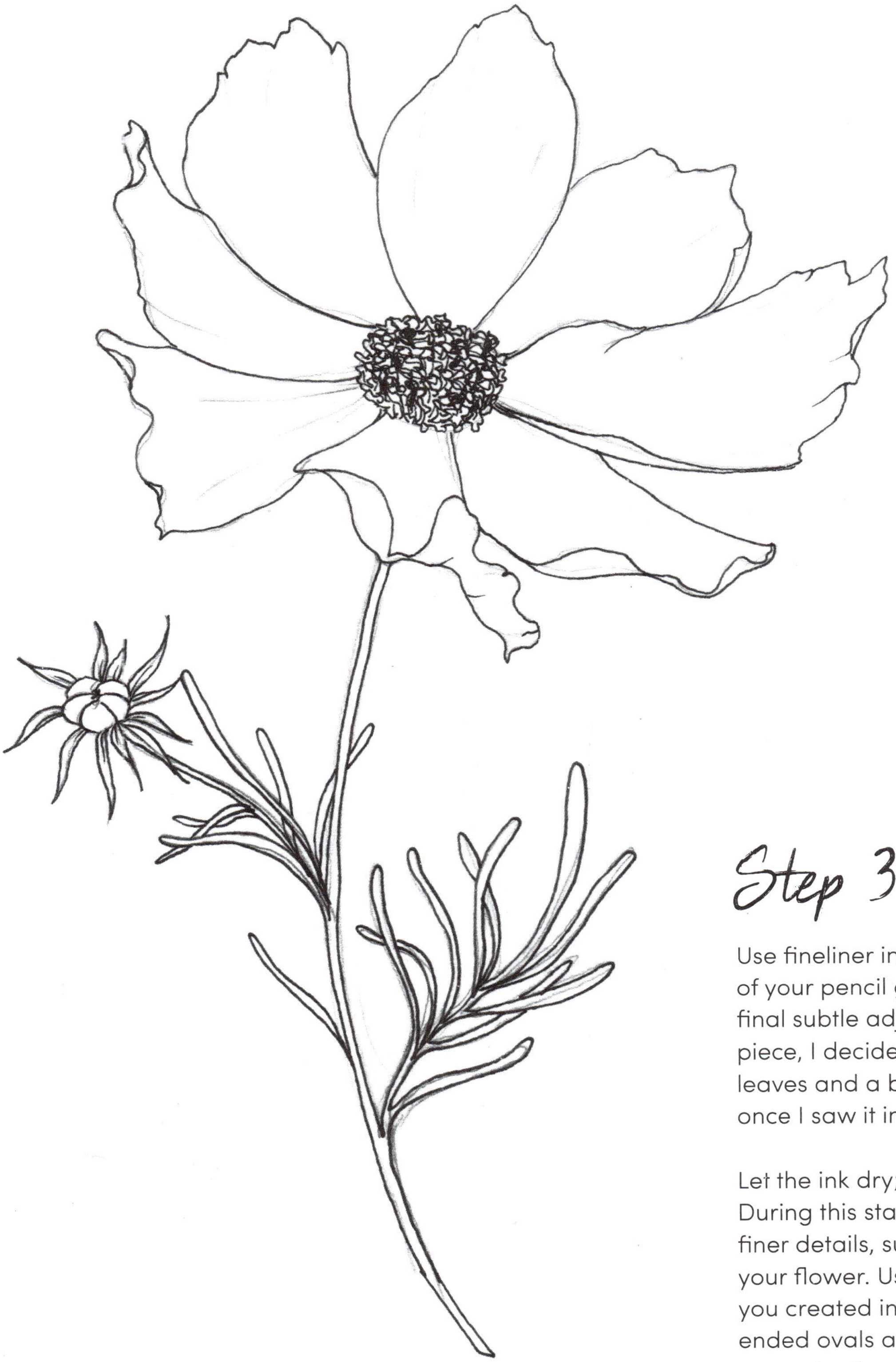

Step 3

Use fineliner ink to go over the lines of your pencil guide, making any final subtle adjustments. For this piece, I decided to add a few more leaves and a bud to my drawing once I saw it in ink.

Let the ink dry; then erase the pencil. During this stage, you can add the finer details, such as the center of your flower. Use the practice strokes you created in step 1, with the open-ended ovals and "C" shapes building on each other.

Step 4

Now that you have a clear view of the outline of your cosmos, you can begin shading. Use the "flick" hatching technique to add subtle curved lines to the petals and straight lines to for shadows on the parts of the petals that lie completely in shade. Single lines extend the length of the stem and petals to add depth.

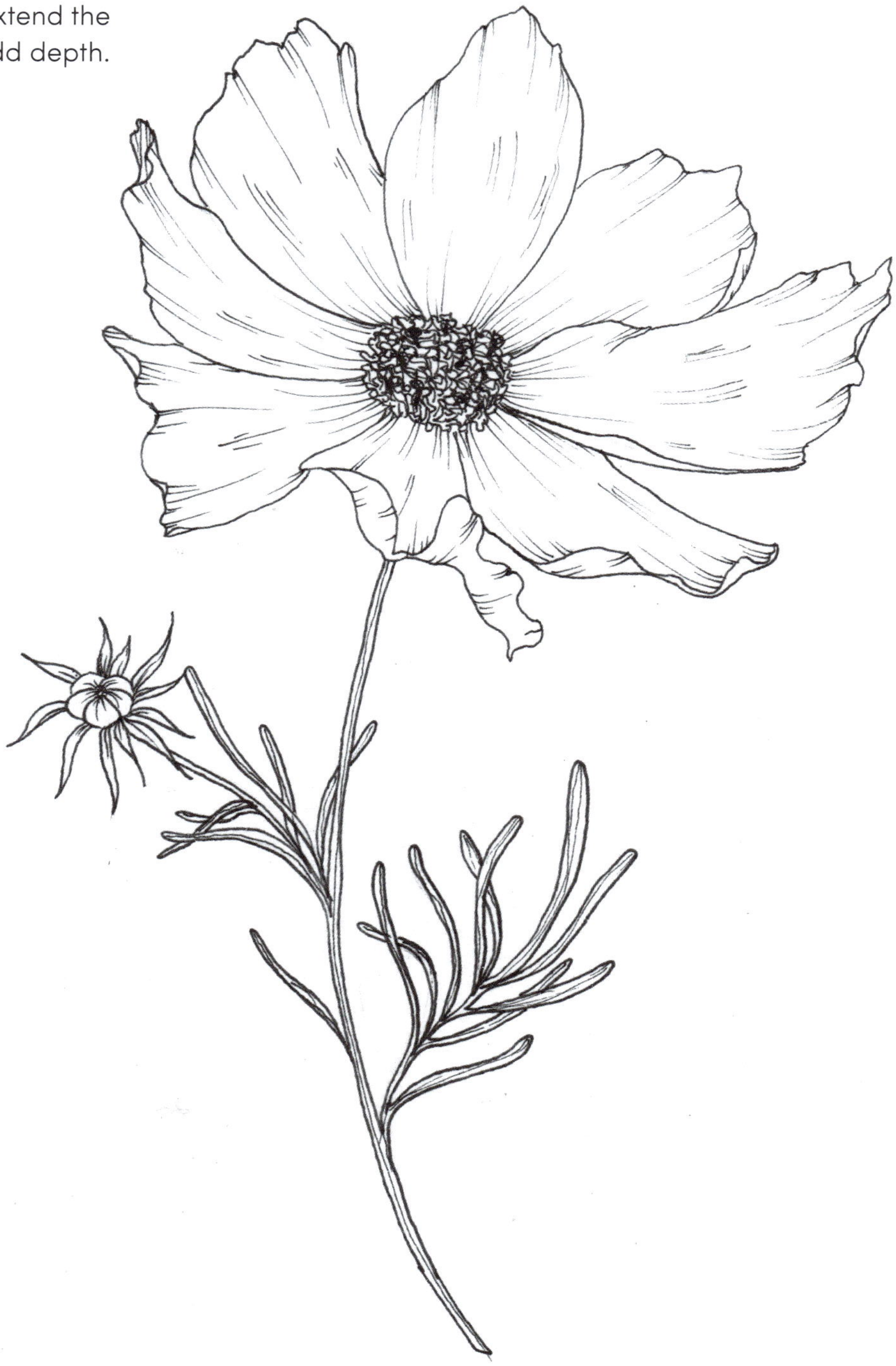

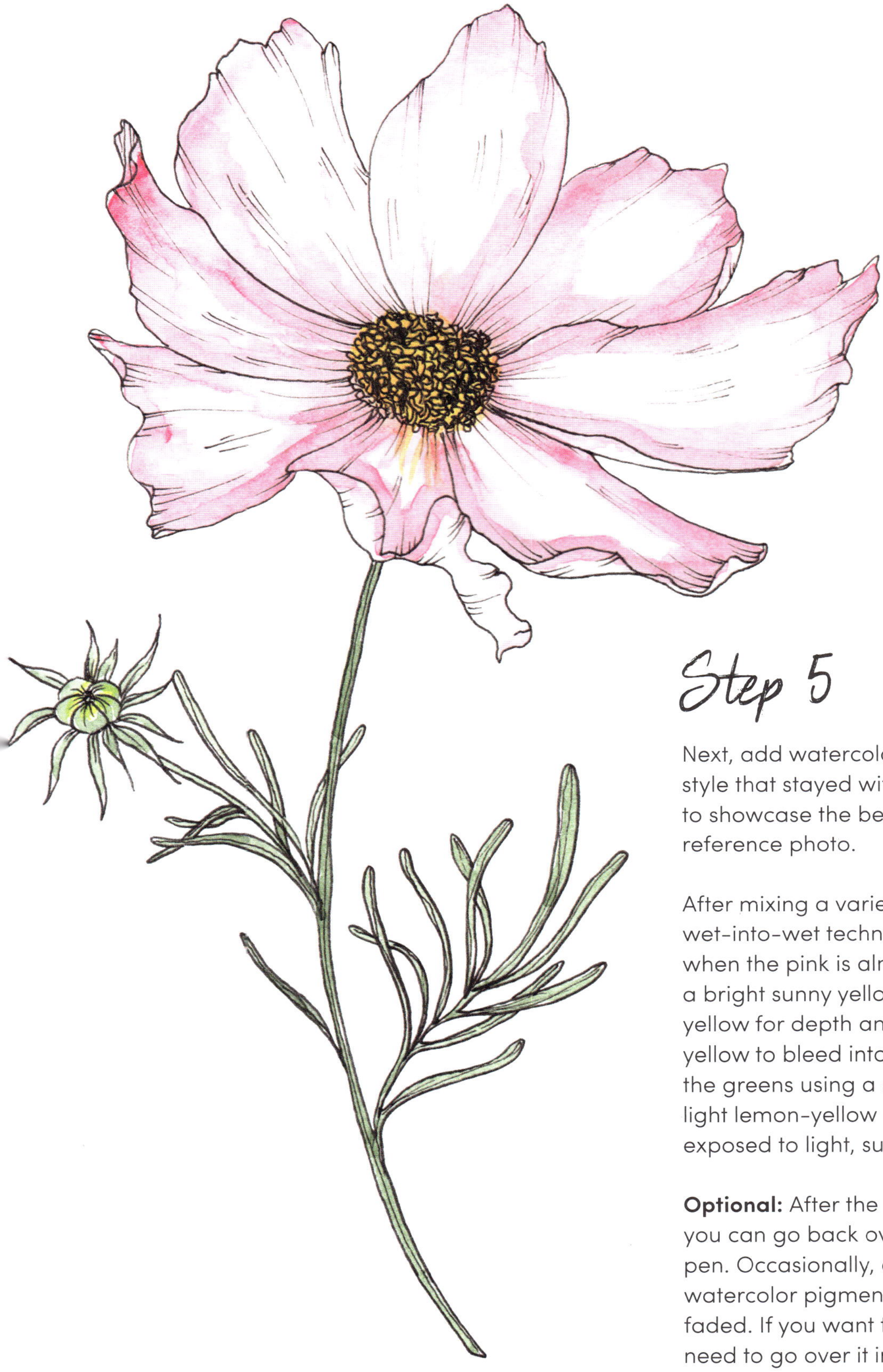

Step 5

Next, add watercolor. I chose a loose watercolor style that stayed within the lines of my ink drawing to showcase the beautiful coloring seen in the reference photo.

After mixing a variety of pinks and white, use the wet-into-wet technique to outline the petals. Next, when the pink is almost dry, paint the center using a bright sunny yellow; then add a darker ochre yellow for depth and dimension. Allow some of the yellow to bleed into the still-barely wet pinks. Paint the greens using a size 2 round brush. Add a very light lemon-yellow layer in the areas that are more exposed to light, such as the bud.

Optional: After the paint has dried completely, you can go back over the center ink with fineliner pen. Occasionally, depending on how dense your watercolor pigment is, the black can appear faded. If you want the black ink to "pop," you may need to go over it in the denser spaces where your watercolor extends past the ink lines.

California Poppy

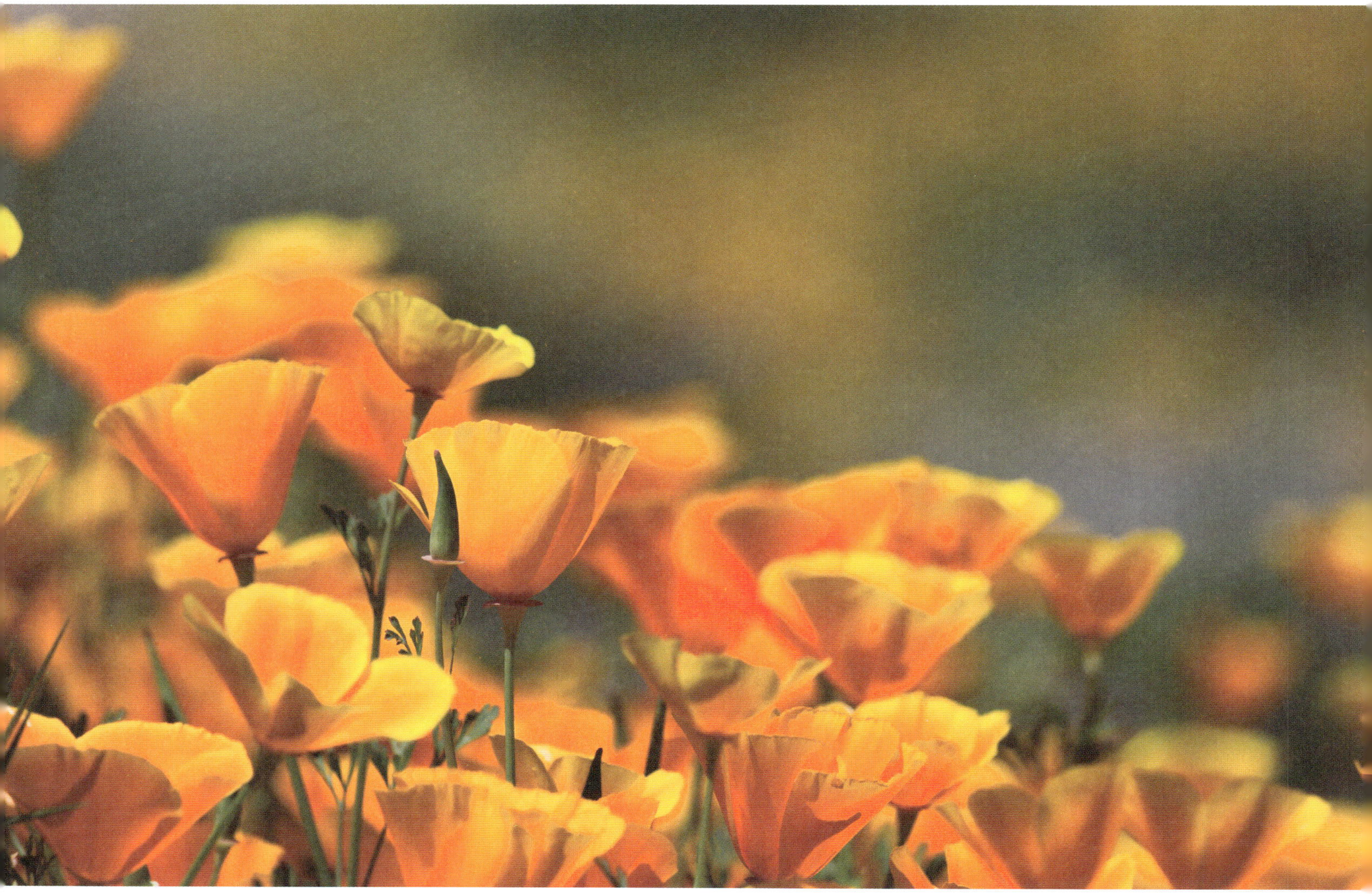

To create a California poppy, you can use this photo, which shows a clustering of California poppies featuring plenty of different angles, shapes, and stages of bloom.

Step 1

Observing your reference photo, practice outlining the petals and leaves from different angles. You may trace over these images using tracing paper, but I recommend that you practice drawing freehand. You can use the practice images provided here as a jumping-off point, but there is truly so much variety that you can create with a California poppy.

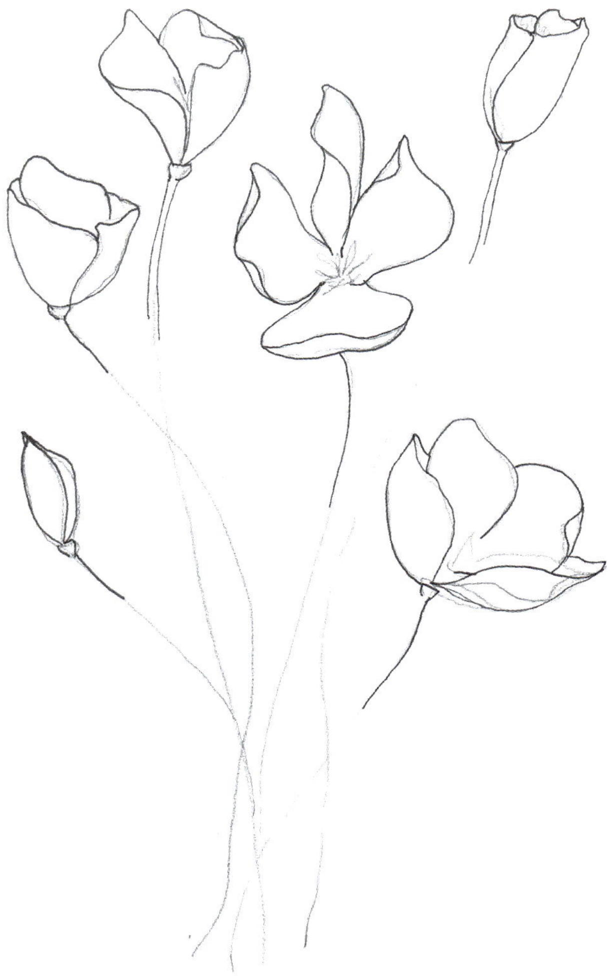

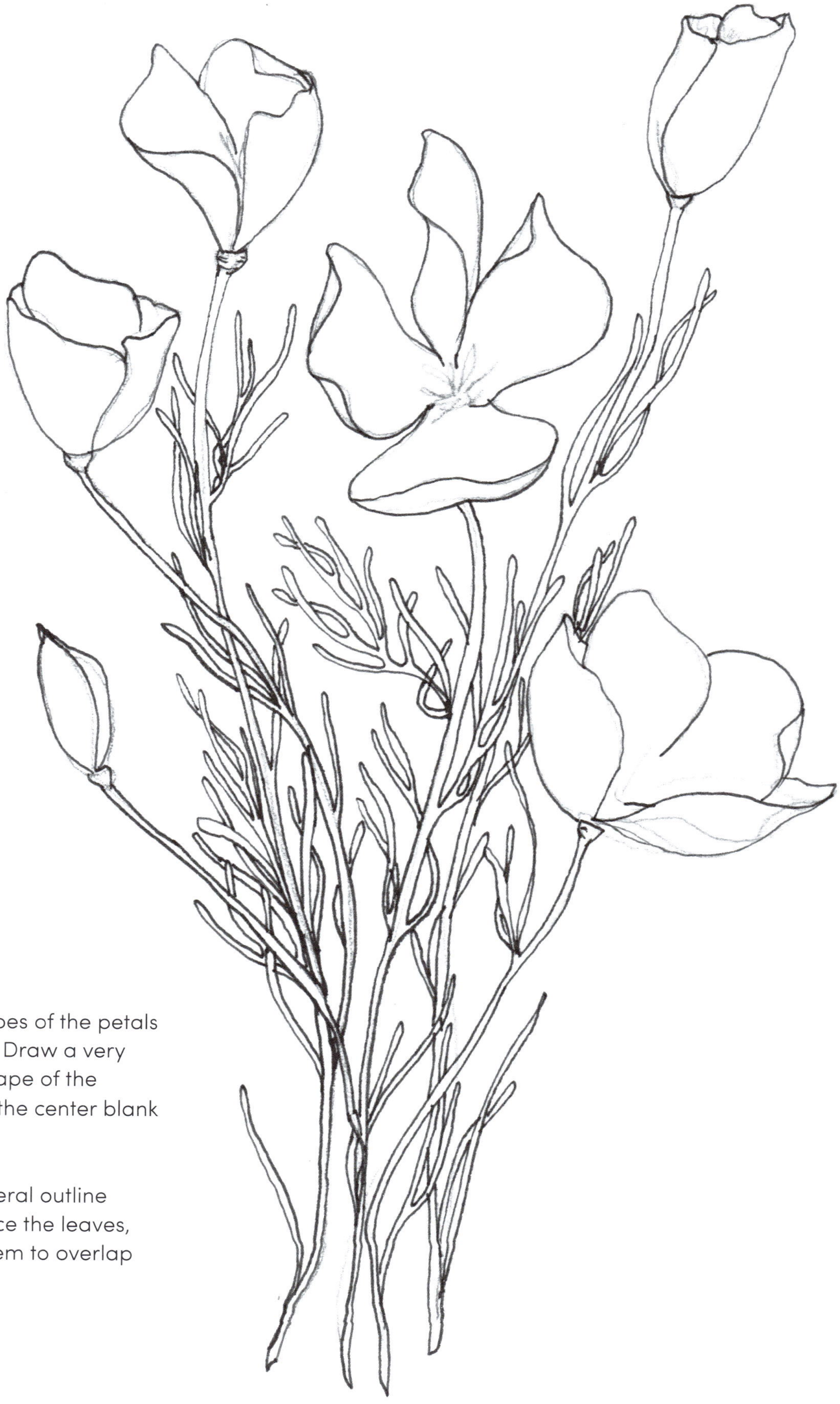

Step 2

Combine the angles and shapes of the petals and leaves in a pencil sketch. Draw a very light outline of the general shape of the clustering of flowers, leaving the center blank to add details later.

Optional: You can add a general outline shape where you want to place the leaves, especially if you would like them to overlap the top of the stems.

The more overlap and curvature you create with your leaves, the more dynamic your piece will feel, creating the illusion of depth and movement.

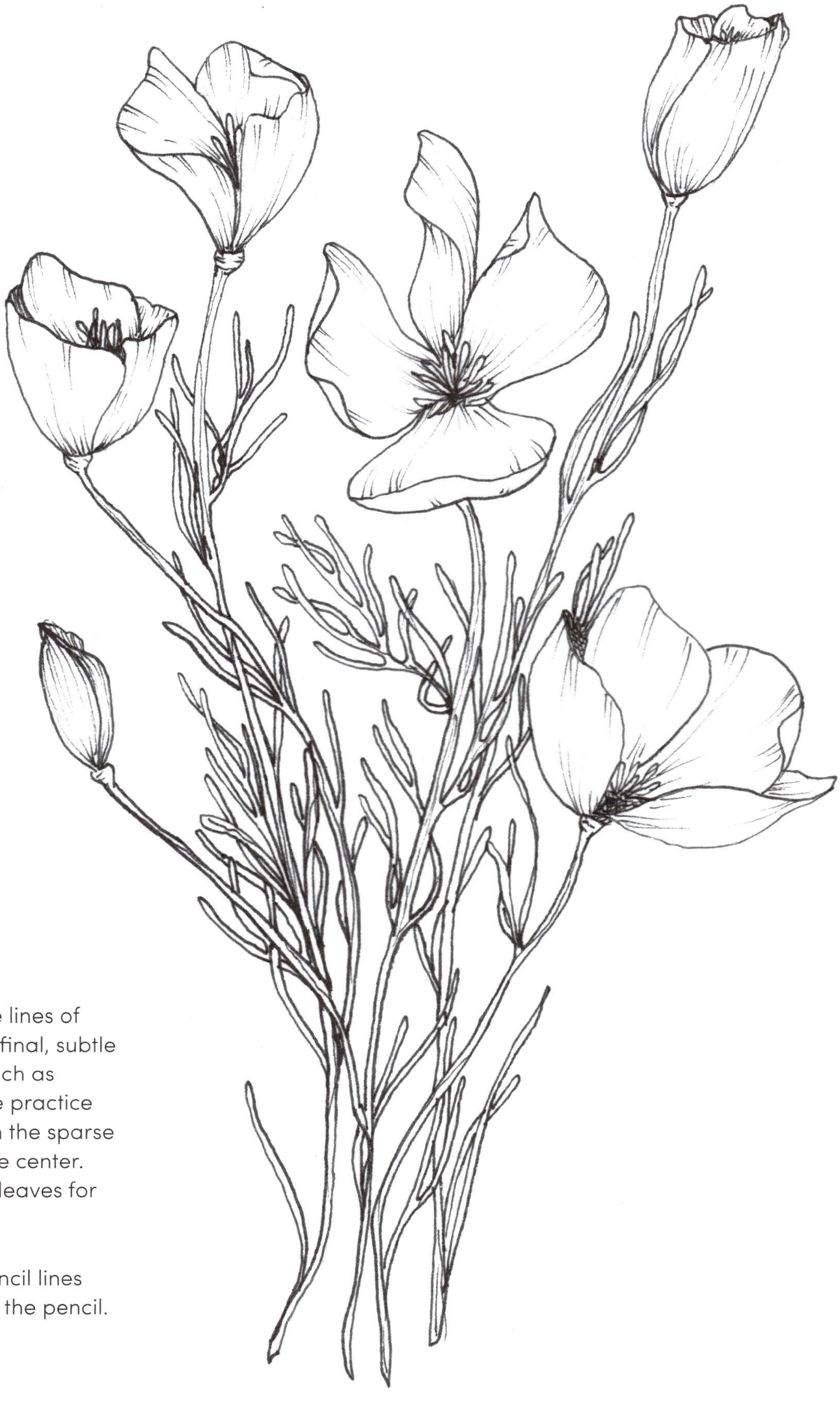

Step 3

Use a fineliner pen to go over the lines of your pencil guide and make any final, subtle adjustments. Add finer details, such as the center of the flower, using the practice strokes you created in step 1, with the sparse long ovals branching out from the center. You can add the outlines of your leaves for more detail.

Once you have gone over the pencil lines and allowed the ink to dry, erase the pencil.

Step 4

Add clean water to the page. Then dab in a mixture of blues, leaving the flower petals clear of water and pigment. Once the paint dries, you can leave the flowers white or add orange.

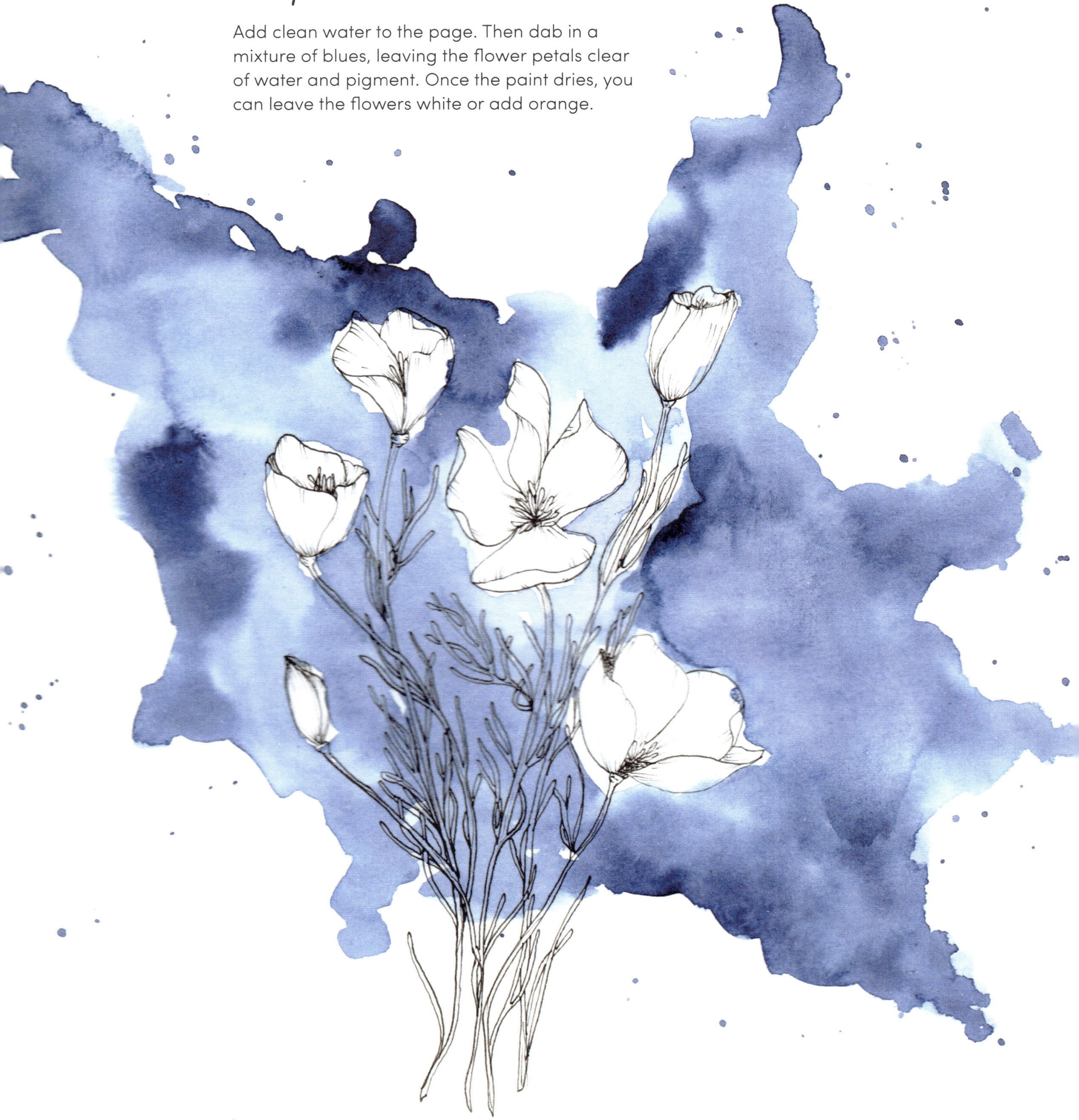

Step 5

Add white flecks to the blue background to mimic a galaxy or sky, and use orange and white in the flower petals.

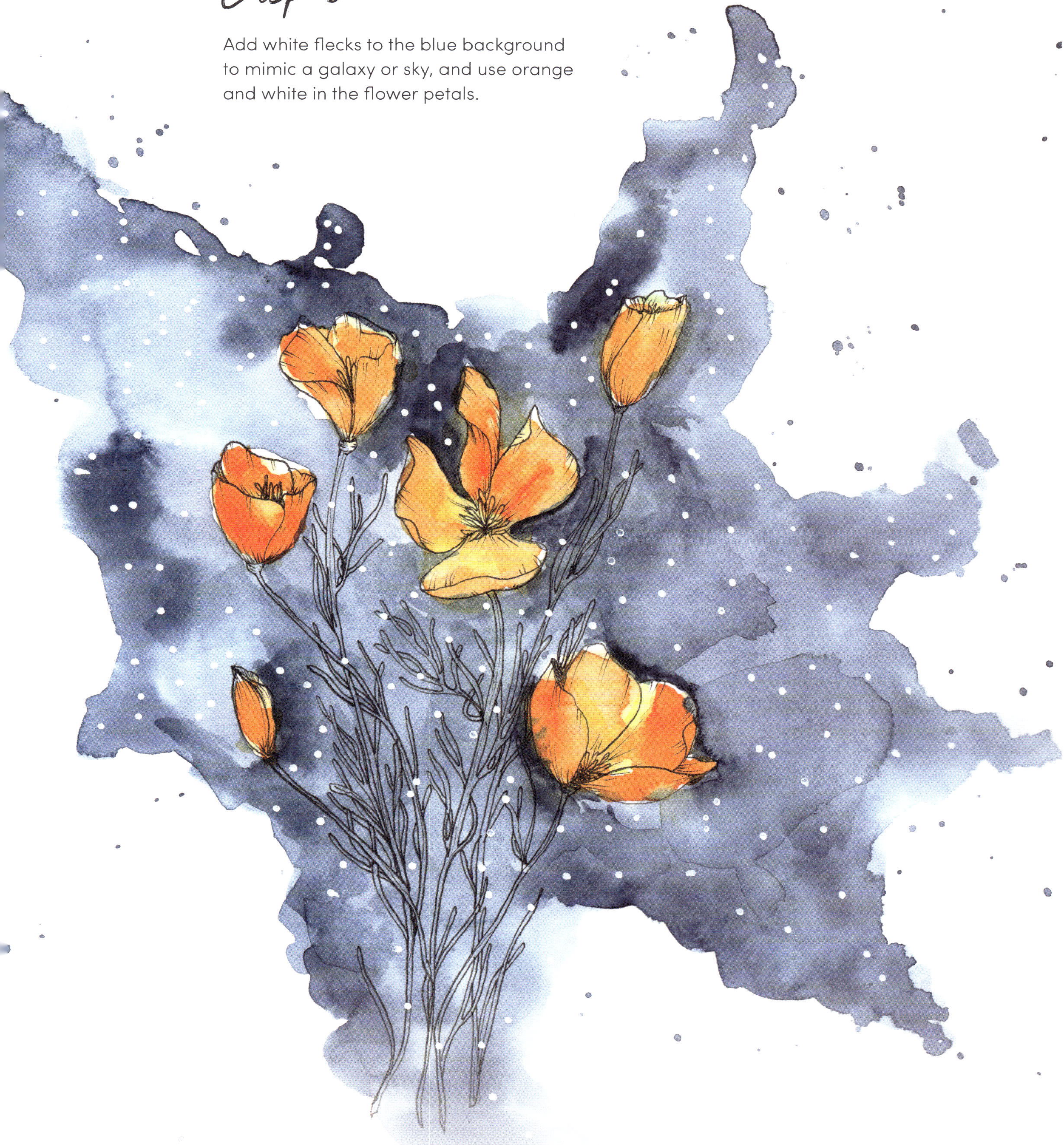

Red Poppy

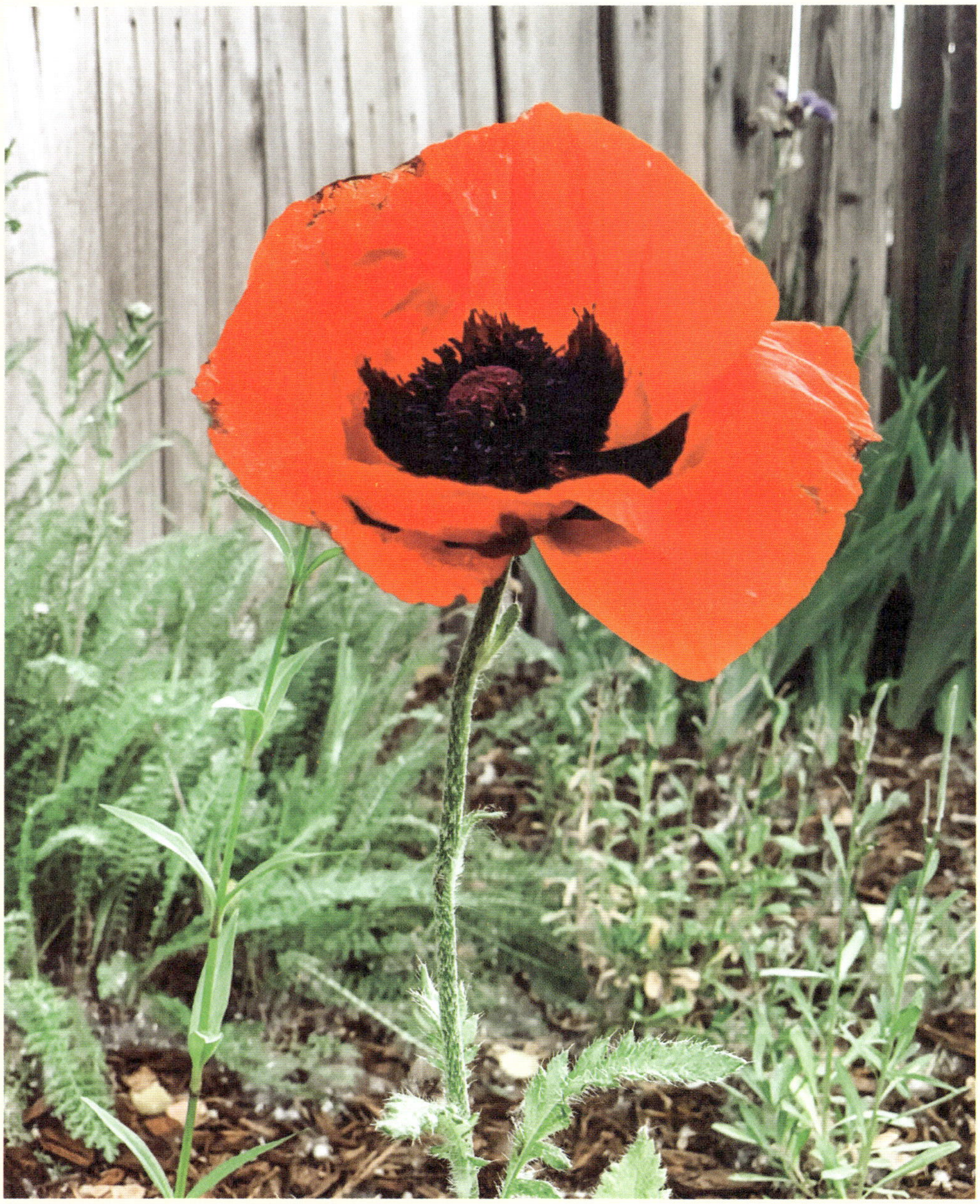

I took this reference photo in my garden this year. It shows the whole flower, the petals, and the detailed center of the poppy. Note the fuzzy little stem!

Step 1

Using the reference photos, practice outlining the petals and leaves from different angles.

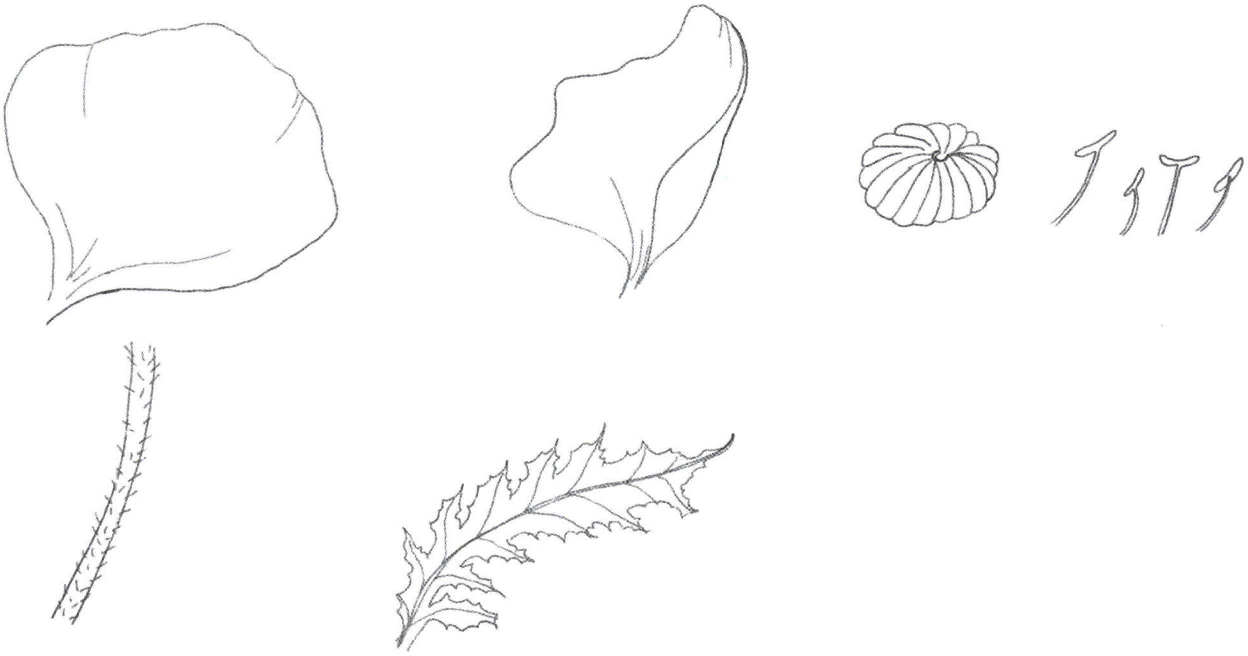

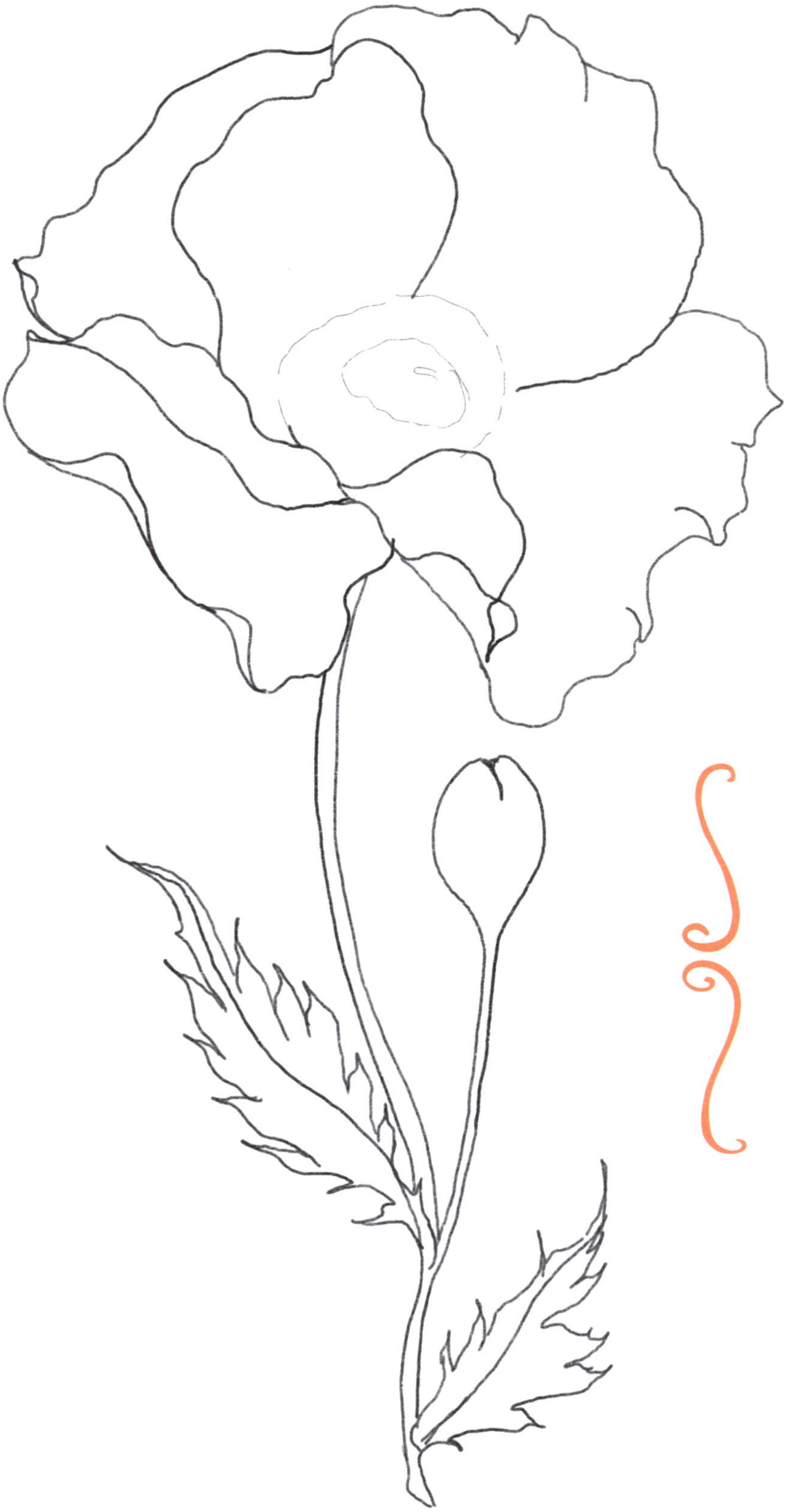

Step 2

Draw a very basic outline of the general shape of the petals, as well as the placement of the leaves and bud. Leave the center blank; you'll add these details later.

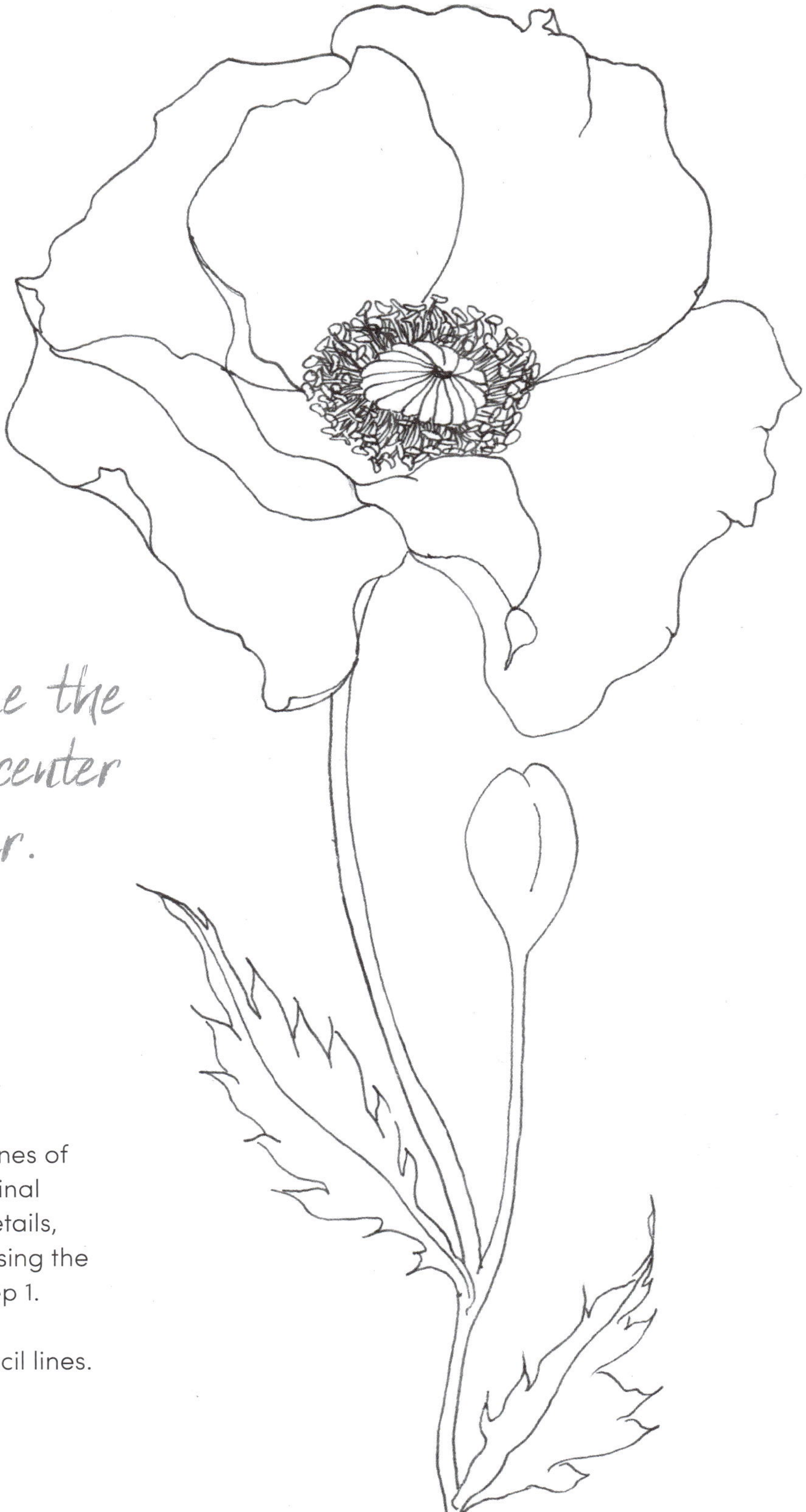

Overlap and intertwine the tendrils around the center part of the flower.

Step 3

With a fineliner pen, go over the lines of your pencil guide and make any final adjustments. Also add the finer details, such as the center of the flower, using the practice strokes you created in step 1.

Let the ink dry; then erase the pencil lines.

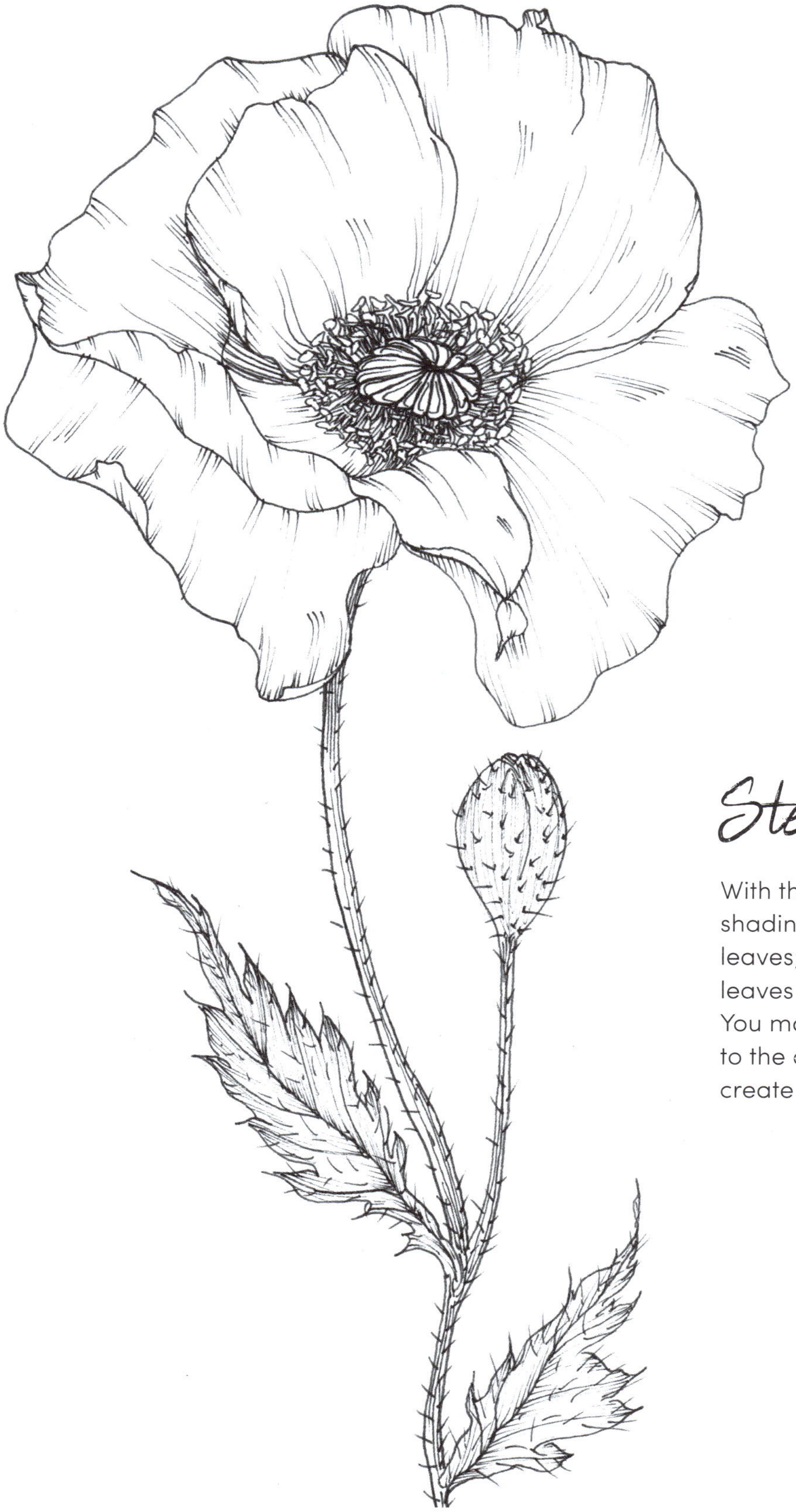

Step 4

With the "flick" hatching technique, add shading to the petals. Sparsely shade the leaves; then add little flicks along the stem and leaves to denote the fuzzy little bits of the plant. You may also want to add some subtle shading to the center of the flower, which will help create density in the middle.

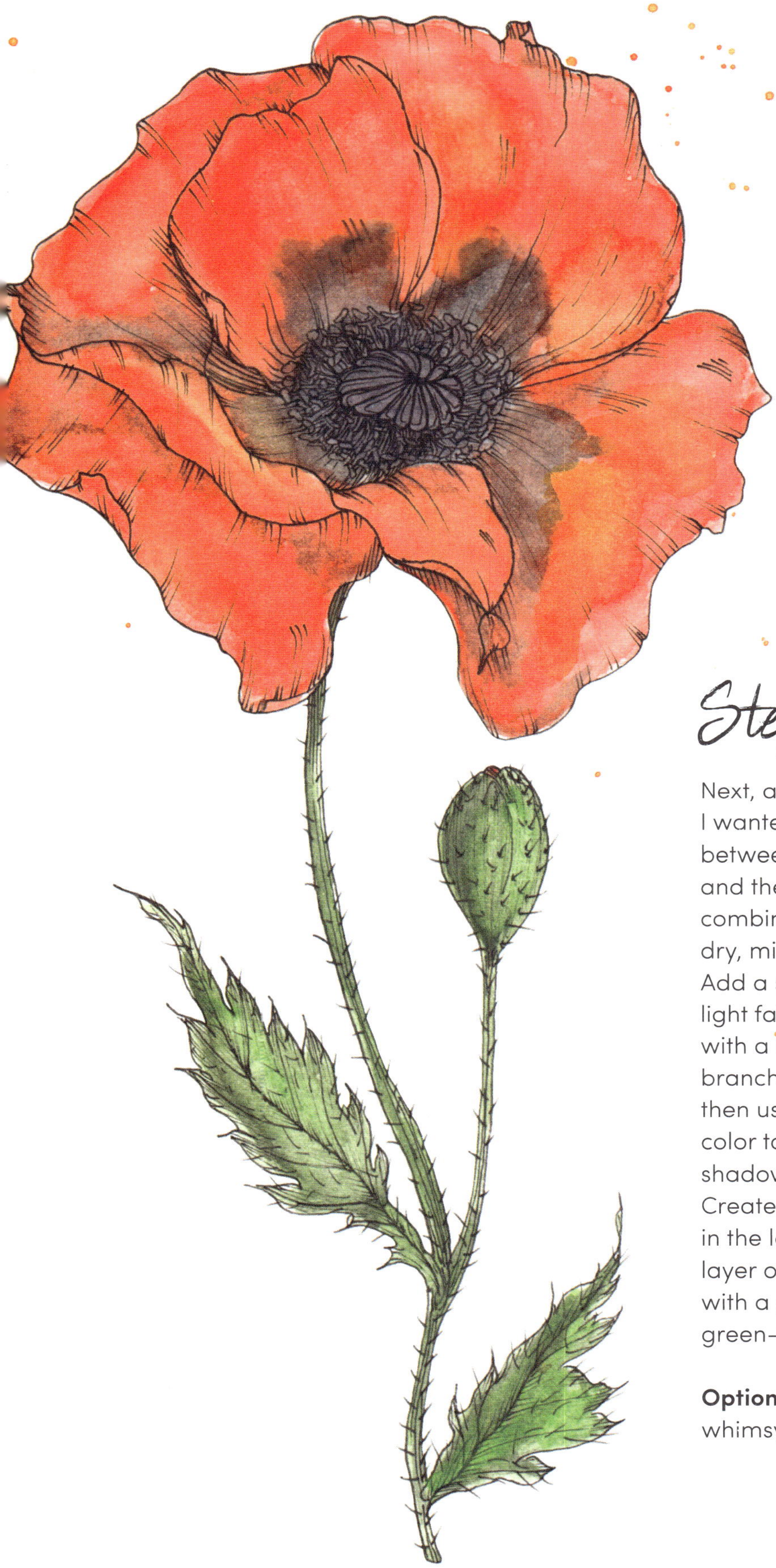

Step 5

Next, add watercolor. For this piece, I wanted to showcase the contrast between the black center of the flower and the surrounding red petals. Using a combination of wet-into-wet and wet-on-dry, mix different reds to create a base. Add a splash of light orange where the light falls on the petals. Paint the center with a dark purple-gray and allow it to branch out into the middle of the petals; then use a lighter version of the center color to extend into the areas where shadows fall densely amongst the petals. Create an interplay of light and shadow in the leaves and bulb by painting a base layer of green. Let it dry; then come in with a gray in the shadows and lighter green-yellow where the light falls.

Optional: Orange-red splashes can add whimsy to this piece.

Anemone

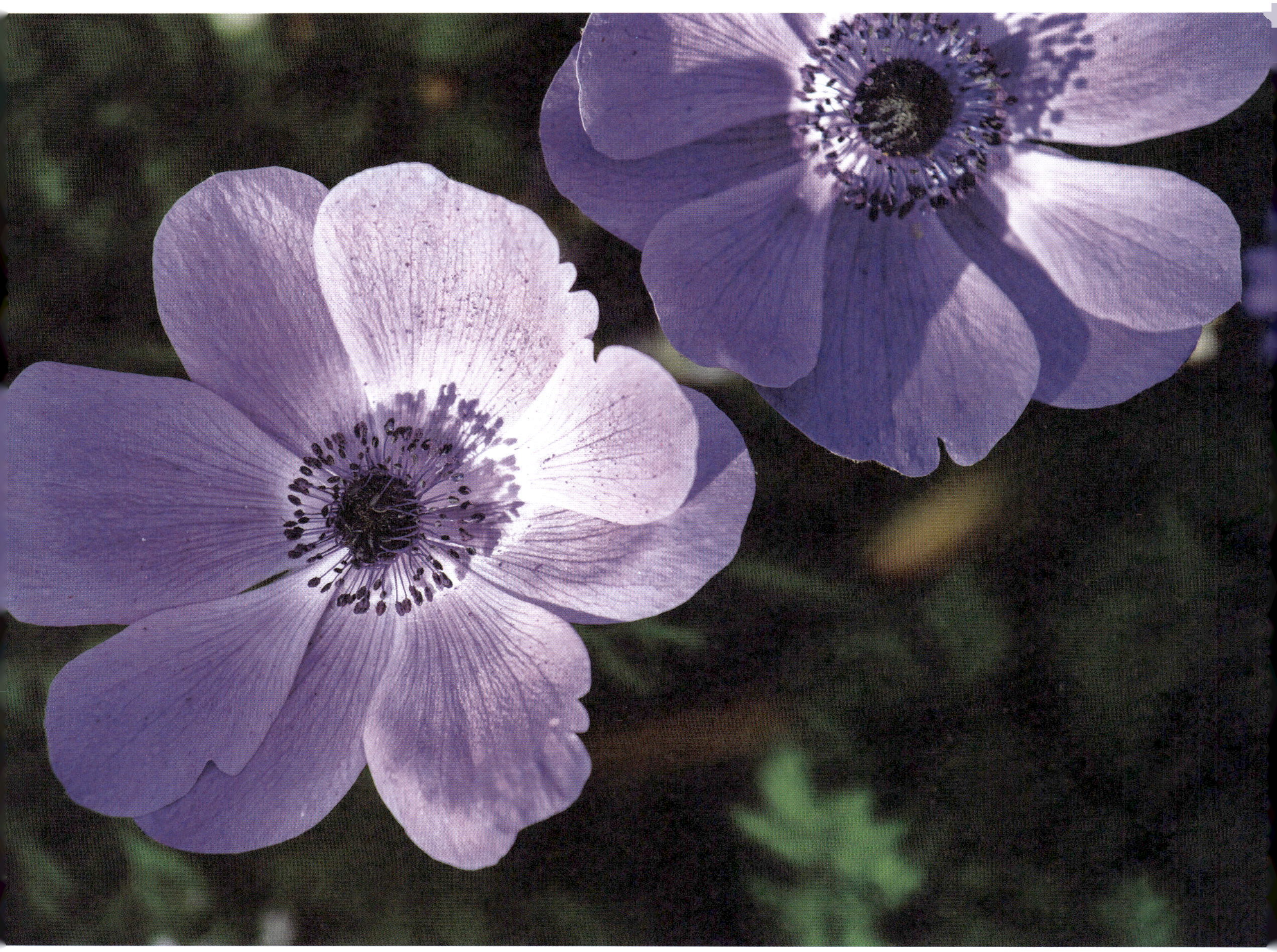

Let's use the shapes from these two reference photos to create anemones. I planted these in my garden last year, but I haven't had any luck getting them to bloom again, sadly.

Step 1

Using your reference photos, practice outlining the petals and leaves from different angles. The petal shape is very straightforward, and you will create the dynamic feeling in these flowers using shading, the angles of the petals, and the detailed centers.

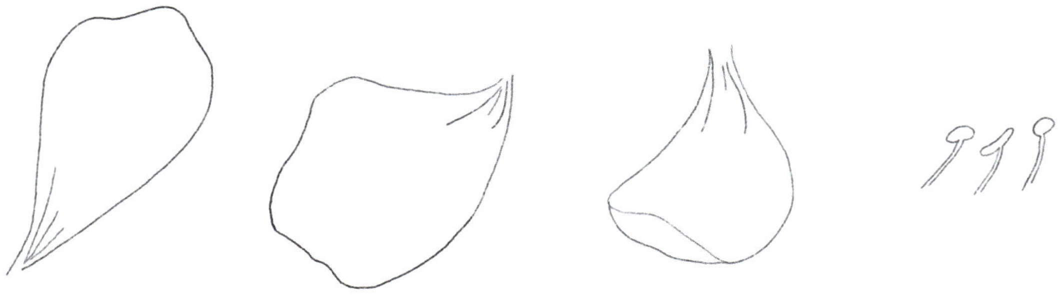

Step 2

Combine the angles and shapes of the anemone petals and centers using a pencil sketch. You can draw a rough outline of the general shape of the petals, leaving the center blank to add details later and placing two circles to note where the two components that make up the center will lie.

At this stage, you can also add a couple of leaves to each flower, though I think they would look equally beautiful without them, depending on the style you want to create.

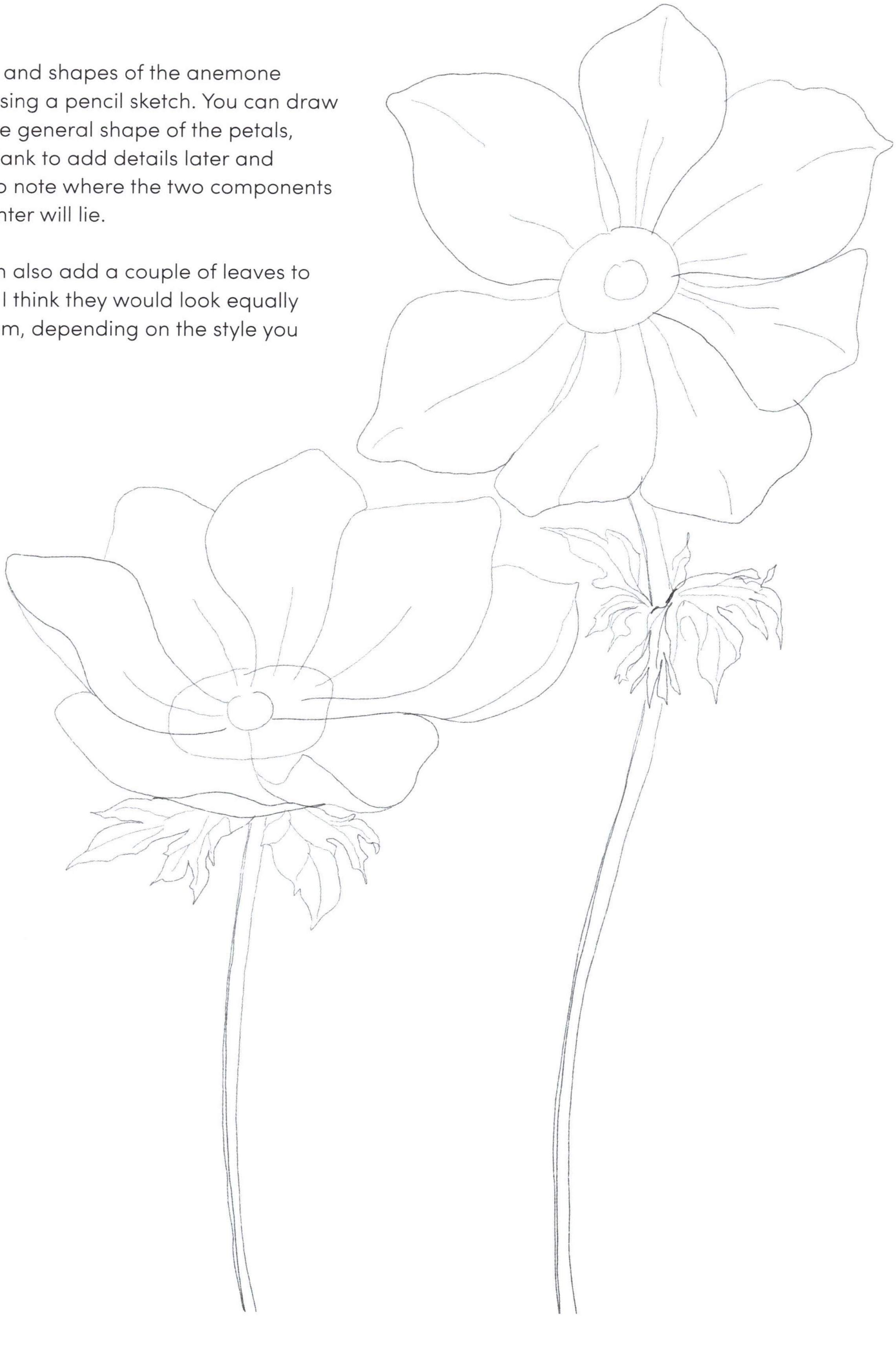

Step 3

Come in with a fineliner pen, going over the lines of your pencil guide and making any final adjustments. Add fine details, such as the center of the flower, with the sparse long ovals branching out from the center. To create the denser center part, use small, upward, overlapping flicks.

Once the ink is dry, erase your pencil marks.

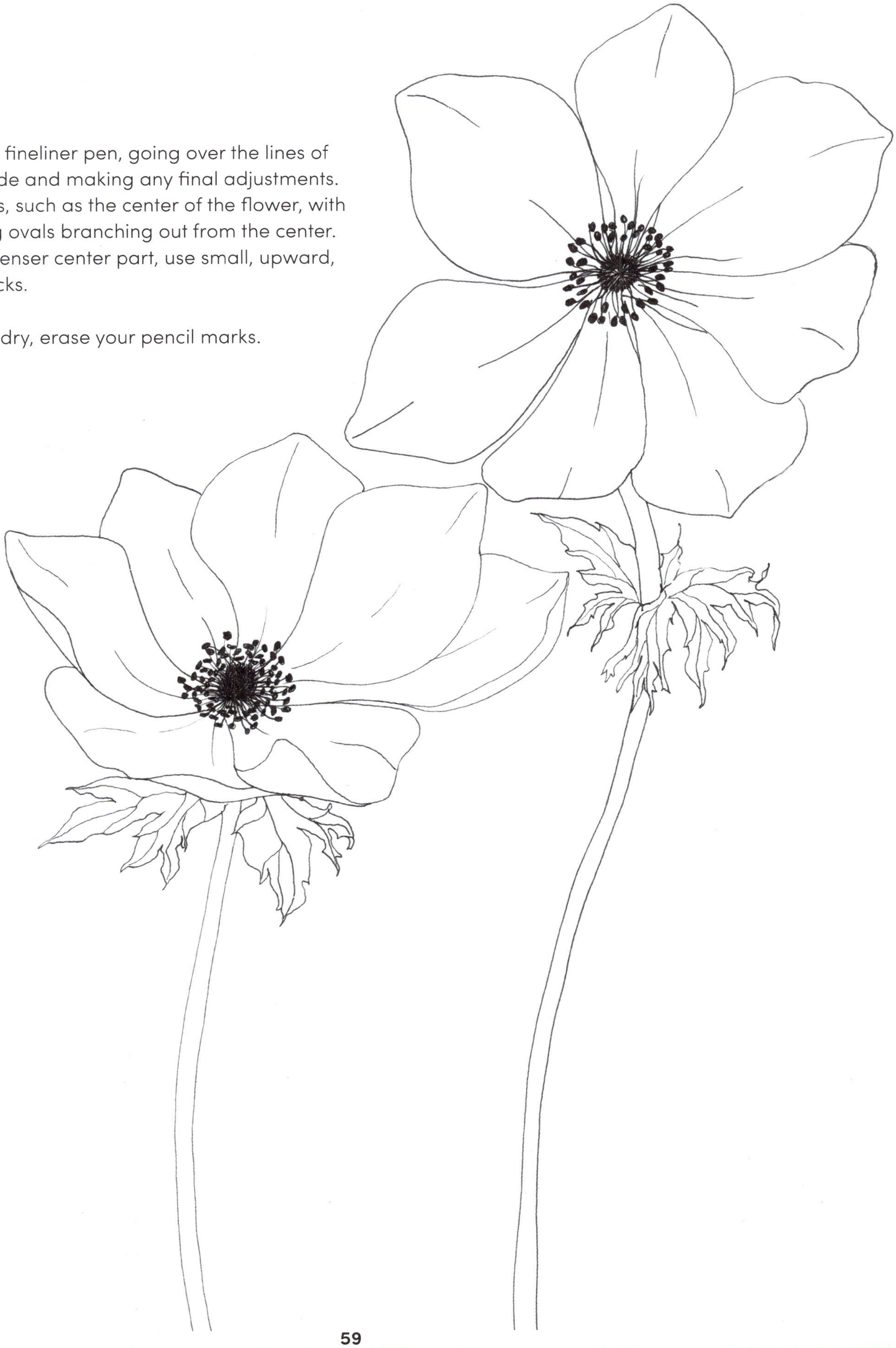

Step 4

Begin shading, ensuring that the curve of the pen flicks follows the lines of the petals. Use sparse shading to convey the flower's delicacy, and avoid adding too much density to the petals, as they will be white. To keep a minimalistic feel, shade the stems with straight, clean lines down the length of the flower, and do not shade the petals beyond the veins of the leaves added in step 3.

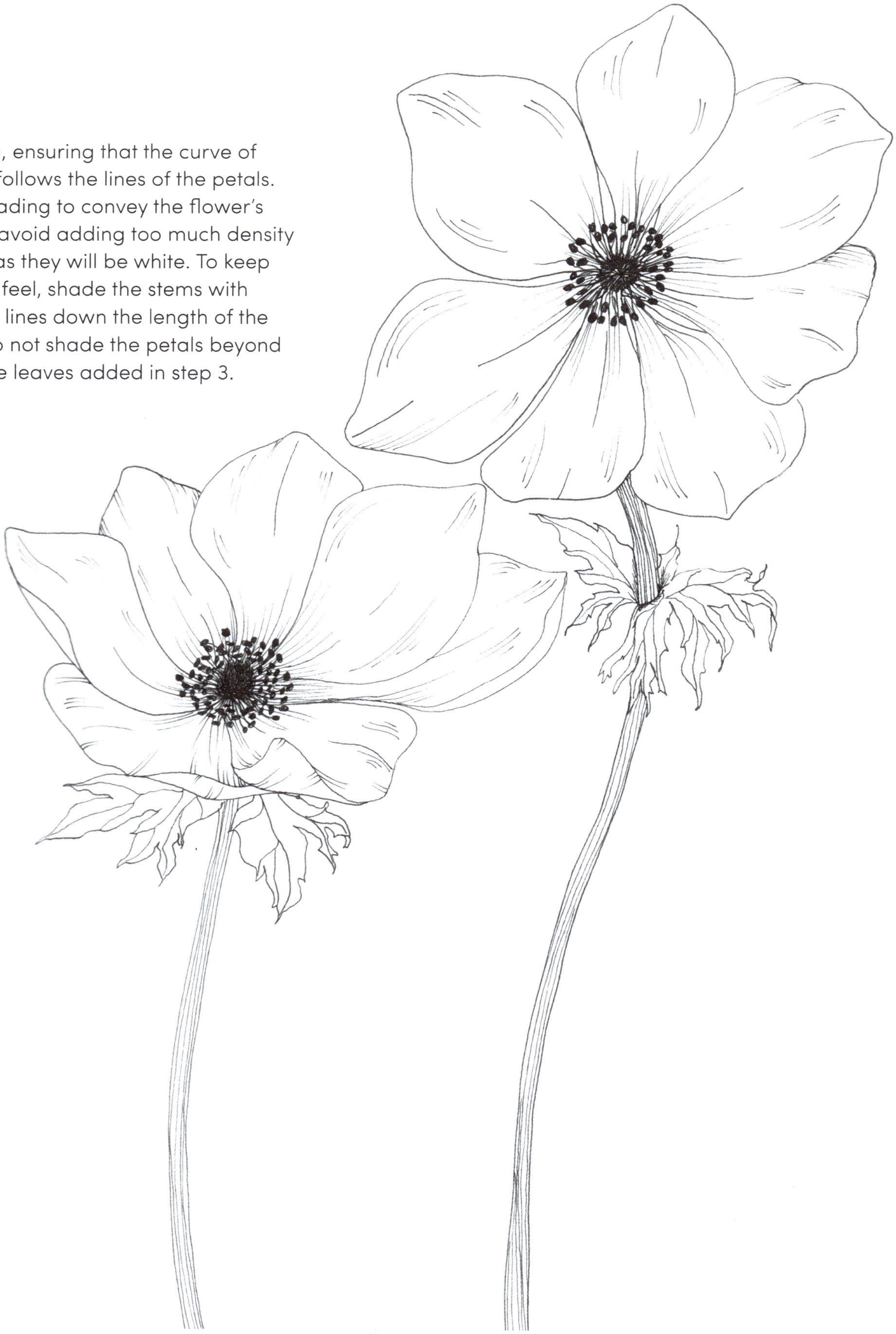

Step 5

Finally, add watercolor. I loved the delicacy and clean, modern feel of this piece and decided to continue this theme by making my anemones white. If you choose to add a brighter color or want to depict a different style, I recommend adding more shading to your anemones so that your ink lines will pop through the color.

I blended Payne's gray with a dab of purple to create subtle shading. Using plenty of water and very little pigment, add pigment to the page using the wet-on-dry technique. Shade the petals depending on where shadows should fall, keeping in mind that subtle works best with white flowers.

Paint the stems inside the lines of the ink drawing. You can create a looser, more whimsical feel by keeping parts of the leaves white.

Optional:
Add watercolor splashes for more whimsy in this piece.

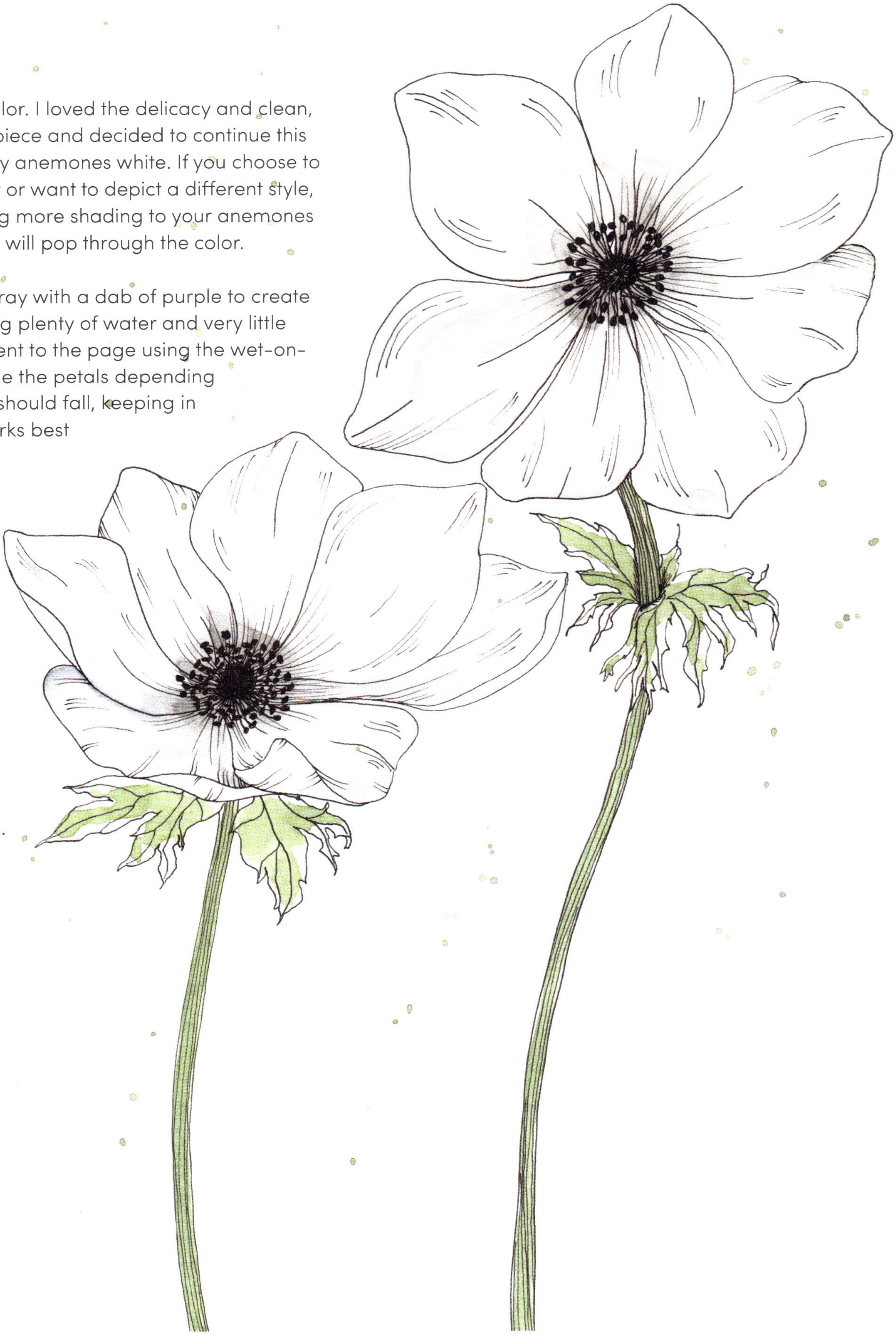

Wild Rose

Use the shapes in these reference photos to create your final piece of a wild rose.

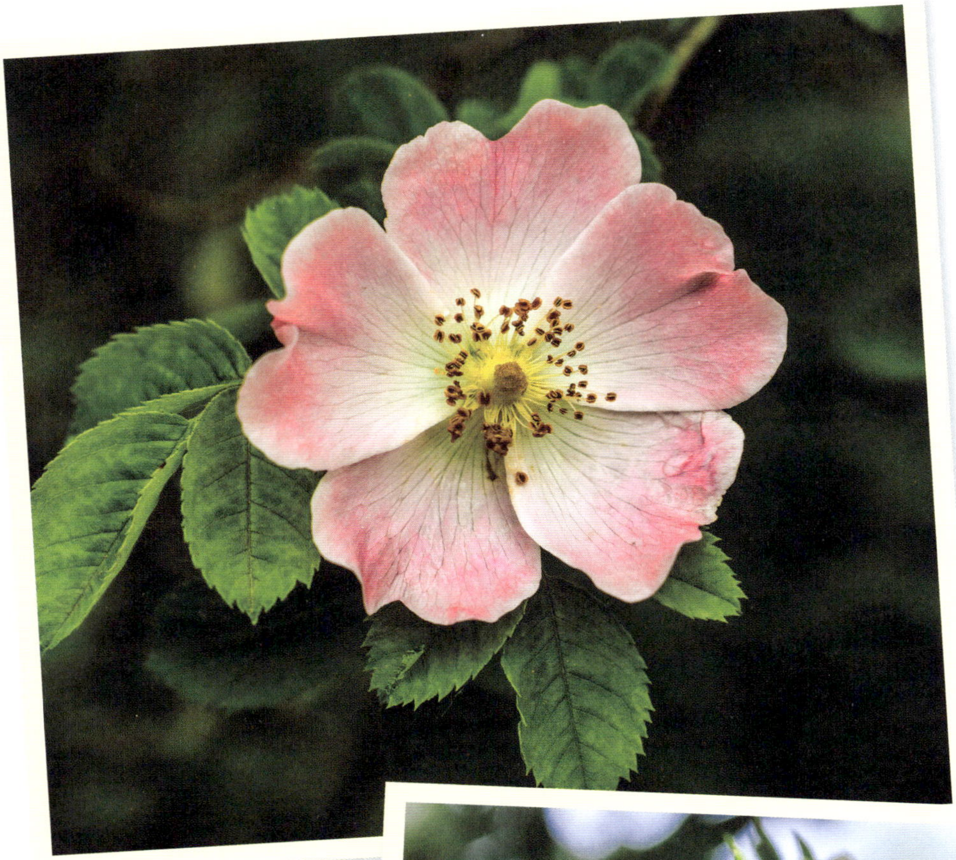

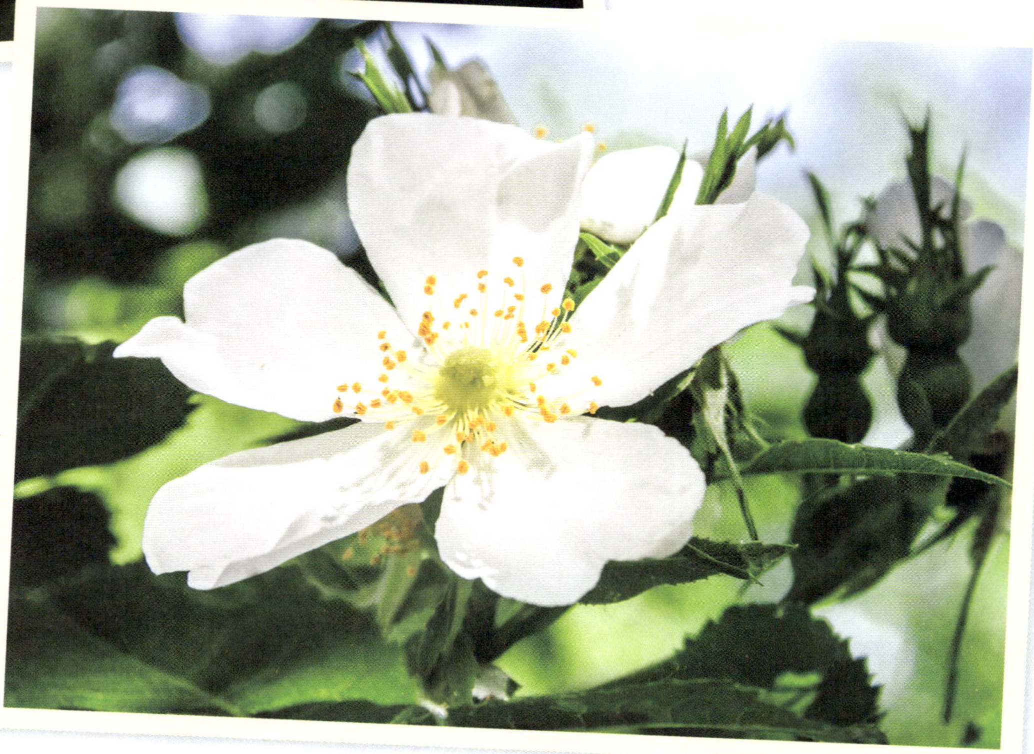

Step 1

Practice outlining the petals and leaves from different angles. The petal shape is very straightforward, and you will create the dynamic feeling in this flower using shading, the angle of the petals, and the detailed center. Note how many leaves branch off each stem.

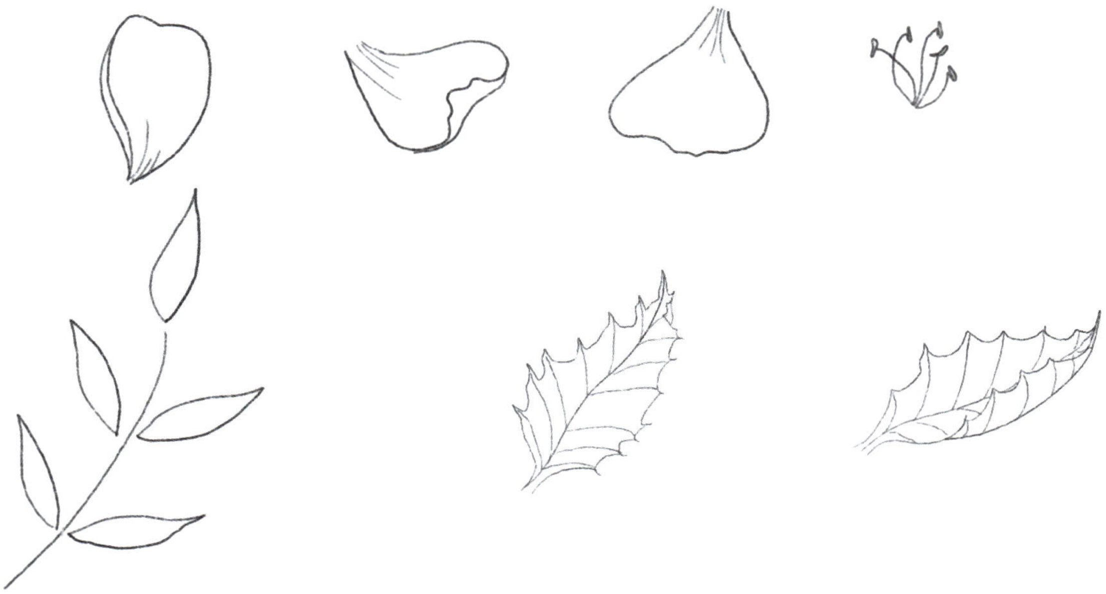

Step 2

With a pencil sketch, combine the basic shapes in a layout of your choosing. I decided to combine the two flowers with relatively sparse leaves in the background. Create a rough sketch of your petals and determine the leaf placement, leaving the center blank to add details when you come in with ink.

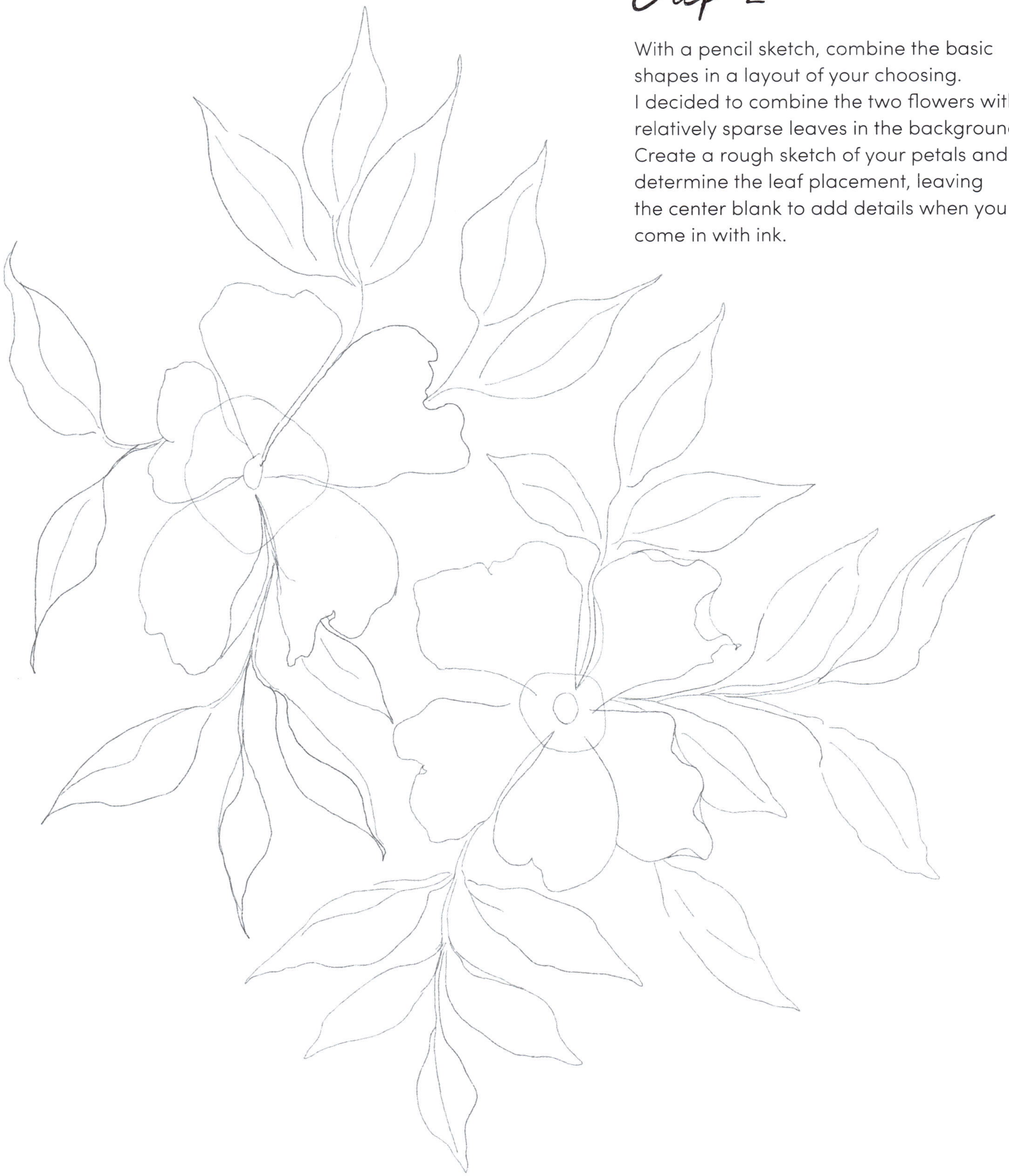

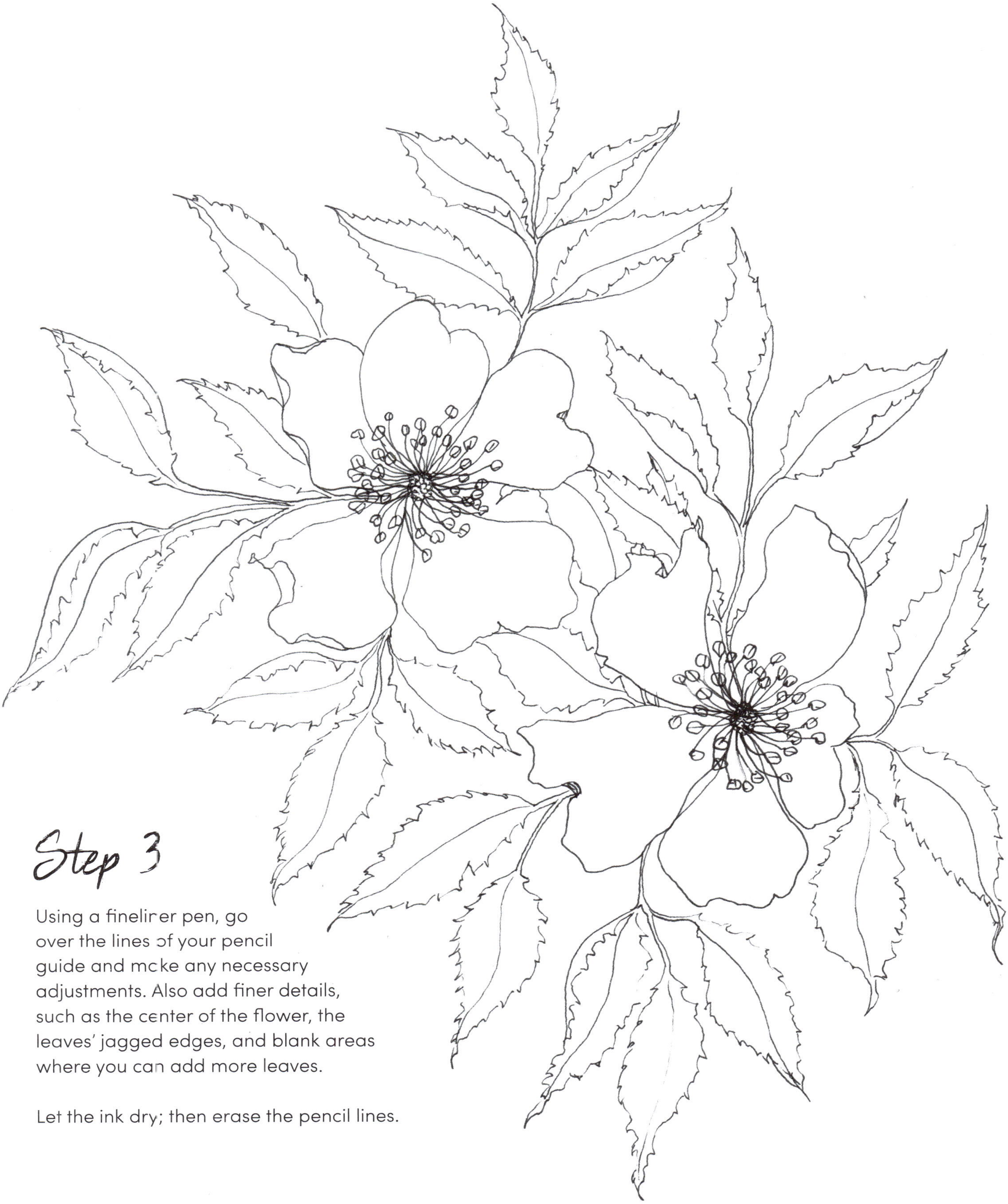

Step 3

Using a fineliner pen, go over the lines of your pencil guide and make any necessary adjustments. Also add finer details, such as the center of the flower, the leaves' jagged edges, and blank areas where you can add more leaves.

Let the ink dry; then erase the pencil lines.

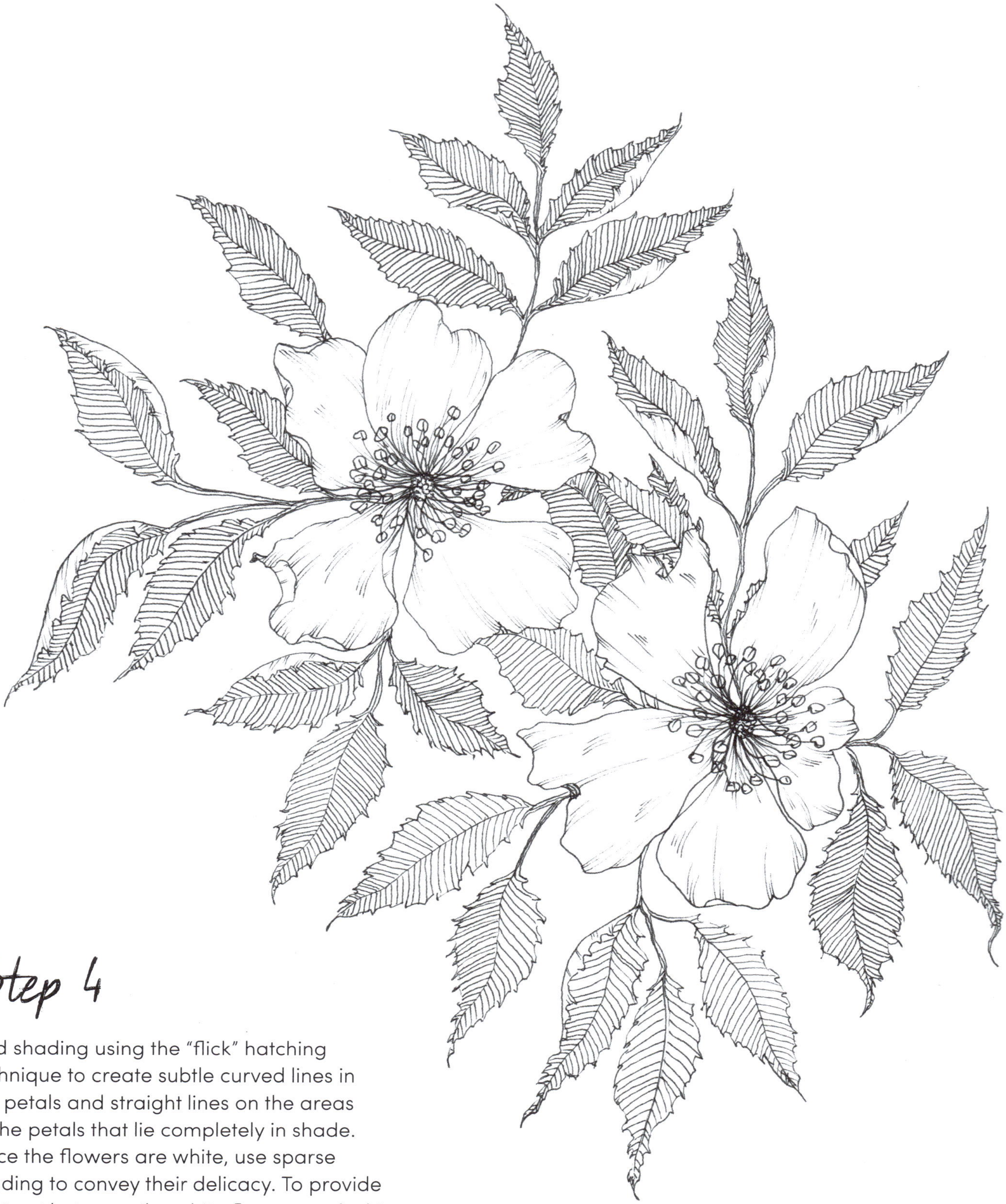

Step 4

Add shading using the "flick" hatching technique to create subtle curved lines in the petals and straight lines on the areas of the petals that lie completely in shade. Since the flowers are white, use sparse shading to convey their delicacy. To provide contrast between the white flowers and white background of the paper, shade the leaves with straight lines that are fairly close together.

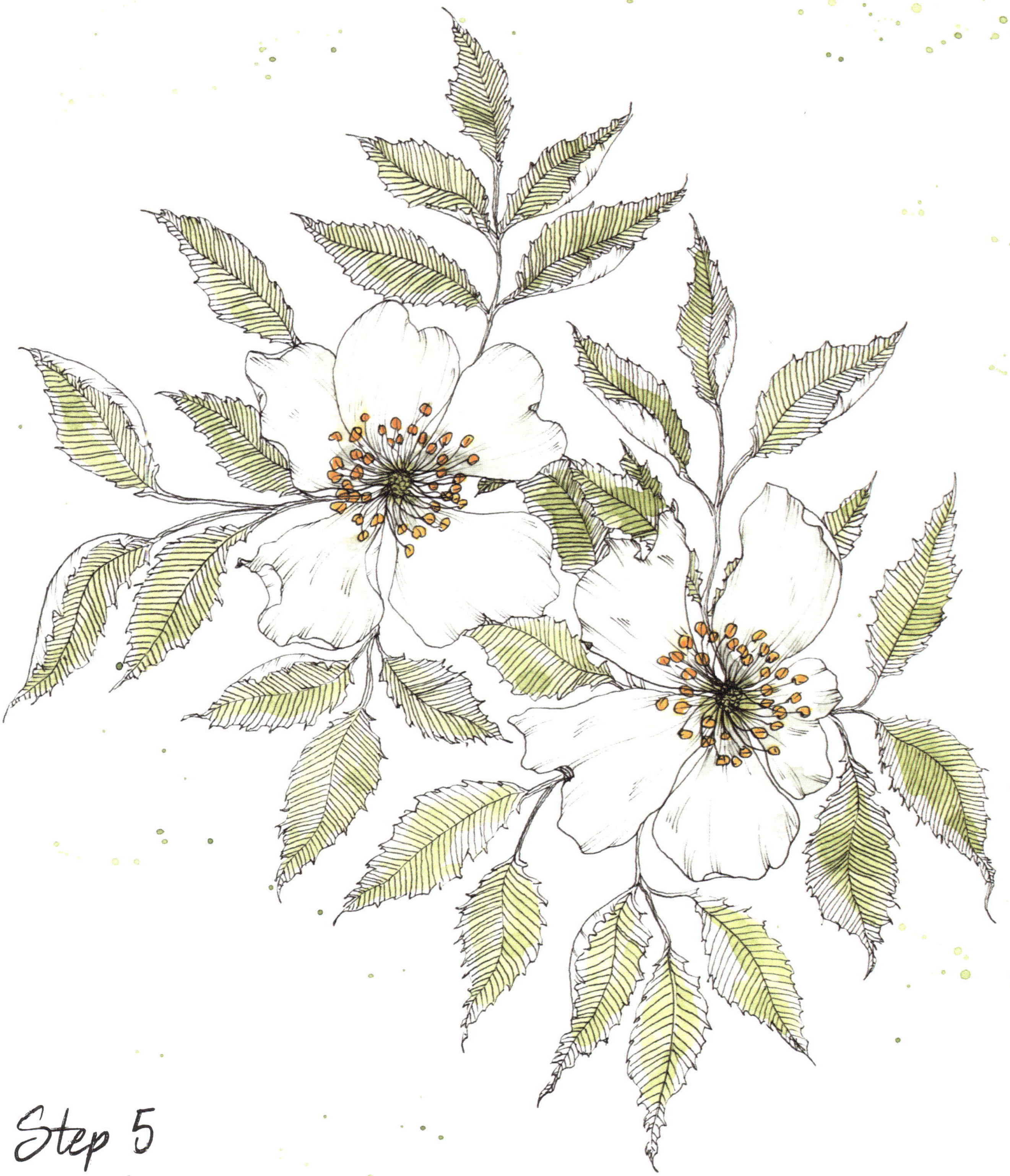

Step 5

I blended Payne's gray watercolor with a dab of yellow to create subtle shading. Using plenty of water, very little pigment, and the wet-on-dry technique, add pigment to the page. Place the shading in the petals where shadows would fall. Then use a size 2 round brush to paint the center details of the flower with a combination of warm, bright yellow and ochre yellow.

Paint the leaves using a mixture of mossy green, Payne's gray, and a touch of lemon yellow.

Optional: Use watercolor splashes to add further whimsy to this piece.

Agapanthus

Begin by reviewing the basic shapes that make up an agapanthus. I used reference images from the internet to determine the shapes in the flower and its globular form, and I chose not to include leaves in this piece and instead to showcase the detailed flower.

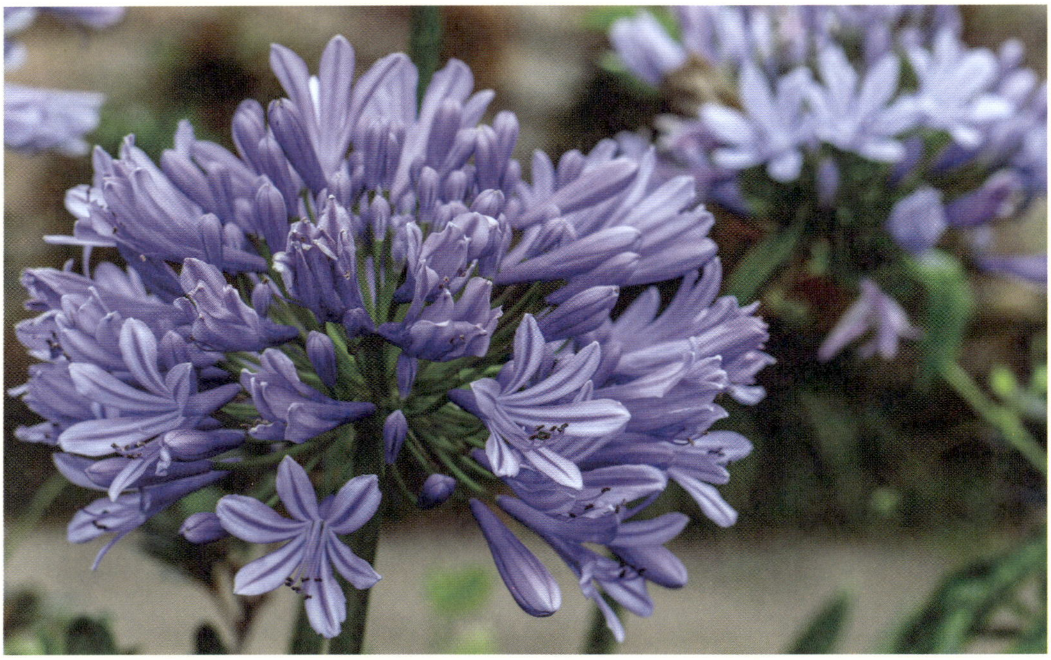

Step 1

Practice outlining the flowers from different angles and at various stages of bloom. The petals have a very straightforward shape, and you will create the dynamic feeling and round shape of this flower using overlapping components.

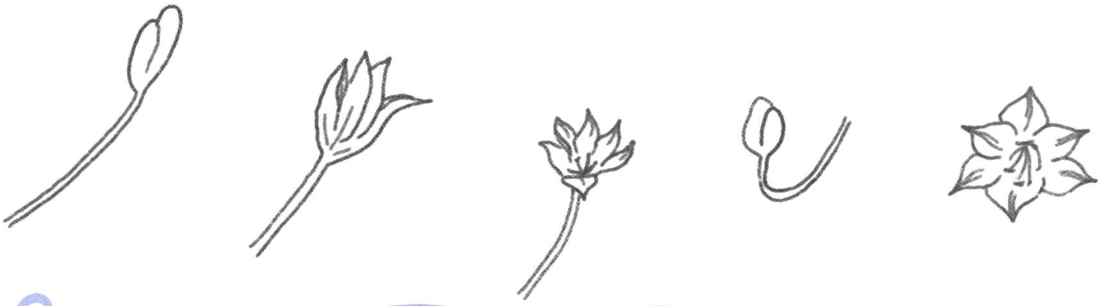

Step 2

Combine the angles and shapes of the agapanthus in a pencil sketch, or if you feel you have a strong understanding of the flower's basic shapes, go straight to ink lines. The flower itself looks complex, but it is made up of simple parts. Start from your center point, and draw all of the individual stem/flower components branching off from there. Alternate their directions, curves, overlap, and stages of flower bloom.

If you create a pencil sketch, add ink lines afterward. Let them dry; then erase the pencil lines.

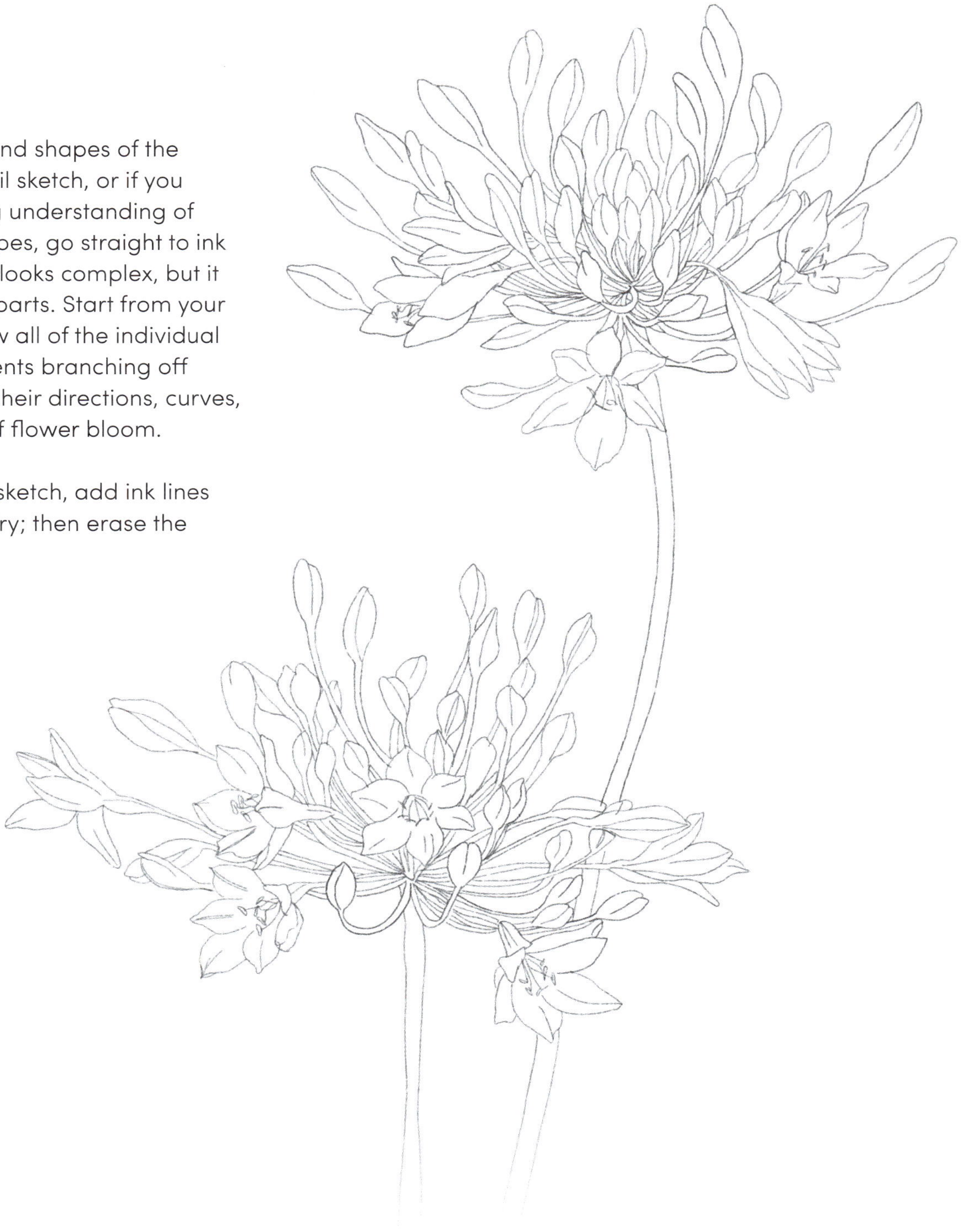

You can use a combination of lighter and darker greens with subtle grays to create the shadow effect here.

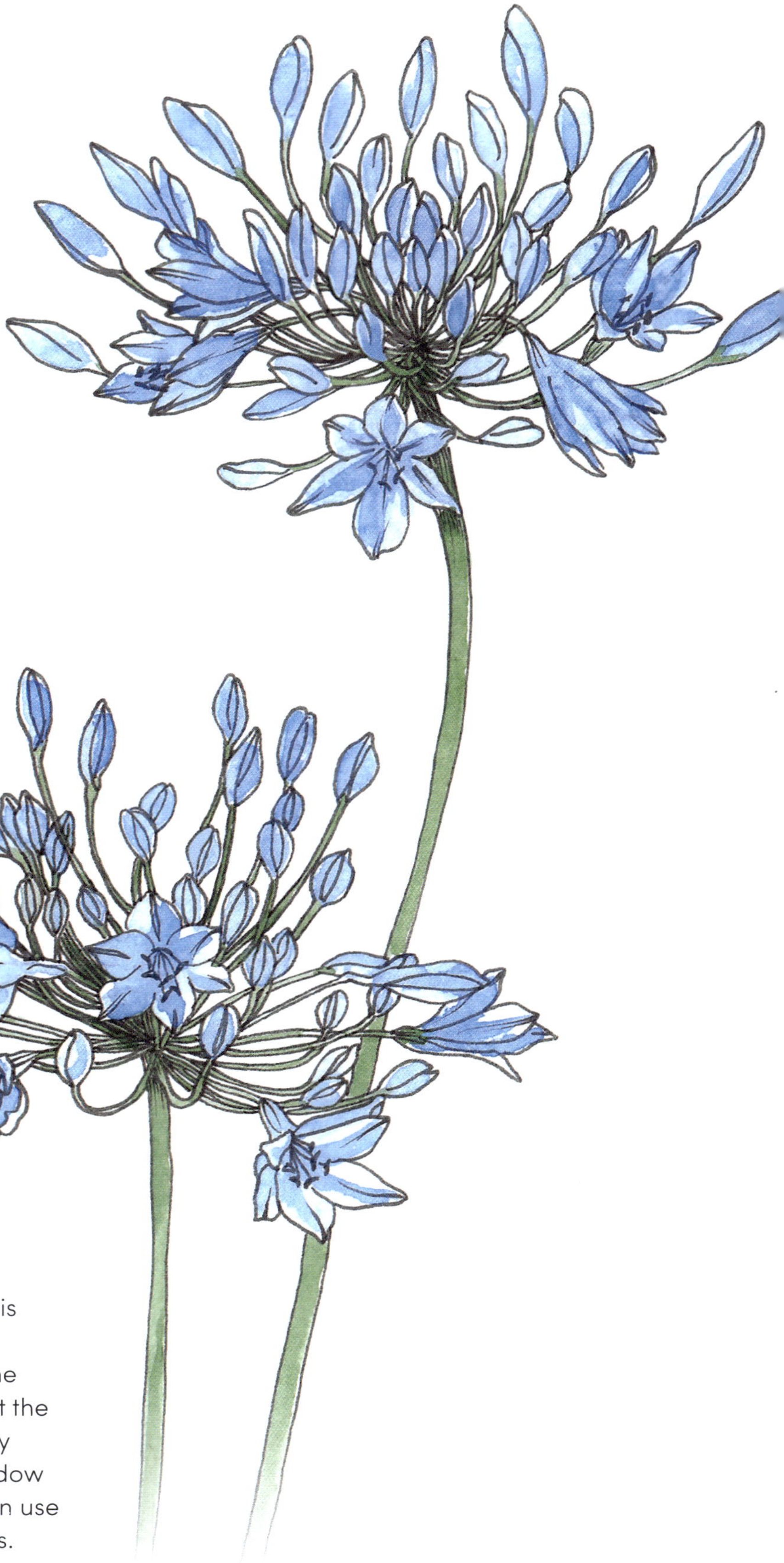

Step 3

Add watercolor. Because of the delicacy of this piece, I wanted to pull out its structures using clean colors. With a size 2 round brush and the wet-on-dry technique for better control, paint the flowers pale blue. Then come in with a slightly darker blue to add a sense of depth and shadow play to the individual flowers. Let this dry; then use the same brush with green paint for the stems.

Step 4

For an extra-modern flare, add a blue wash using a wet-into-wet technique in the background. To mimic stars, add spots of white acrylic paint once the watercolor dries.

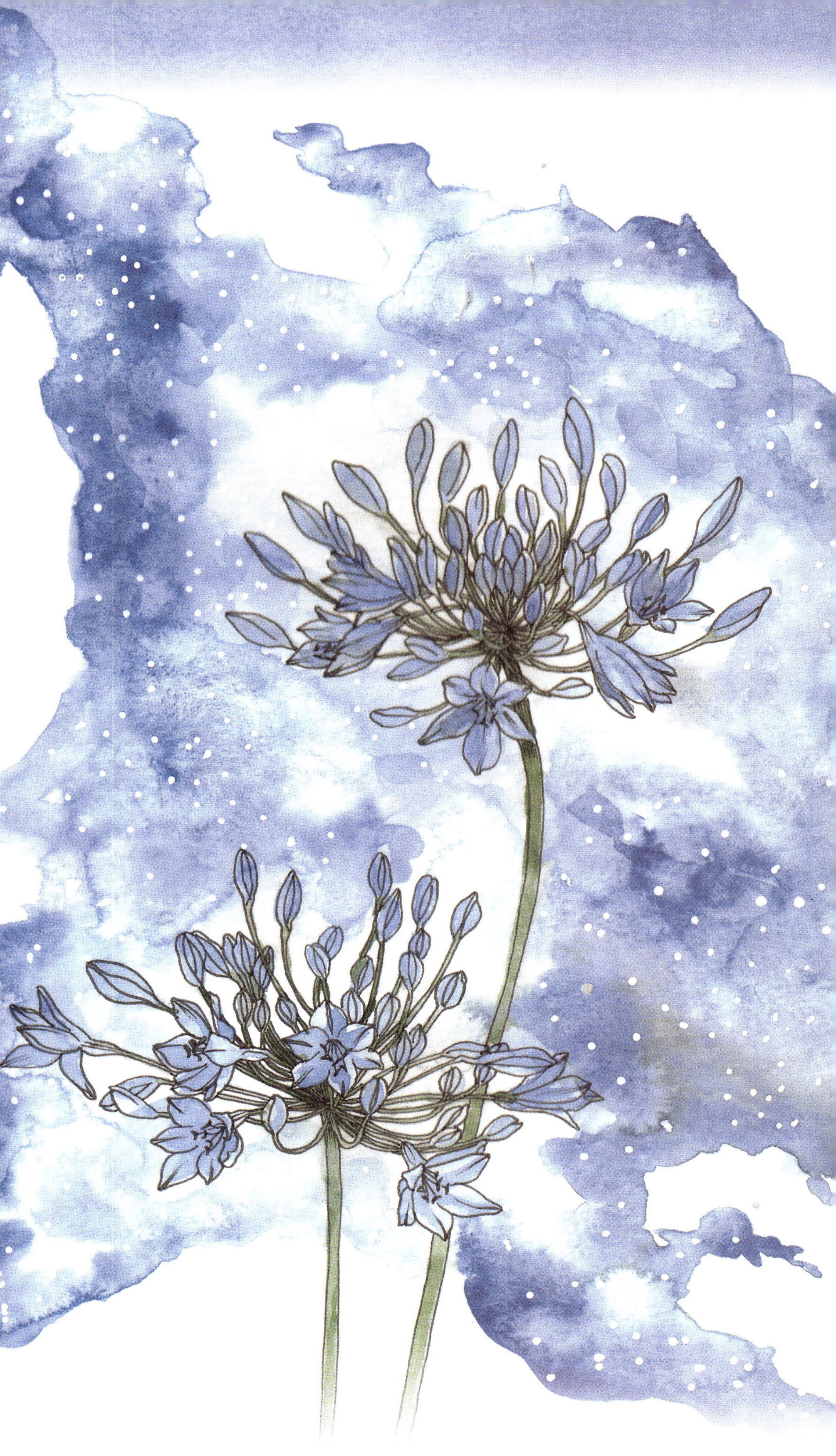

Lily

To create this lily from memory, I used a combination of live observation and internet searches. If you prefer to use a reference photo for practice, I recommend doing an image search on the internet and finding different angles of leaves and petals.

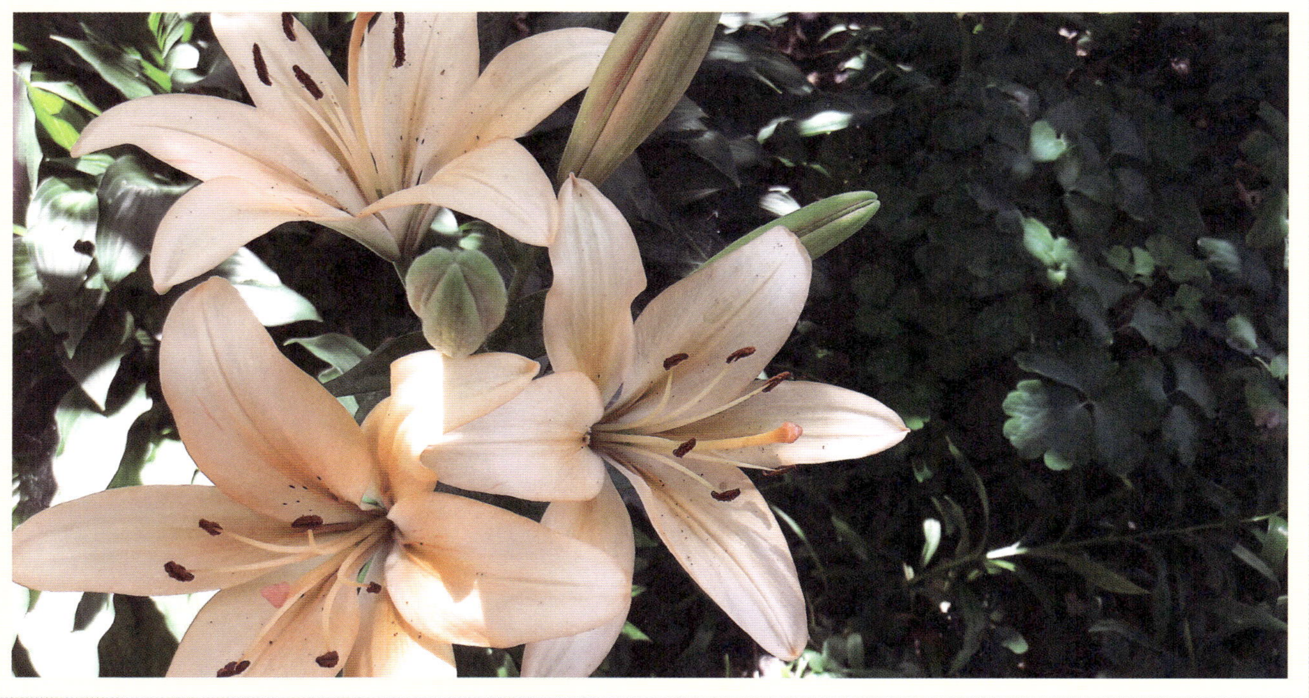

Step 1

Practice outlining the petals and leaves from different angles.

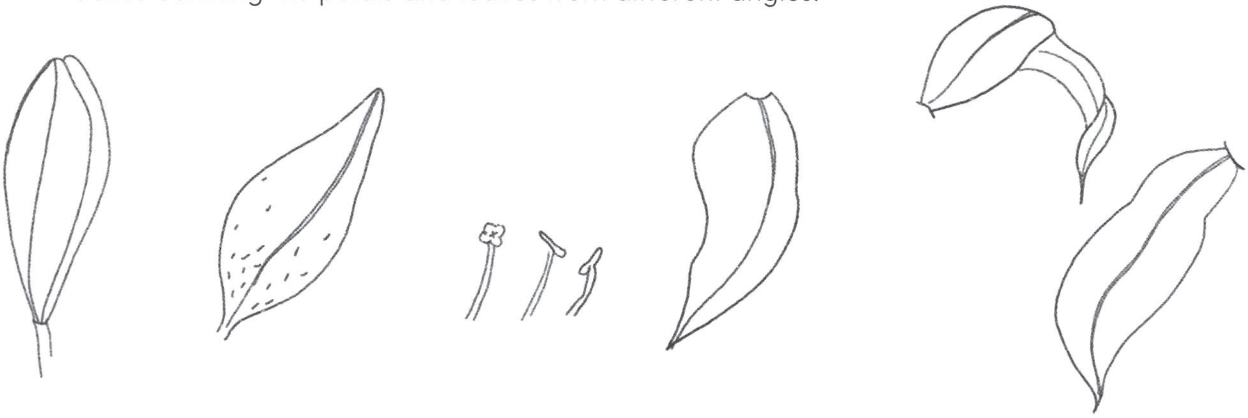

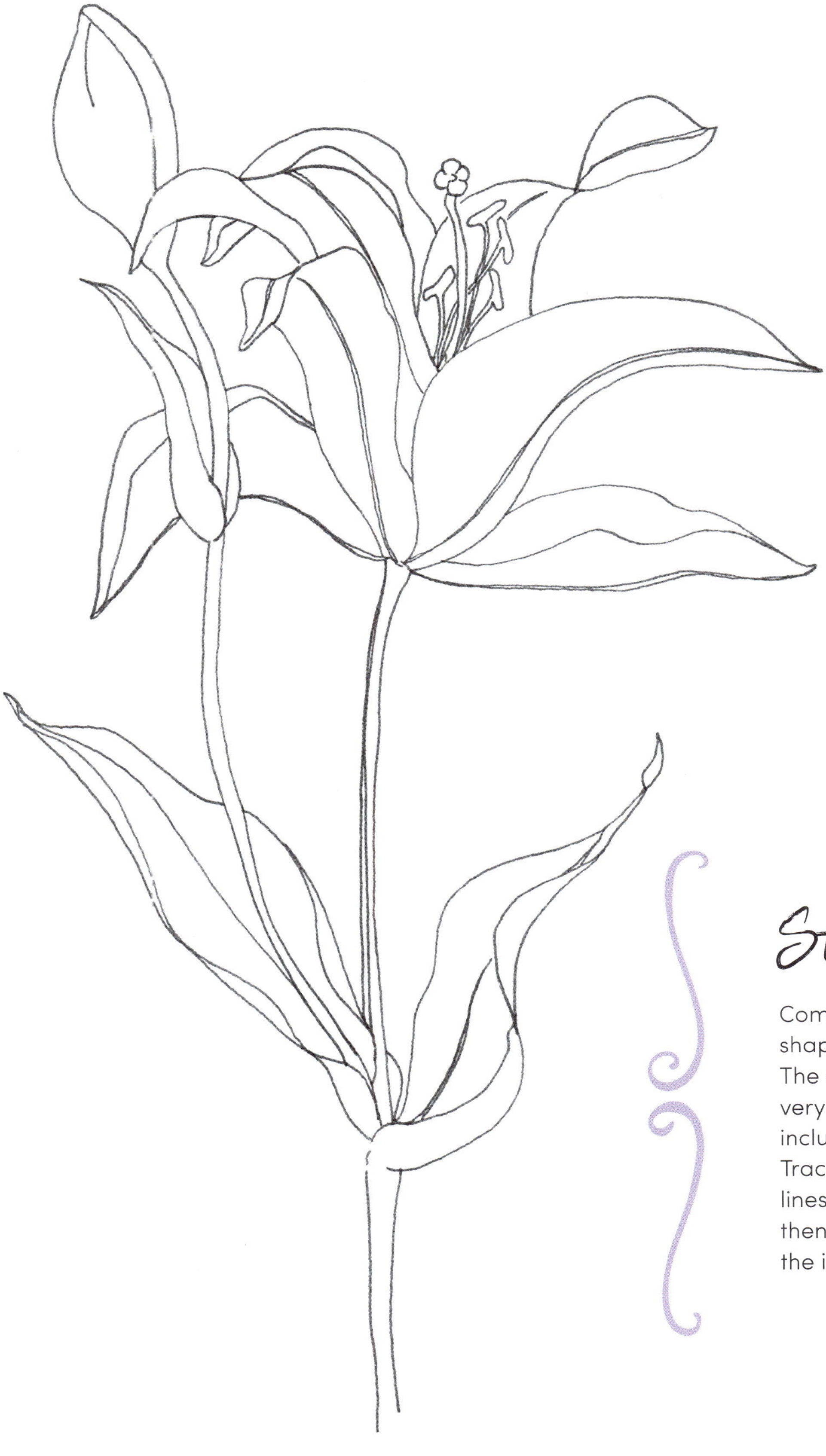

Step 2

Combine the angles and shapes in a pencil sketch. The center of a lily is not very complex, so you can include that part as well. Trace over your pencil lines with a fineliner pen; then erase the pencil once the ink is dry.

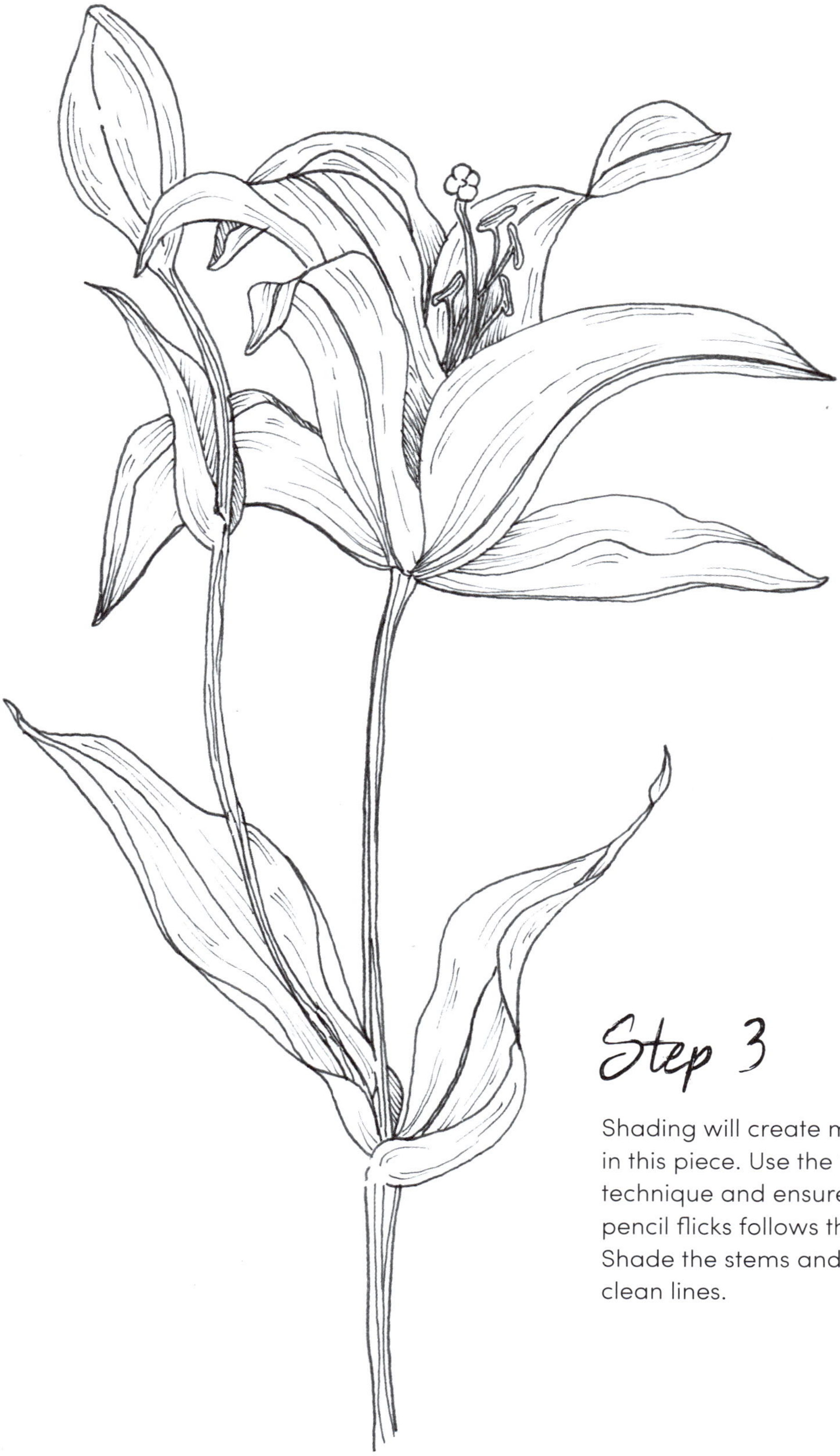

Step 3

Shading will create movement and depth in this piece. Use the "flick" hatching technique and ensure that the curve of the pencil flicks follows the lines of the petals. Shade the stems and stamens with long, clean lines.

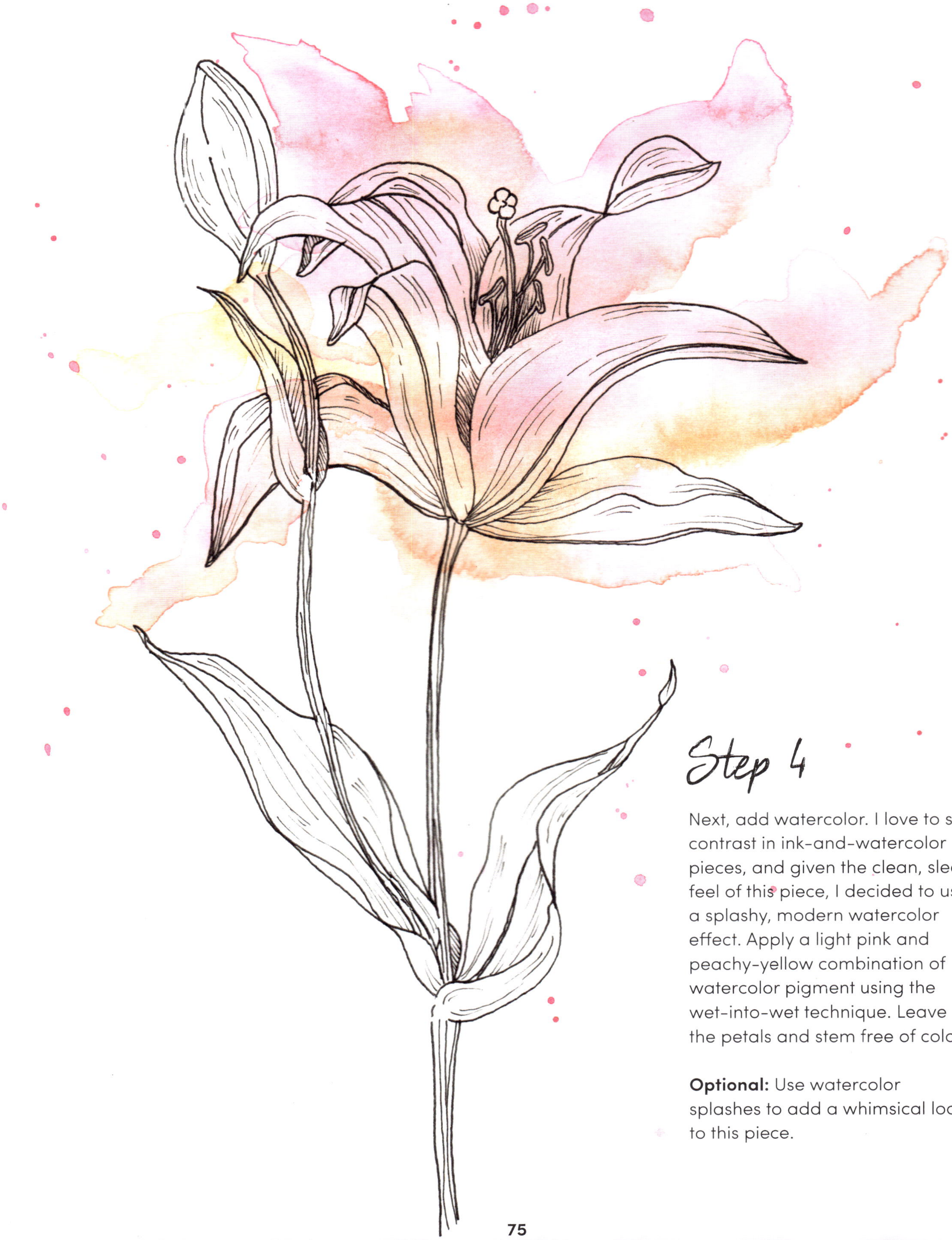

Step 4

Next, add watercolor. I love to see contrast in ink-and-watercolor pieces, and given the clean, sleek feel of this piece, I decided to use a splashy, modern watercolor effect. Apply a light pink and peachy-yellow combination of watercolor pigment using the wet-into-wet technique. Leave the petals and stem free of color.

Optional: Use watercolor splashes to add a whimsical look to this piece.

Freesia

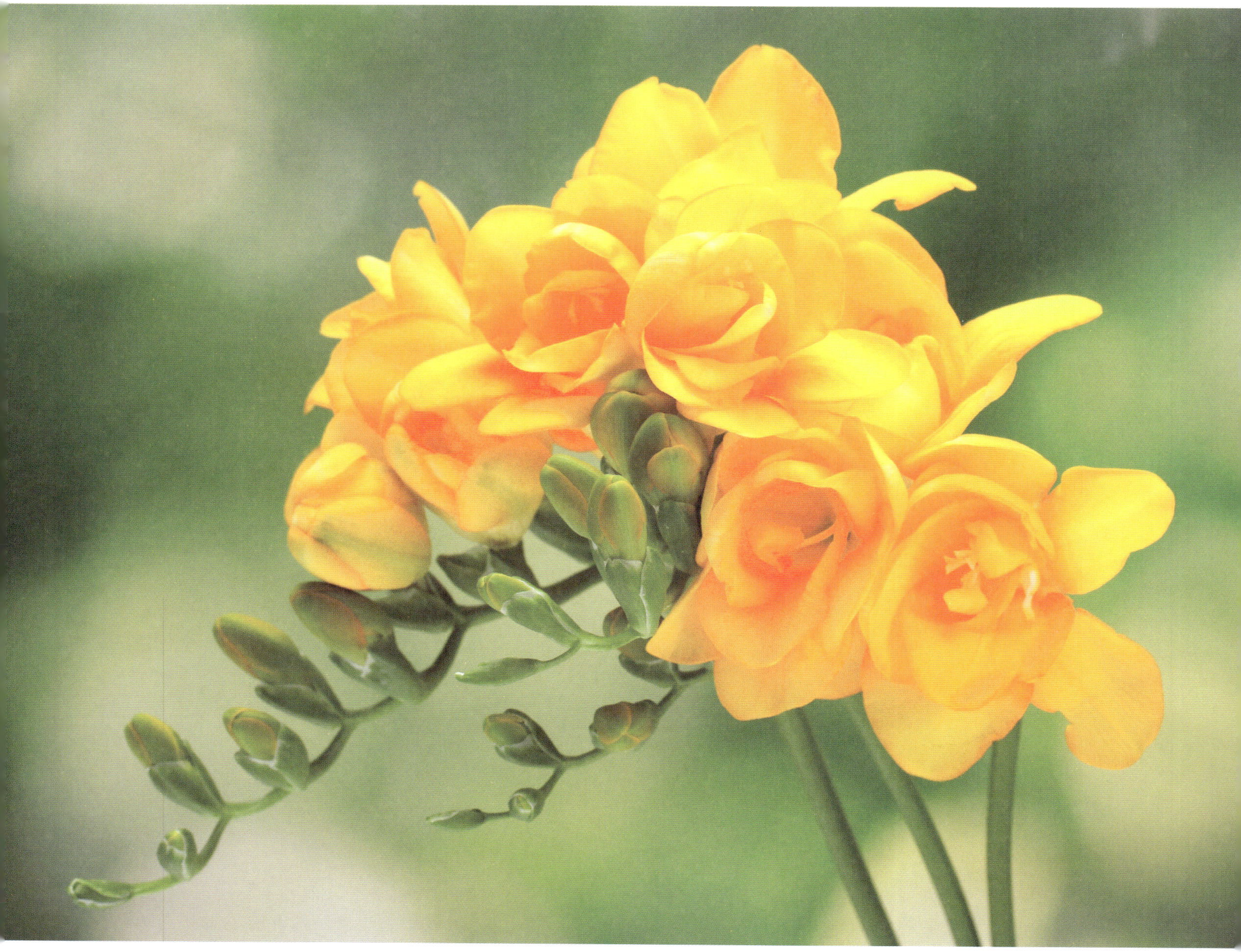

Freesias are beautiful—and great for practicing drawing the different stages of a flower, from bud to full bloom. Not only does this flower allow you to easily experiment with different layouts and angles, but it also gives you the opportunity to work with a simple petal shape that, when drawn in multiples, can look more complex.

Step 1

Look at various reference images to familiarize yourself with freesias. Once you know their general shape and feel, you will easily be able to build any number of freesias.

As you begin sketching your layout, have fun! Try different angles, with some flowers facing you openly and others turned away or at an angle. You can experiment with different petal directions too, with some curving inward and others splayed out.

Roughly sketch the outline of the petals, leaving an empty space in the middle where the stamens will go. Consider the center of each flower so that you can draw petals coming off the center.

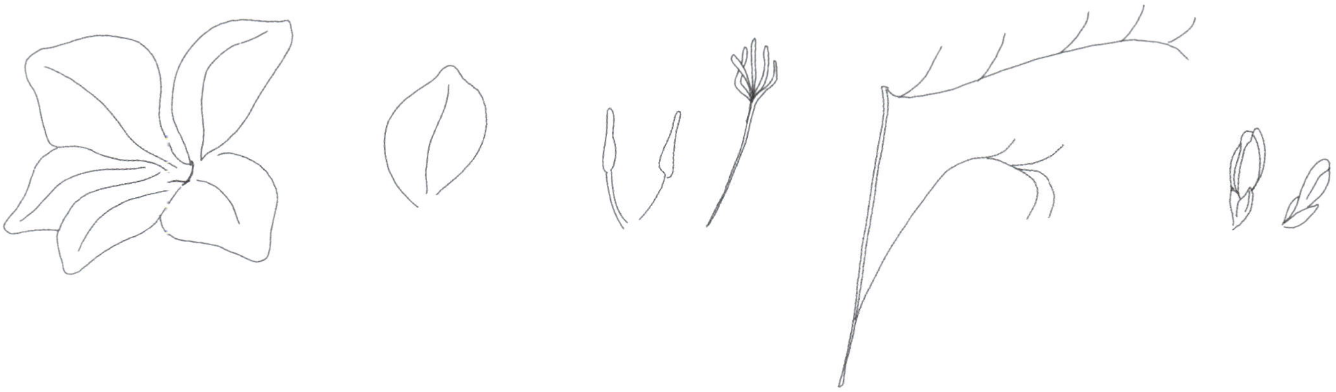

Freesia leaves have a similar structure to the snowdrop (pages 34–37) and gladiolus (pages 82–87), so take a peek at those tutorials as well for even more practice!

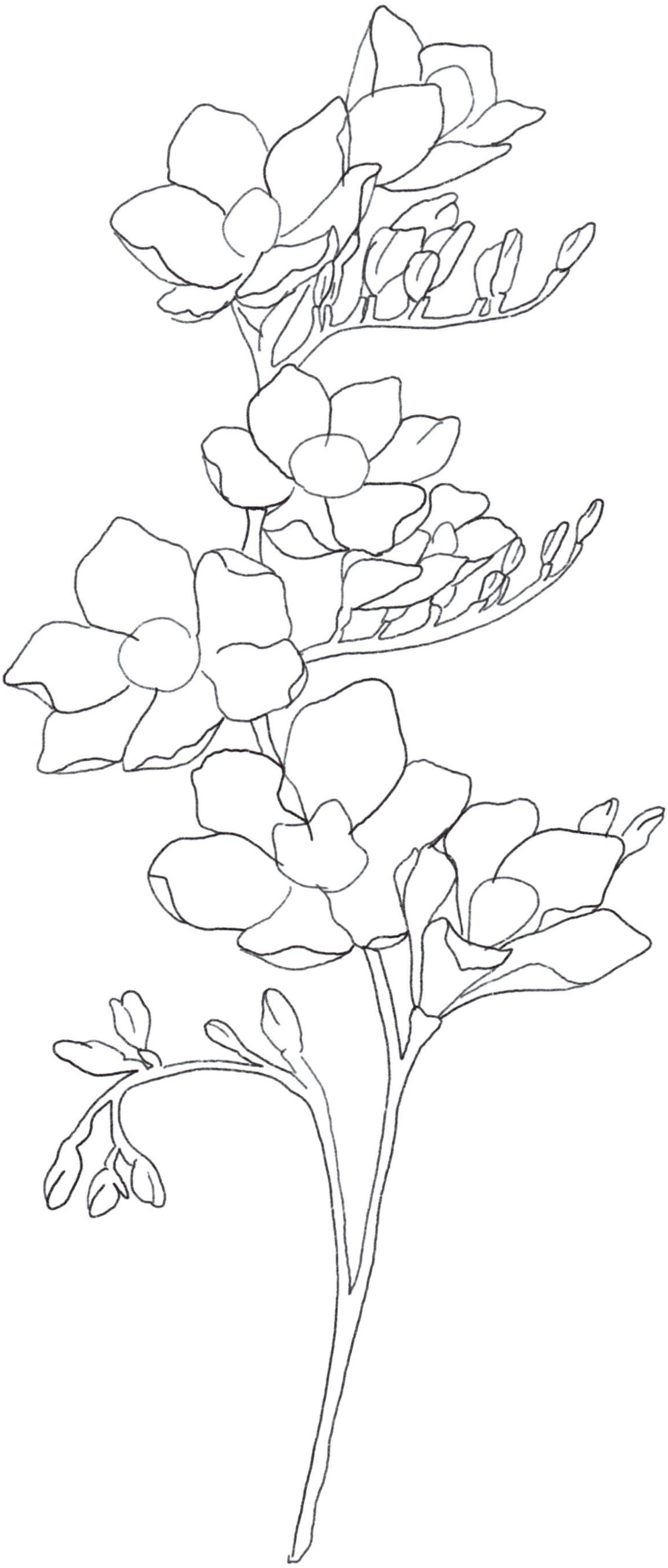

Step 2

Use a fineliner pen and the "flick" technique to shade and create subtle curved lines along the petals.

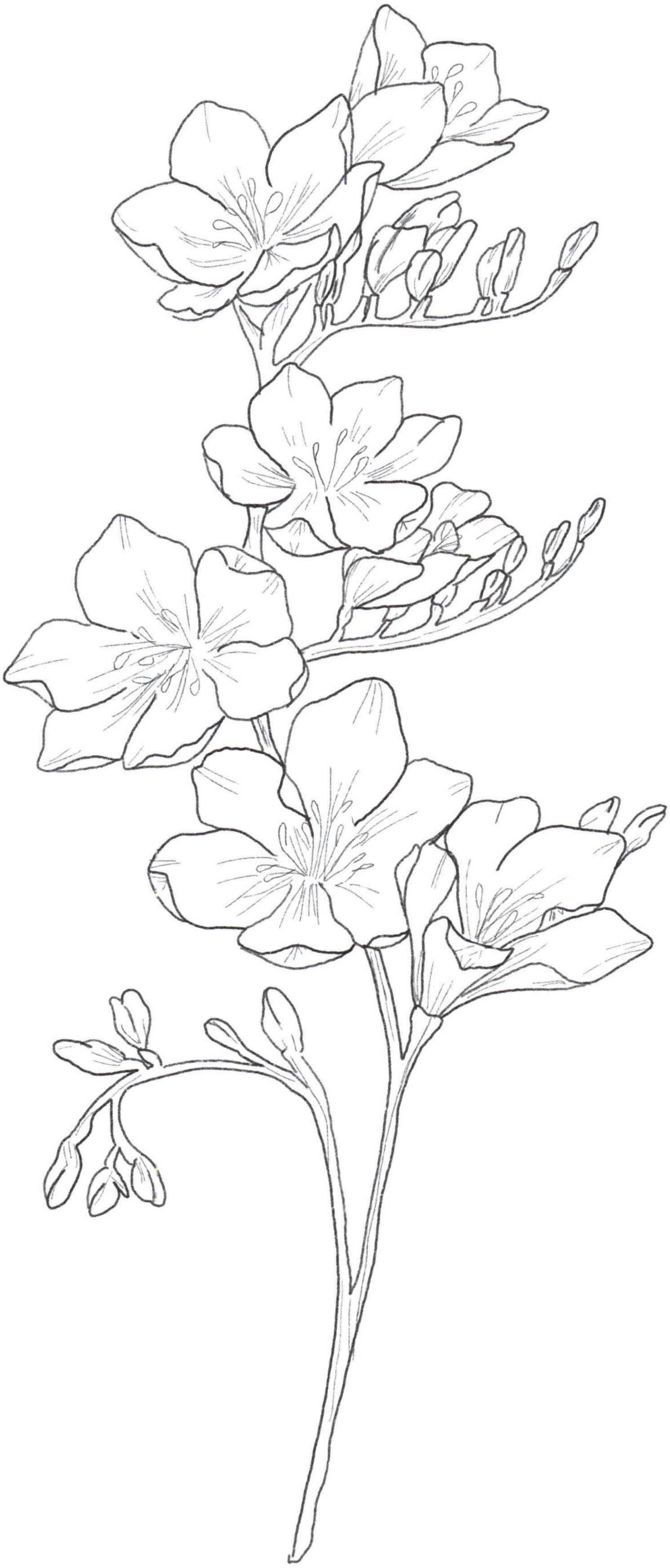

Step 3

You can use a subtle hatching technique to create shadows in the deeper parts of the petals that lie completely in shade. Make small, horizontal marks in a slight downward-facing direction to shade the stem and give it a three-dimensional shape.

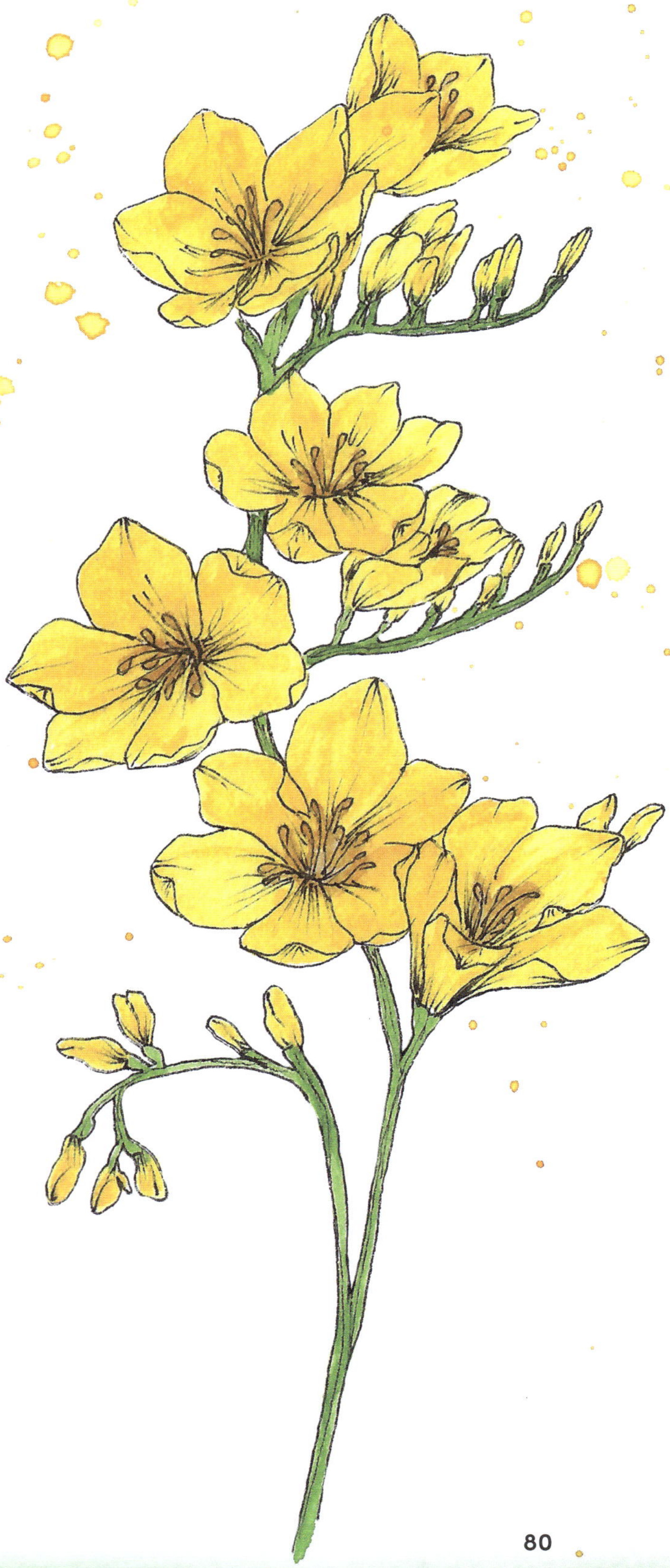

I kept my watercolor loose within the confines of the ink to continue with the whimsical feel of this modern style.

Step 4

Finish by adding watercolor. I wanted to create a whimsical but linear look, as this flower has such a wonderful shape and I didn't want to distract from that with a looser modern watercolor splash.

Freesias come in all sorts of colors, from shades of white and pink to yellows and purples, and I encourage you to explore and pick the color you love. Have fun with this! This project is a great one for practicing creating a bouquet, using all the different colors of freesias.

Using a wet-on-dry technique, paint a very pale underlayer of yellow on the flowers, as well as pale green on the stem and petals. While that paint is wet, come in with slightly darker yellows and greens, creating a mild wet-into-wet technique as the darker colors blend with the initial layer. You can also use grays and add shadow details.

Gladiolus

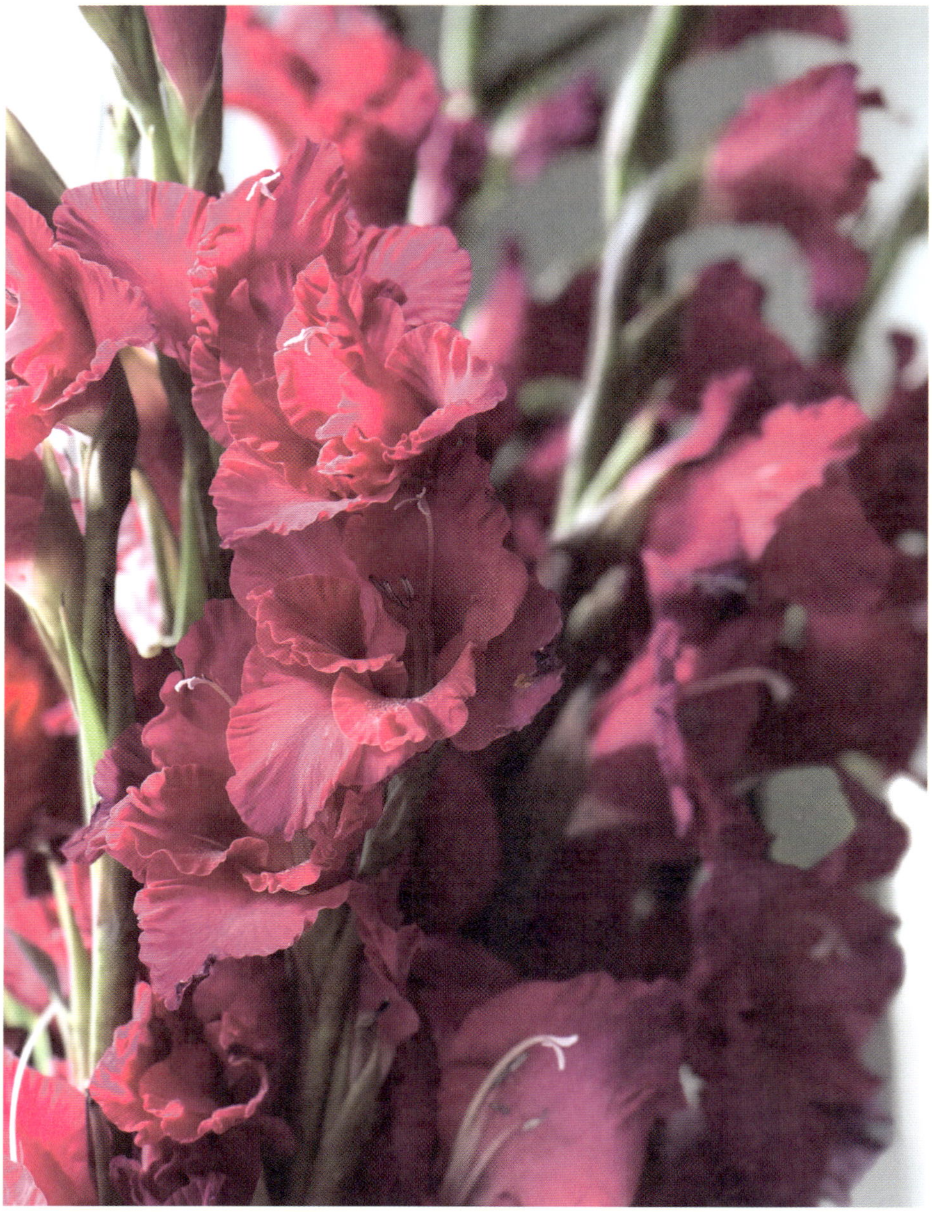

The gorgeous gladiolus is a great plant for beginners seeking to delve into more complicated-looking flowers. The gladiolus features a very simple flower and petal shape layered to create the appearance of a more complex flower. You can see this beautifully in the reference photo.

Step 1

To begin, let's review the basic shapes of the petals and leaves you will use to create the gladiolus.

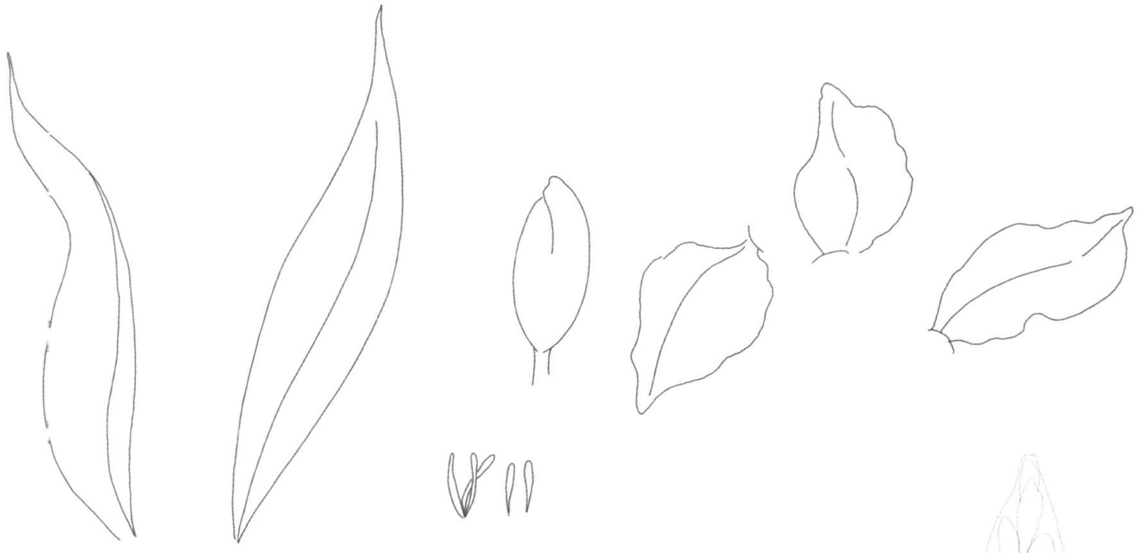

Step 2

Once you've drawn several of the florals in this book, you may want to experiment with slightly freer styles of mapping out your flowers. The more you practice and the more flowers you draw, the more a specific style of approaching layout and floral design will stand out to you. So, let's start experimenting!

Because this flower is both simple and complex, I felt confident that I would be able to draw the flower without first sketching every tiny detail. I created a pencil sketch of the overall shape of the flower, and within that, I included circles for rough placement (and overlap) of my flowers and where the buds should fall on top.

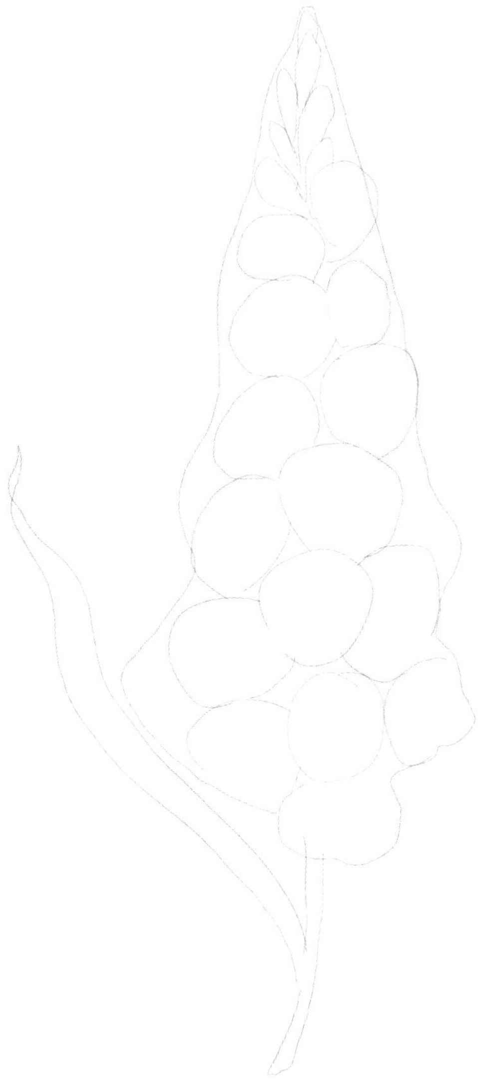

Step 3

This is a simple way to gain a lot of information before you start adding your flowers using pen. Keeping in mind that each individual flower of a gladiolus has five petals and a center, start to build your flowers on top of each other. You can also start to outline and define the leaves.

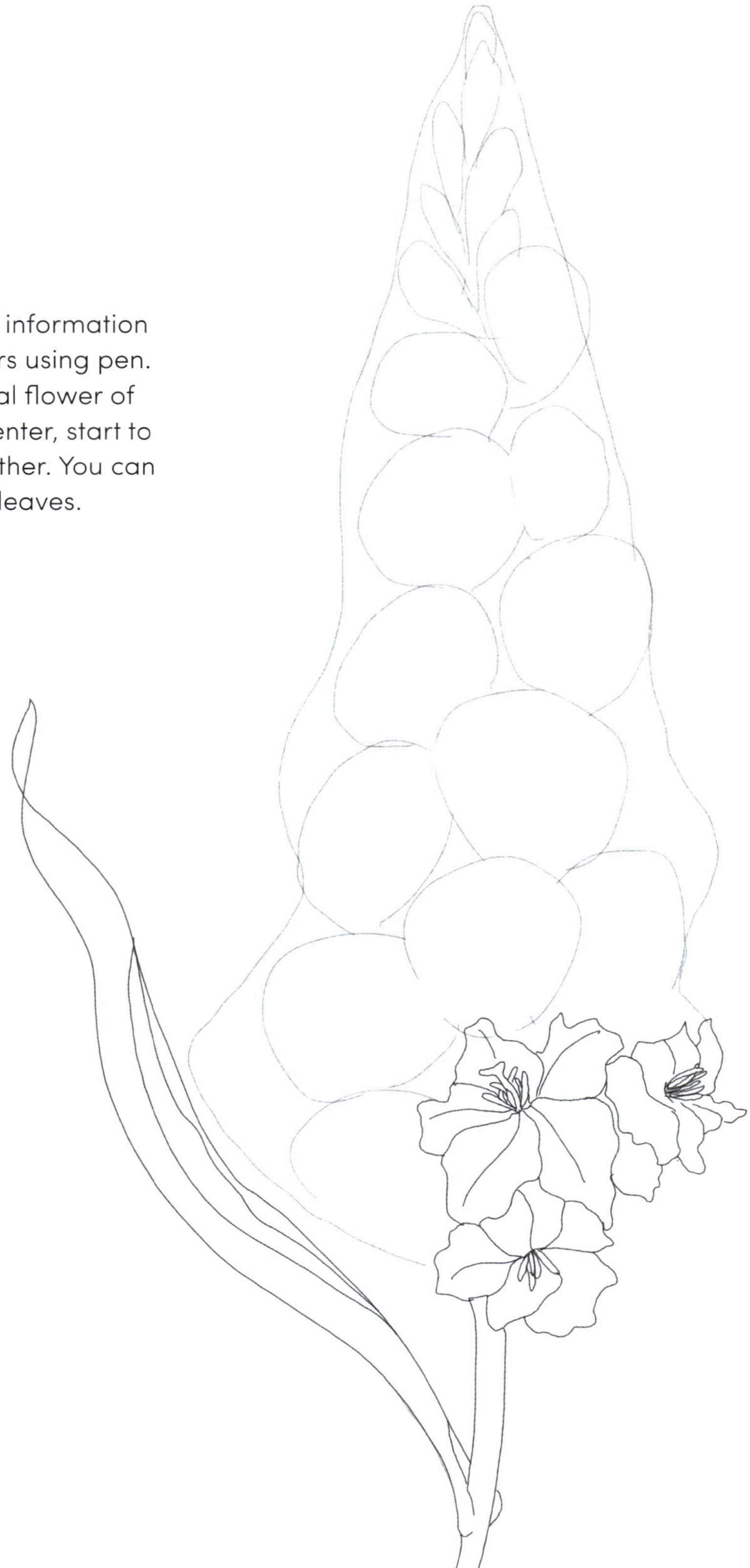

Step 4

Continue to build up the flowers, changing their directions and overlapping them. To overlap each flower, you simply need to draw up to the point of the neighboring petal. This is where your pencil circles come in handy, and you can experiment with how you want to denote which will go on top or beneath the one next to it. For example, if you first want to draw all the petals in the front, you may do that too.

Draw the centers and single-line guides within your petals to show you which direction to shade later. The more complex your flower, the more helpful this step can be.

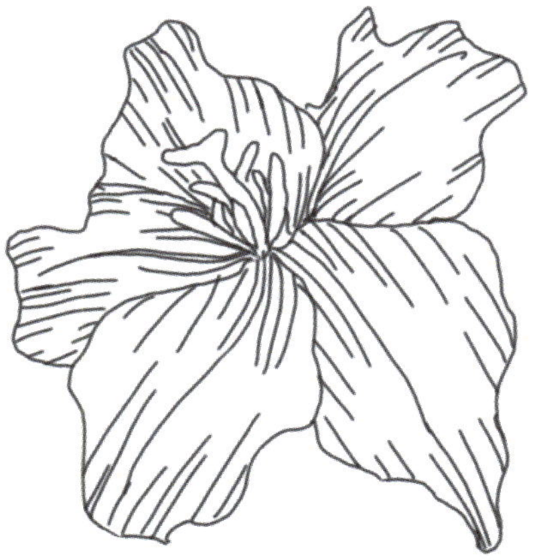

I like beginning at the widest point and working in or up toward the narrowest part of the flower, as this gives me more control over the overall shape.

Step 5

Now you've created a complex-looking flower—and see how simple it was! This is the joy of understanding the parts that make up a flower: the petal shapes that you practiced before, knowing how many petals you need to draw in each flower, and realizing that it's a simple five-petal flower all clustered together and overlapping in a cone shape. See? It's simple!

Now you get to add color!

I wanted to add flowing and whimsical watercolor to offset the detailed complexity of the gladiolus. Using the wet-into-wet technique, apply clean water with a large round brush (size 10 or 12) where you want the watercolor pigment to flow. To this same brush, add color and dab it in your wet areas. I also added yellow accents in watercolor here and there.

Optional: Add paint spatter to create even more whimsy and fun. Saturate your large round brush with water and pigment and tap the brush about 5 to 10 inches over the page.

I added yellow to the stamens digitally, but you could easily use a small paintbrush once your main color paint has dried to add some color to brighten and accent the center areas.

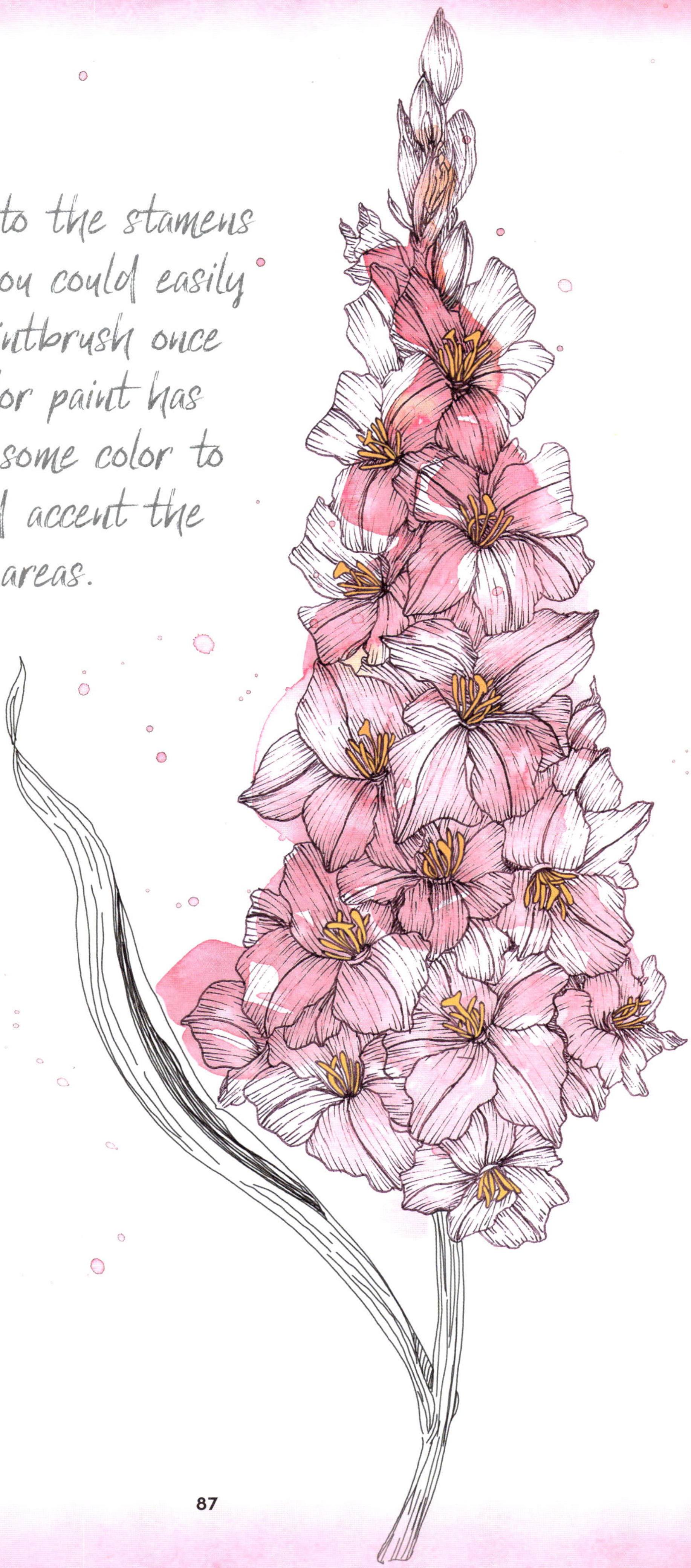

Iris

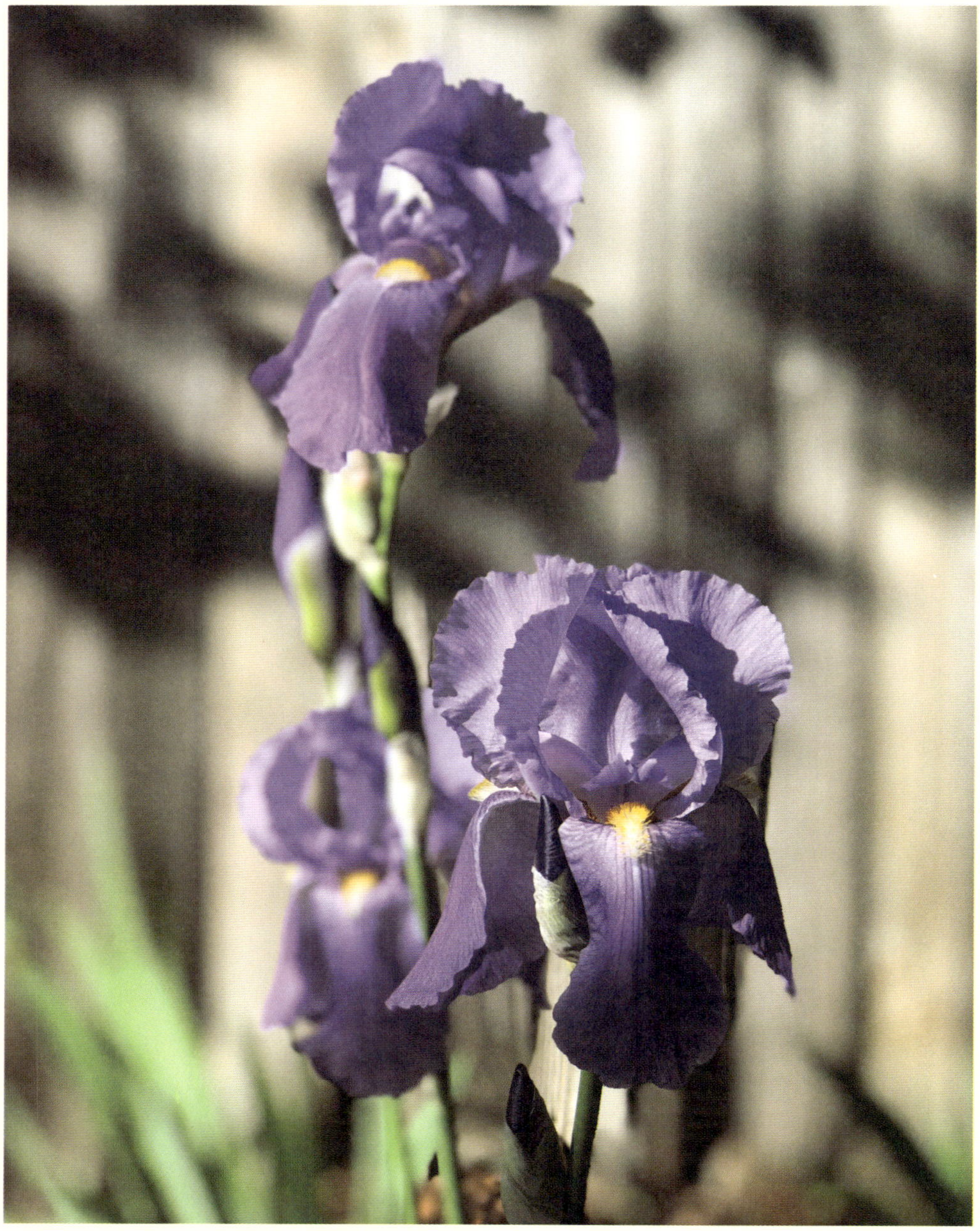

In Greek, the word "iris" means "rainbow." As you can imagine, this beautiful flower comes in an array of colors, brightening those early spring days and helping us forget the cold, snowy, wintry ones.

The inspiration for this project comes from the beautiful blue irises that grow under the cottonwood tree in my backyard. They're bold and stand so tall, it's difficult not to admire them!

Step 1

The traditional iris shape is outlined roughly here on the far right, but as you can see in the reference photo and in the final image on page 93, you can play around with angles and whether you want the full wide front of the petal or its frilly edges to take the lead for your top petals.

Play with the angles of your iris. If the top petals are shown from the side, the bottom petal in the middle will showcase its width with the fuzzy yellow center showing boldly in the middle. Conversely, if the top petals are shown at their widest, the bottom petals will be seen from their sides.

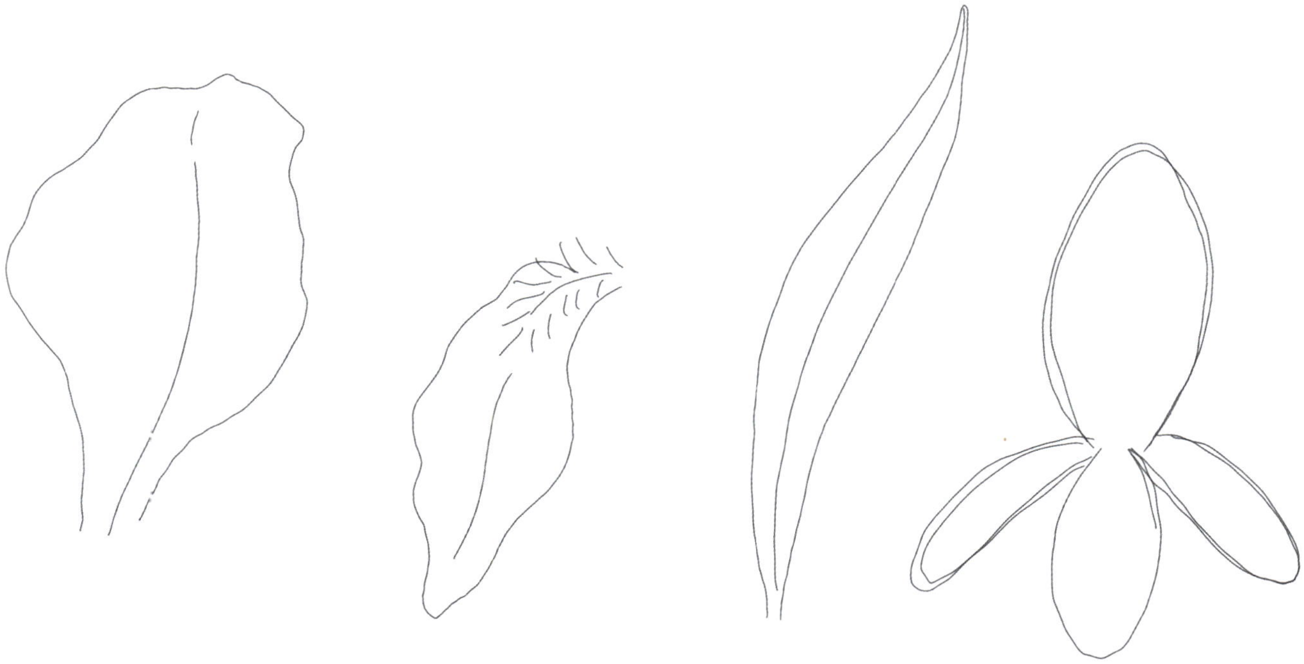

Drawing an iris is a lovely process because you get to try out all of the angles, making this a more complex flower for experimentation.

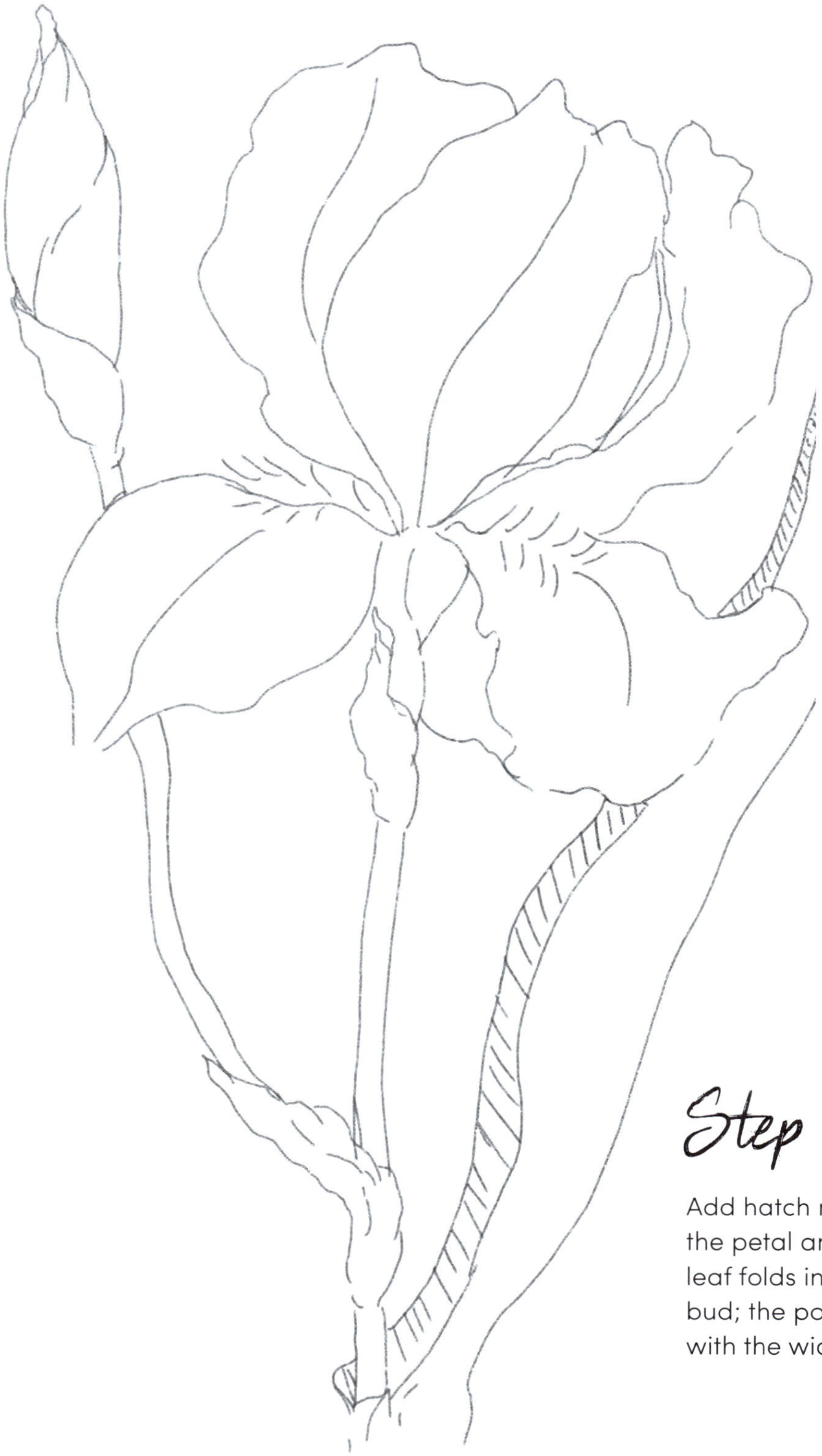

Step 2

Add hatch marks to indicate the shadow of the petal and give the impression that the leaf folds in half toward itself. Also add a bud; the pointy shape contrasts beautifully with the wide frills of the open petals.

Step 3

Begin adding shaded lines to the flowers as you decide how detailed you want to be at this stage. You can create a beautiful ink drawing with more complex shading or a lighter drawing using fewer shade lines.

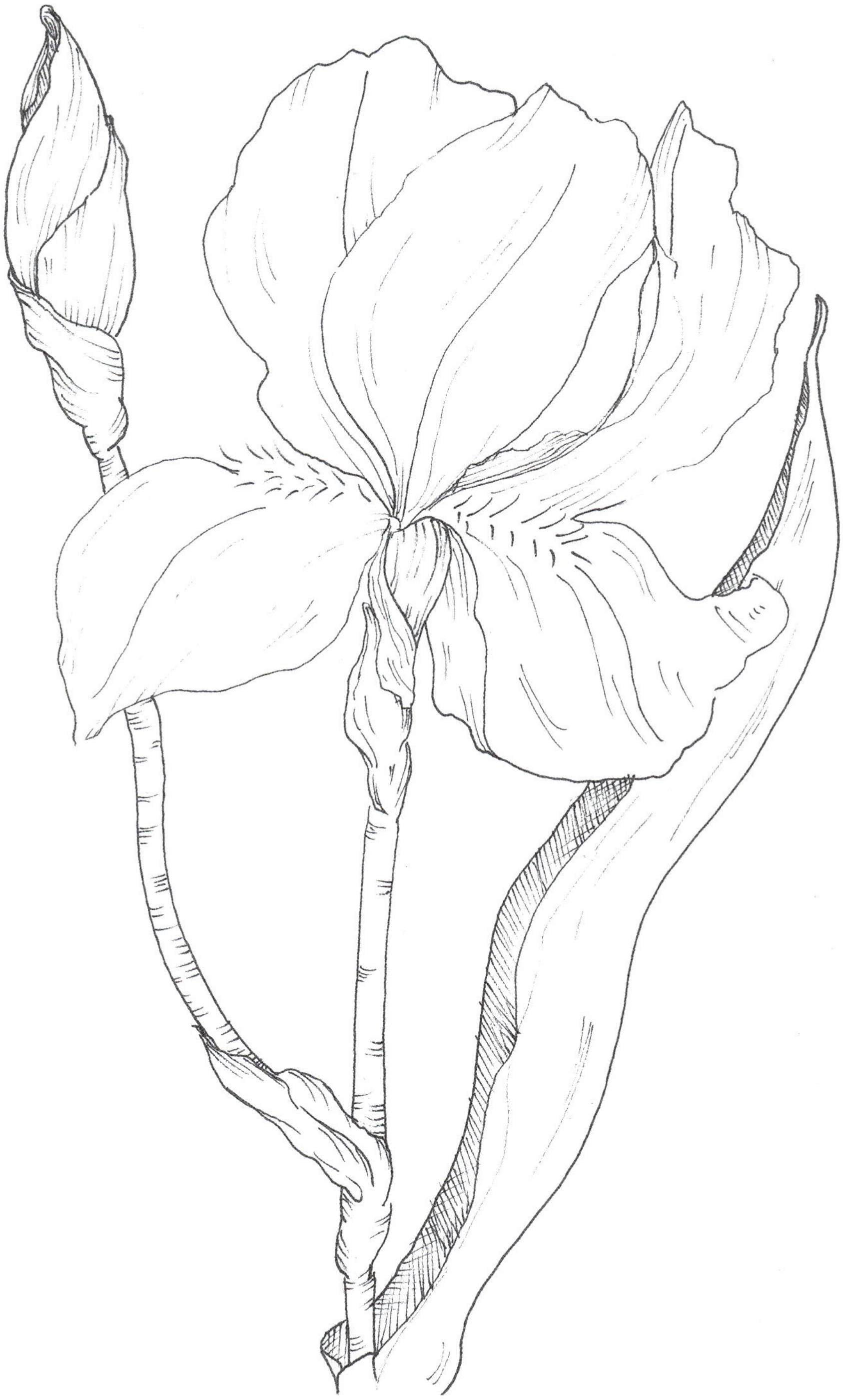

Whatever you choose to do (see step 3), make sure that you keep your shading lines moving with the ever-changing angles of your petals. If you do not pay attention, you will lose some of the flow and dance of your petals, which will detract from the overall feel of the iris.

Step 4

The iris is one of my favorite flowers to paint because you can add such a variety of colors and really let each one "pop" with its wide petals.

Use a large round brush (size 10 or 12) and begin with a wet or dry layer of a pale purple for the petals. While the paint is still wet, add areas of darker purples and pinks to give the impression of a wet-into-wet technique (which, in reality, is wet paint on wet paint as opposed to wet paint on water).

Let these layers dry a bit before coming in with purple mixed with Payne's gray for the shadowy areas. While the purple is still slightly dry, add a bold yellow to the fuzzy bits of the blue iris. Letting it bleed slightly into the surrounding purple creates a bit of yellow glow surrounding the petals.

For the petals, use a combination of light green, darker green, and Payne's gray with the techniques outlined above. Once these greens are almost dry, add lemon yellow to the top layer to help bring out the yellow of the iris and complement the purplish-blue of the petals.

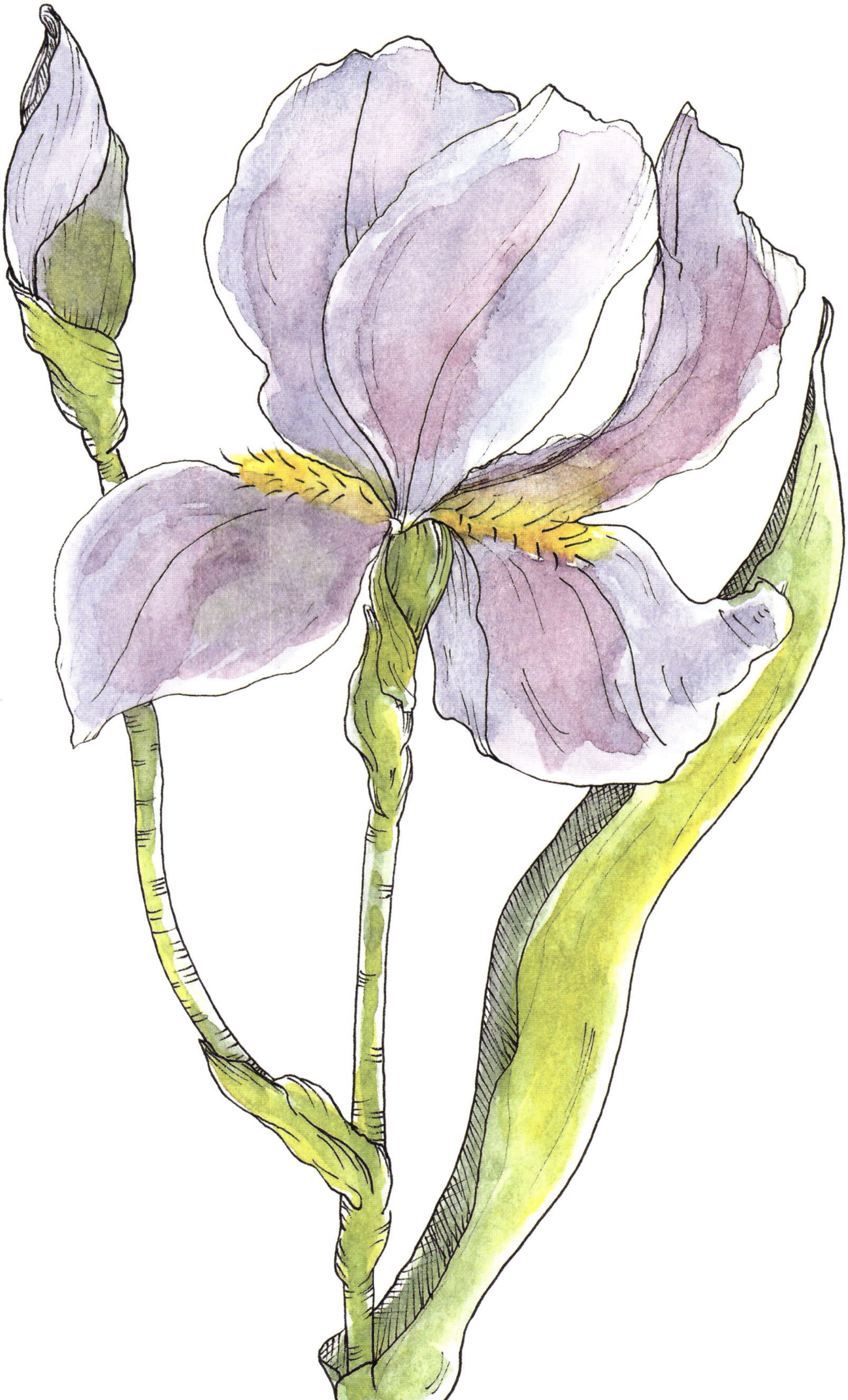

Hollyhock

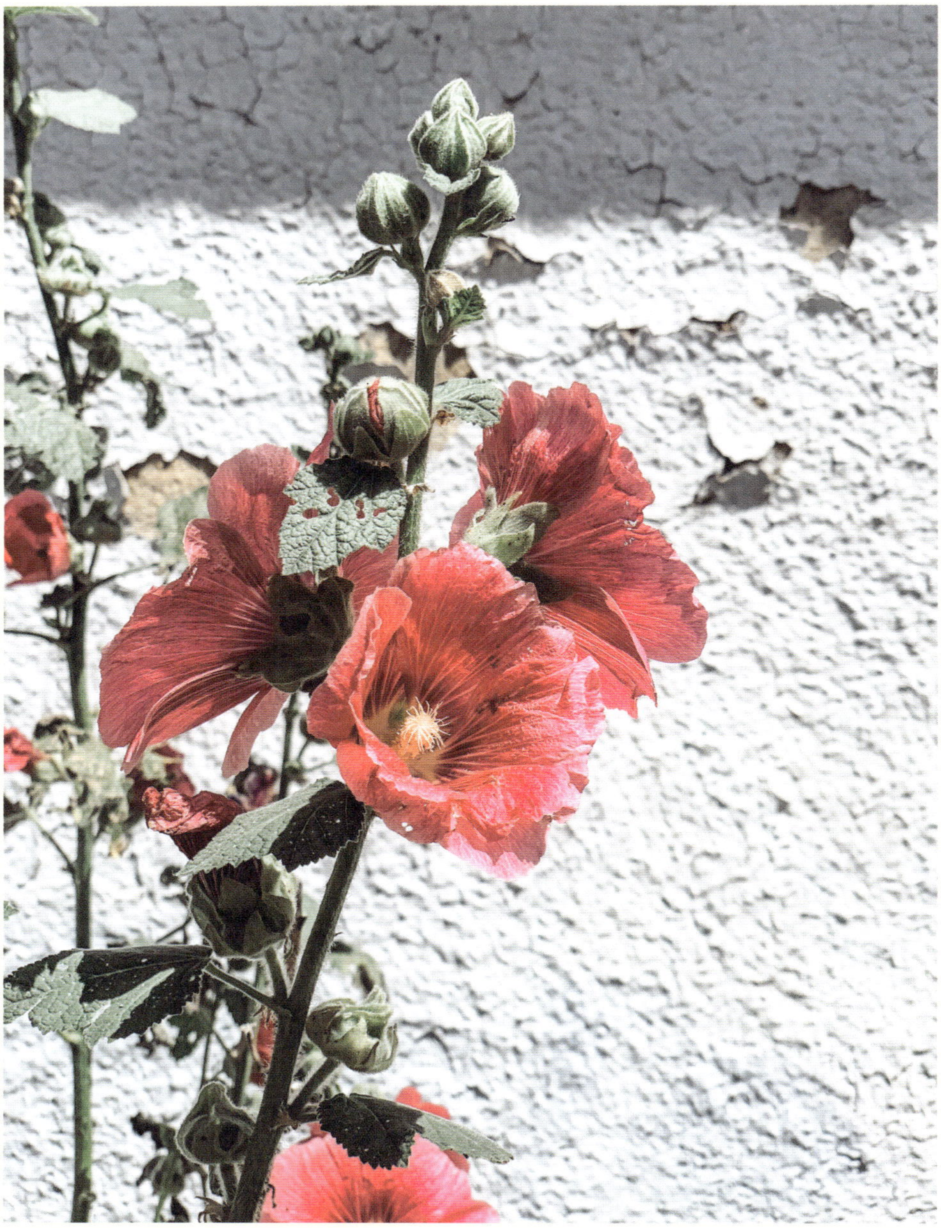

The hollyhock is a gorgeous flower, and we are going to have some fun with this one! It's easy to get lost in the minute details of the hollyhock and all that this stunning flower has to offer. But I'd like you to challenge yourself differently here by embracing a loose style of ink and watercolor. This can be a fun way to gain insight into your style, but it may be harder to do than it sounds. To create a beautiful, loose floral piece, you'll need a strong sense of layout and shape since you will not include every tiny detail when portraying your flower. Challenge your eye—and that of your viewer. It will feel so liberating!

Step 1

To begin, let's review the basic shapes of the petals and leaves you will use to create the hollyhock. Note the rough shape outlined on the far right for a traditional hollyhock. Let's experiment! Try different angles of flower petals and varying ways to overlap them.

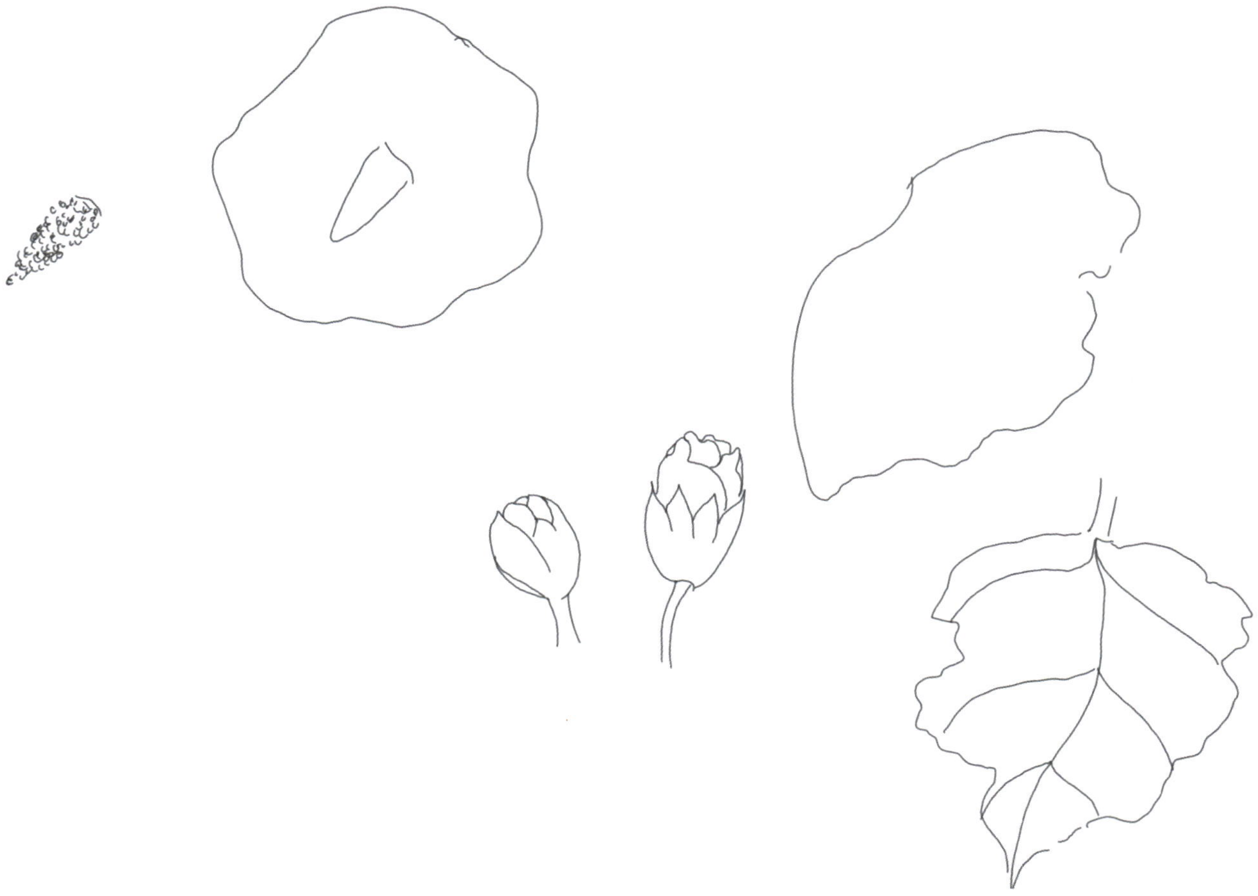

Step 2

Similar to the approach you took with the gladiolus (pages 82–87), the initial sketch of your hollyhock should serve as a very rough outline that tells you more about layout than detail. With the gladiolus, you did this because the flowers hold so much detail that it's better to leave those minutiae for the inking step.

With the hollyhock, the opposite is true. You will include such loose, minimal detail that drawing an overly complex pencil sketch would constrain the drawing and detract from its style.

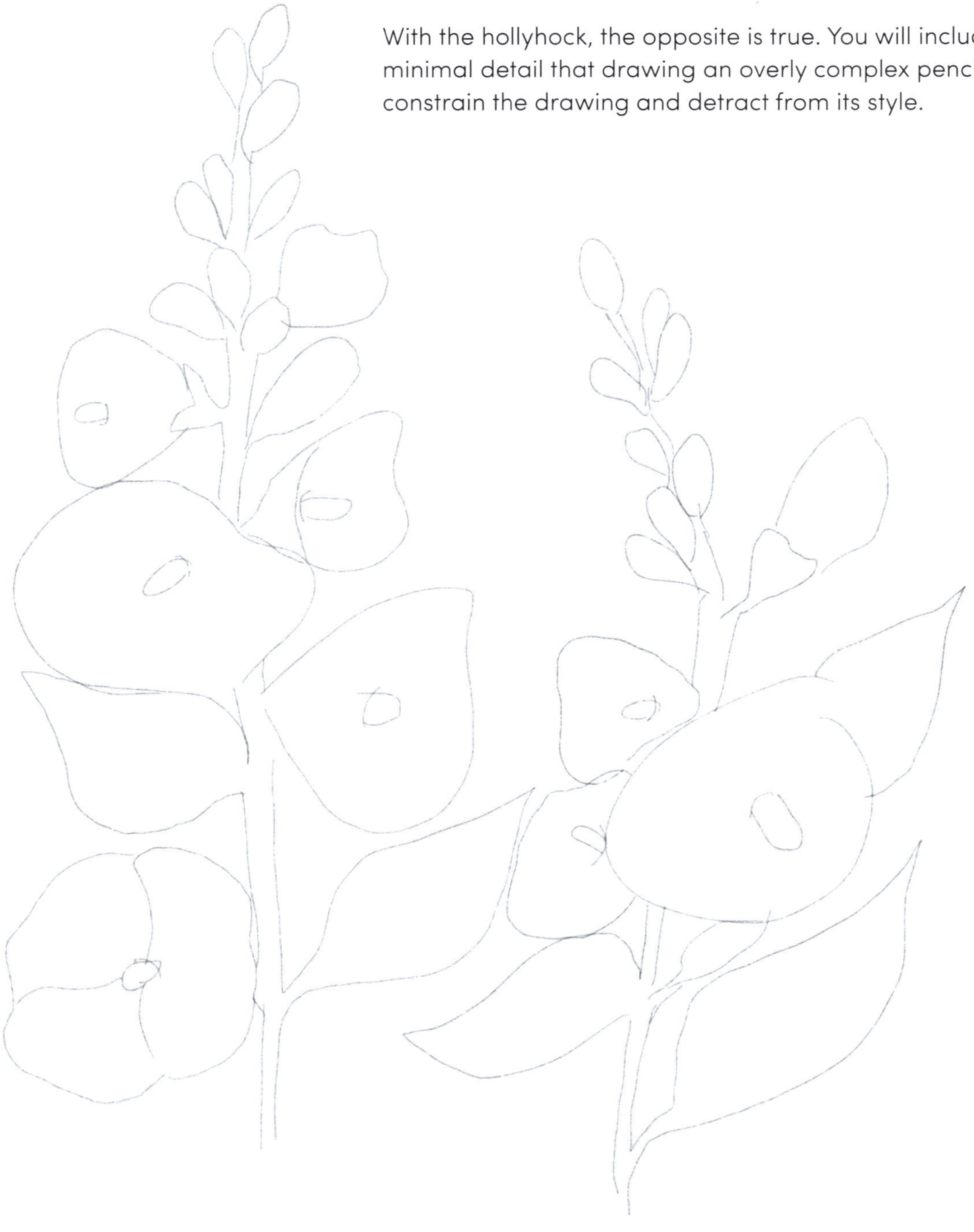

Step 3

Your goal when you add ink is to keep your lines loose and free. This does not mean that you lack control, however. When attempting a loose style with ink, use a loose grip and a light touch on the page while remaining in control of the direction of your lines. While your drawing mimics a sketched appearance, still outline each flower, leaf, and bud to ensure that your artwork doesn't look too messy in the end.

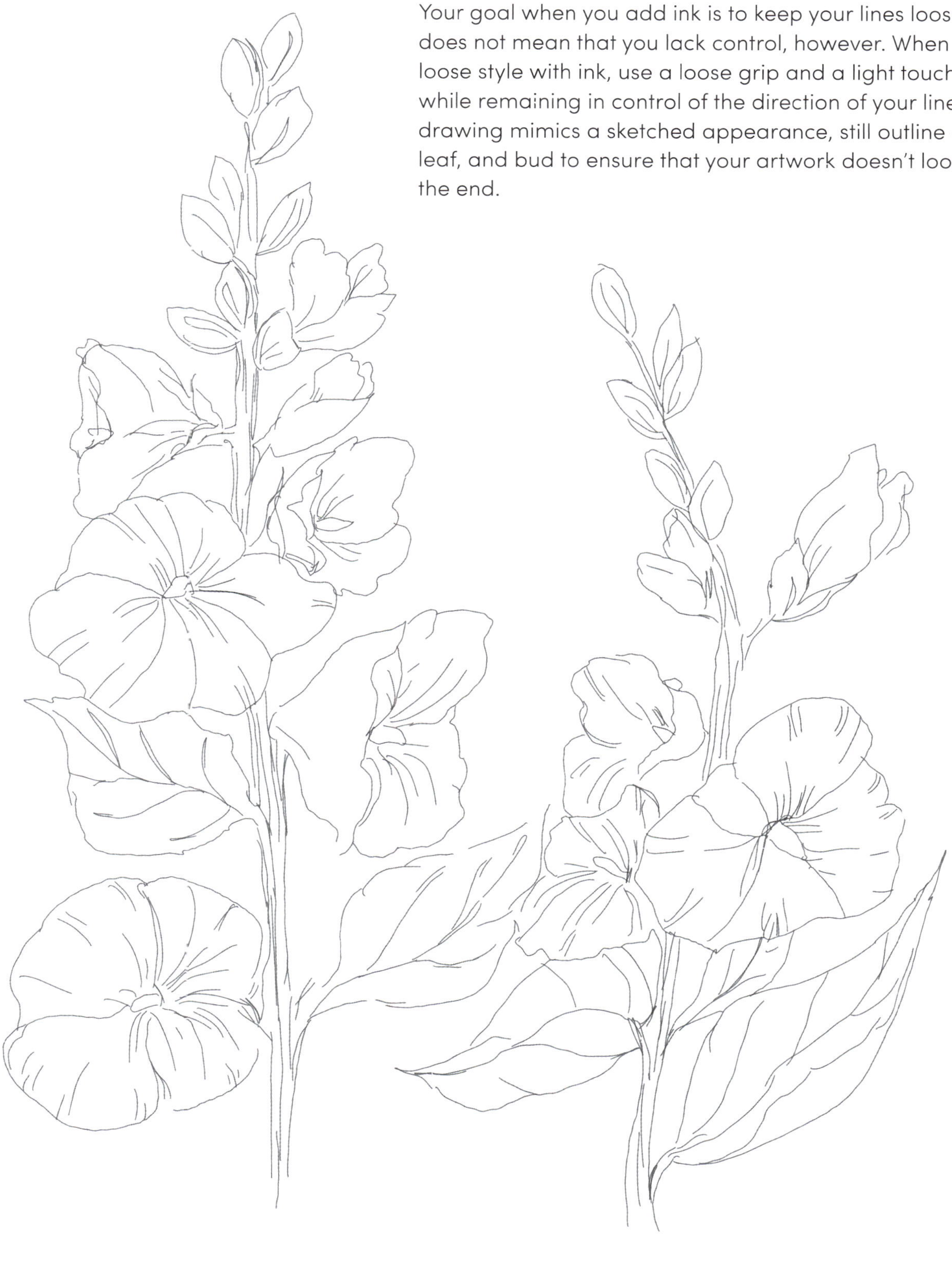

Step 4

When considering colors for this loose style, you will want to keep a few things in mind. If you look at hollyhocks, you'll find a variety of colors to choose from. The trick with this looser style is to give the illusion of shape and color without overdoing it.

For this style, painting wet-into-wet is the best technique. Stay mostly within your outlines, and use white space to your advantage to create a loose and whimsical feel in your hollyhocks.

I chose to use pale pink and darker pink (for shadow effects), as well as darker mossy green with a lemon-yellow overlay. Add yellow to the centers of your flowers after letting the primary flower color dry, unless you want it to bleed into the surrounding colors.

Optional: Add whimsical splashes to your final painting. Especially with a looser style, splashes help add movement to a final piece, almost as if the wind is blowing through the petals and pollen is flowing in the air.

Saturate a large round brush (size 10 or 12) with water and watercolor pigment. Holding it approximately 5 to 10 inches above the page, tap on the end of your paintbrush, near the bristles, and move it around above the page to disperse splashy watercolor drops.

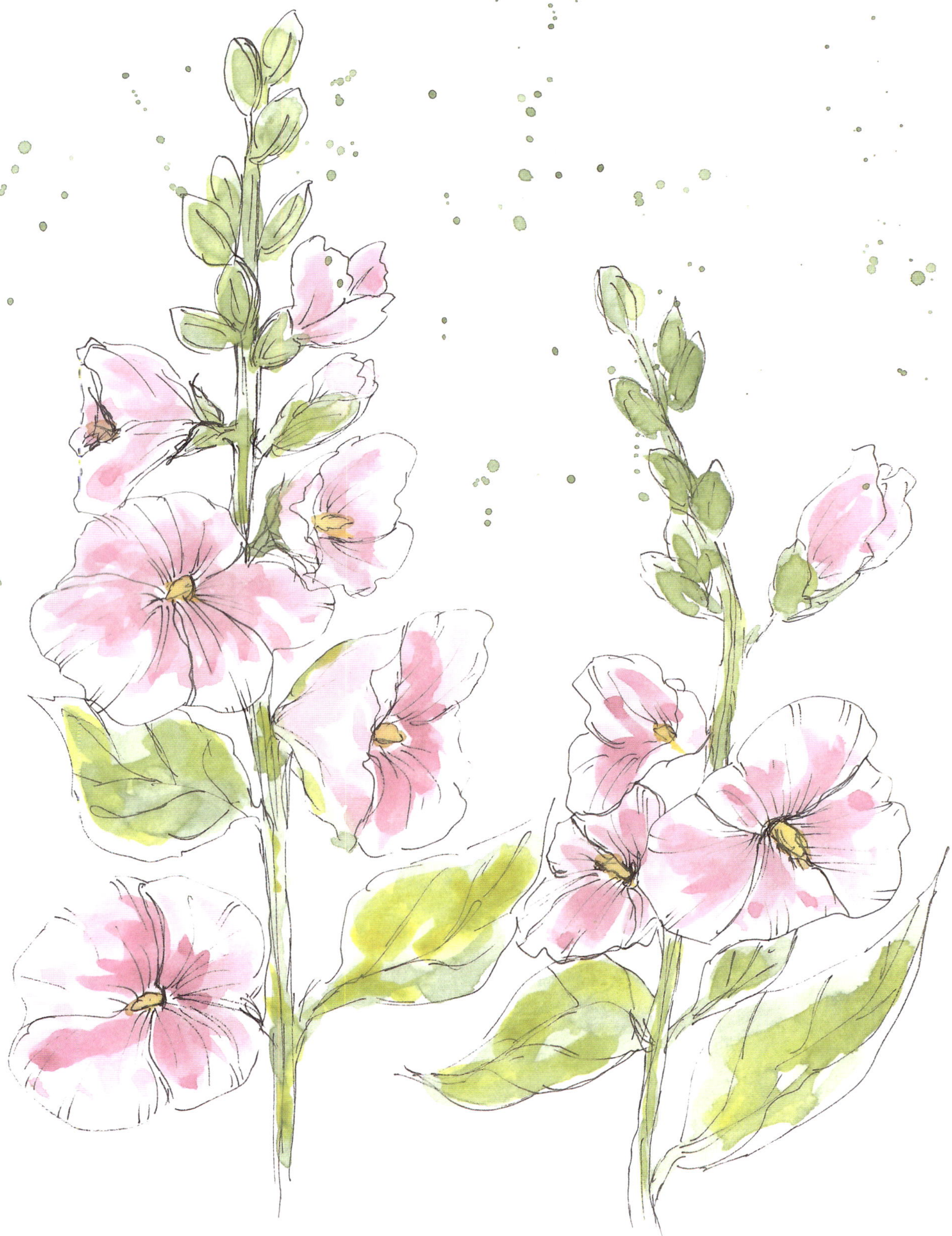

Peony

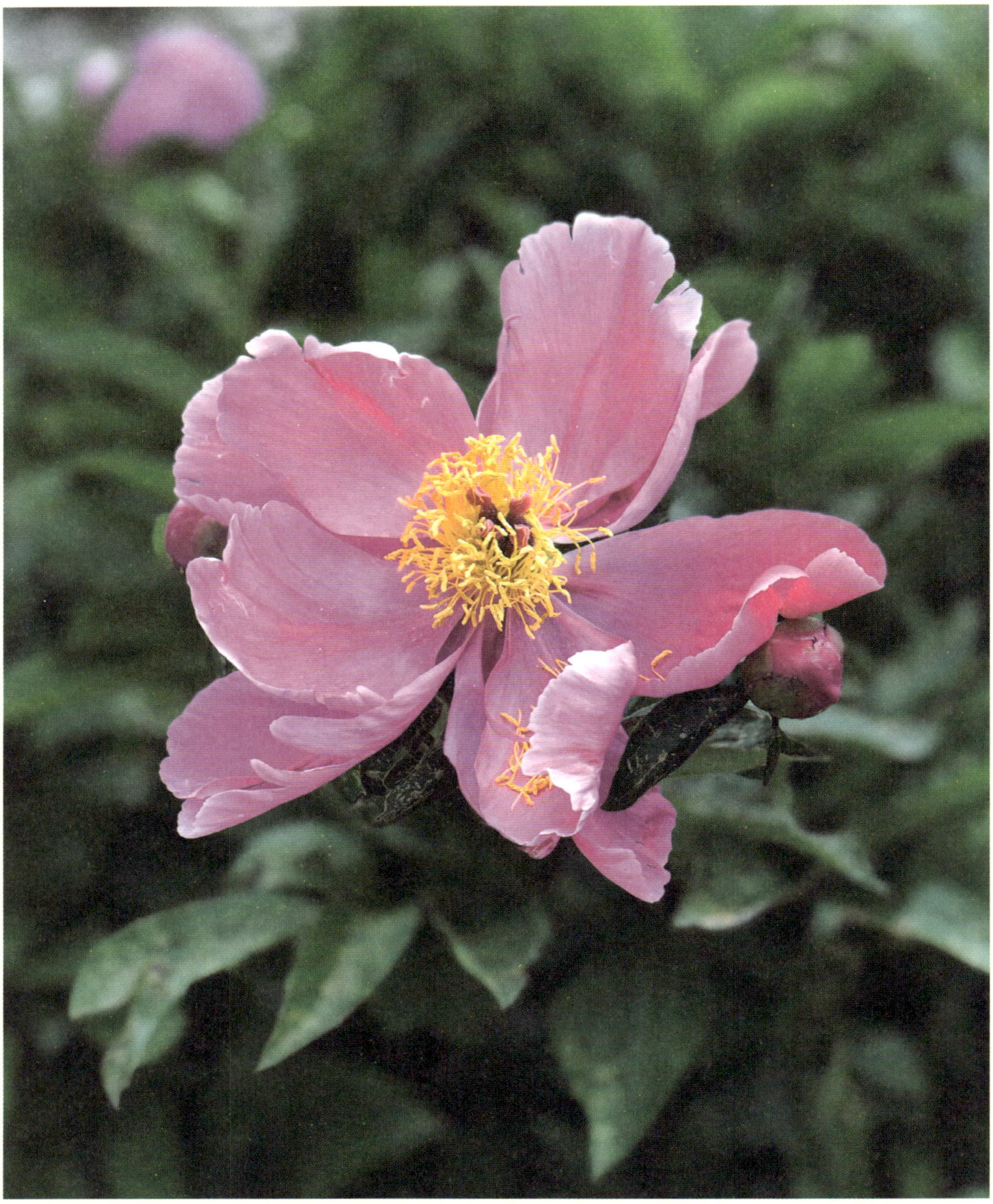

Once again, begin by reviewing the basic shapes of the petals and leaves that you will use to create your floral—in this case, a peony. There are many varieties of peonies, so be sure to practice the specific variety you choose to capture, as they do not all look the same. If you wish, you can model your artwork on this gorgeous peony from my garden! I always enjoy using a photograph that I took of a flower as a reference.

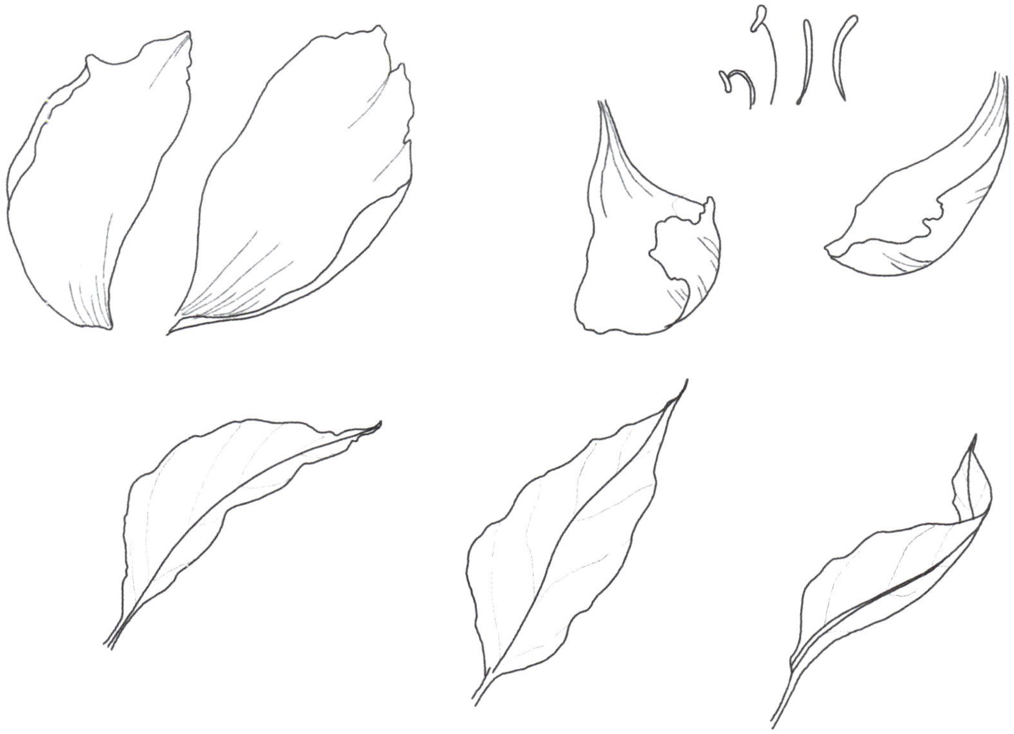

Step 1

Practice outlining your petals and leaves from different angles. You can also practice the different tendrils you will add to the center of the peony. Then trace over your sketches using tracing paper, or draw freehand.

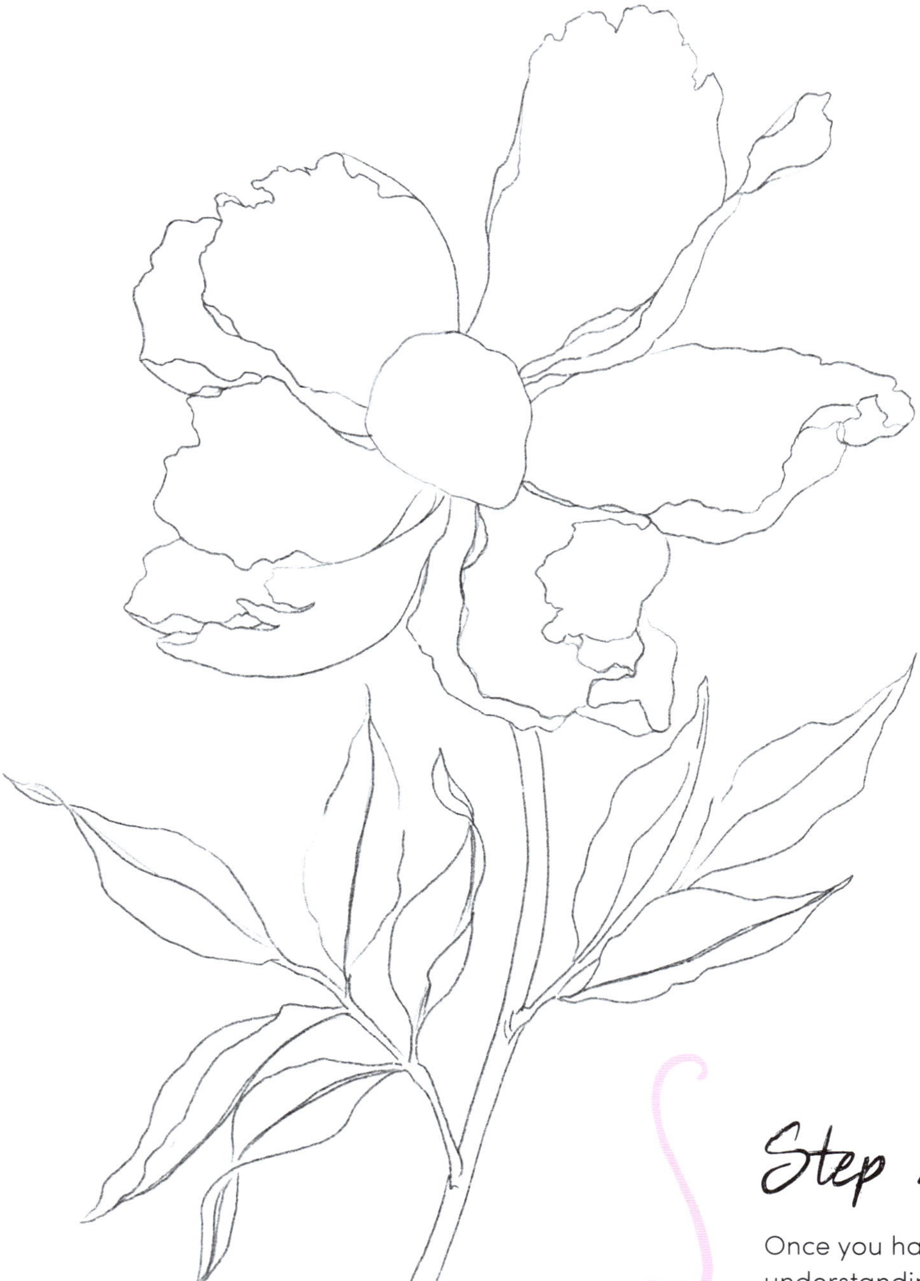

Step 2

Once you have a basic understanding of the angles and shapes of the petals and leaves of a peony, put them together in a pencil sketch. Due to the complexity of the center of this peony, draw a pencil circle where the details will go and do not add details at this stage.

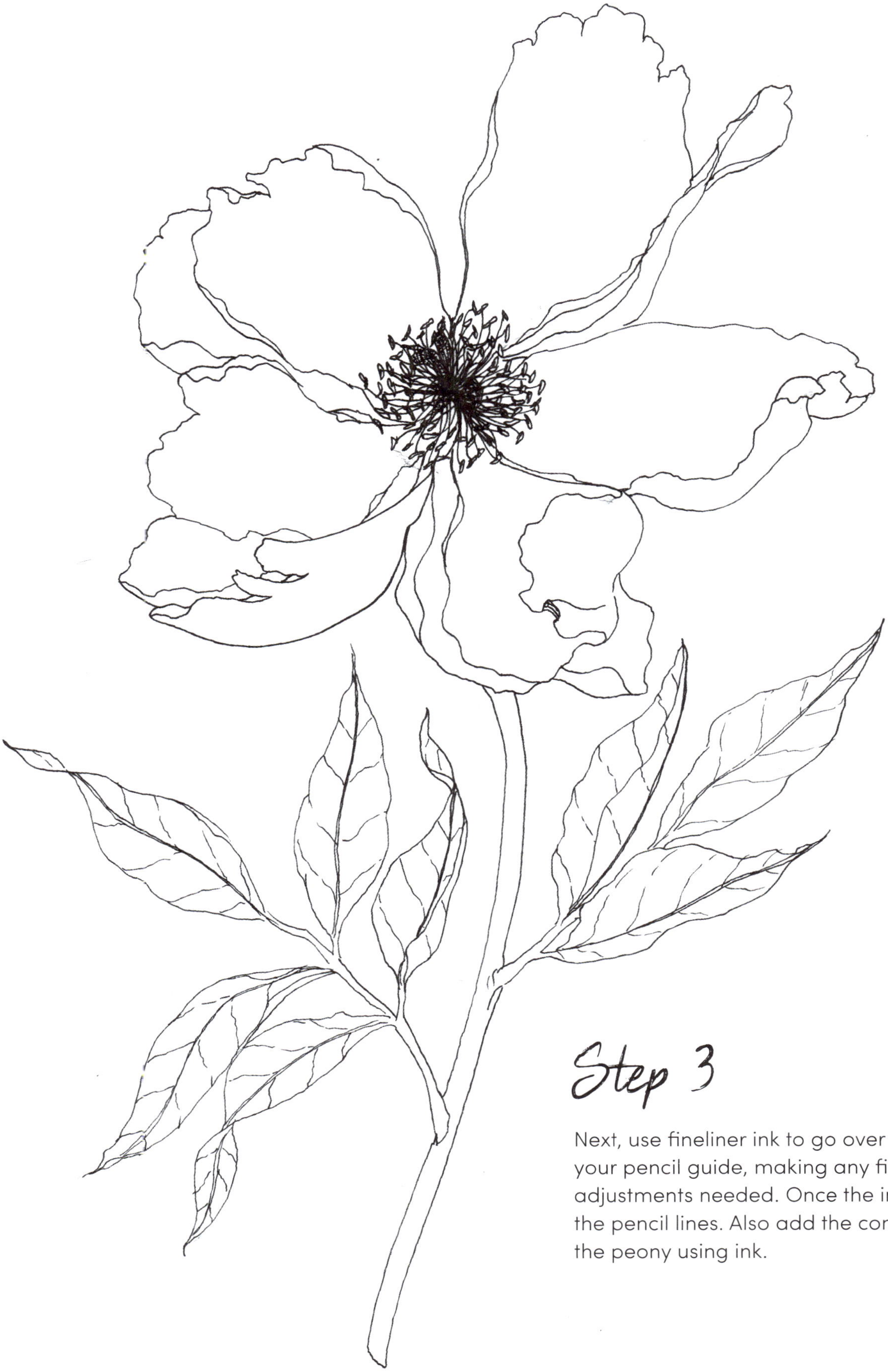

Step 3

Next, use fineliner ink to go over the lines of your pencil guide, making any final, subtle adjustments needed. Once the ink is dry, erase the pencil lines. Also add the complex center of the peony using ink.

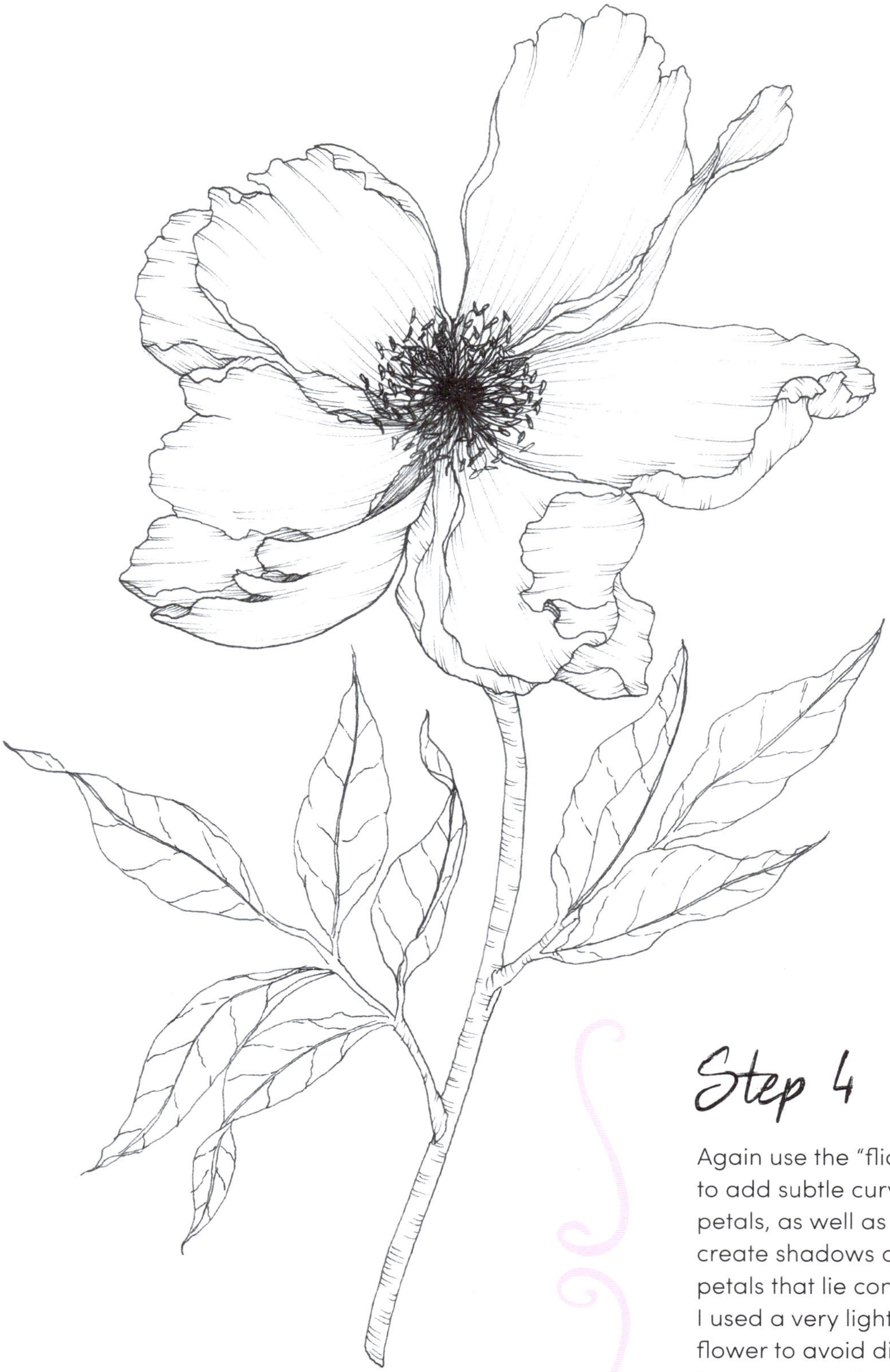

Step 4

Again use the "flick" technique to add subtle curved lines to the petals, as well as straight lines to create shadows on the parts of the petals that lie completely in shade. I used a very light line to shade this flower to avoid distracting from the gorgeous lines of the petals, but you should feel free to shade more liberally and create a darker image if you prefer.

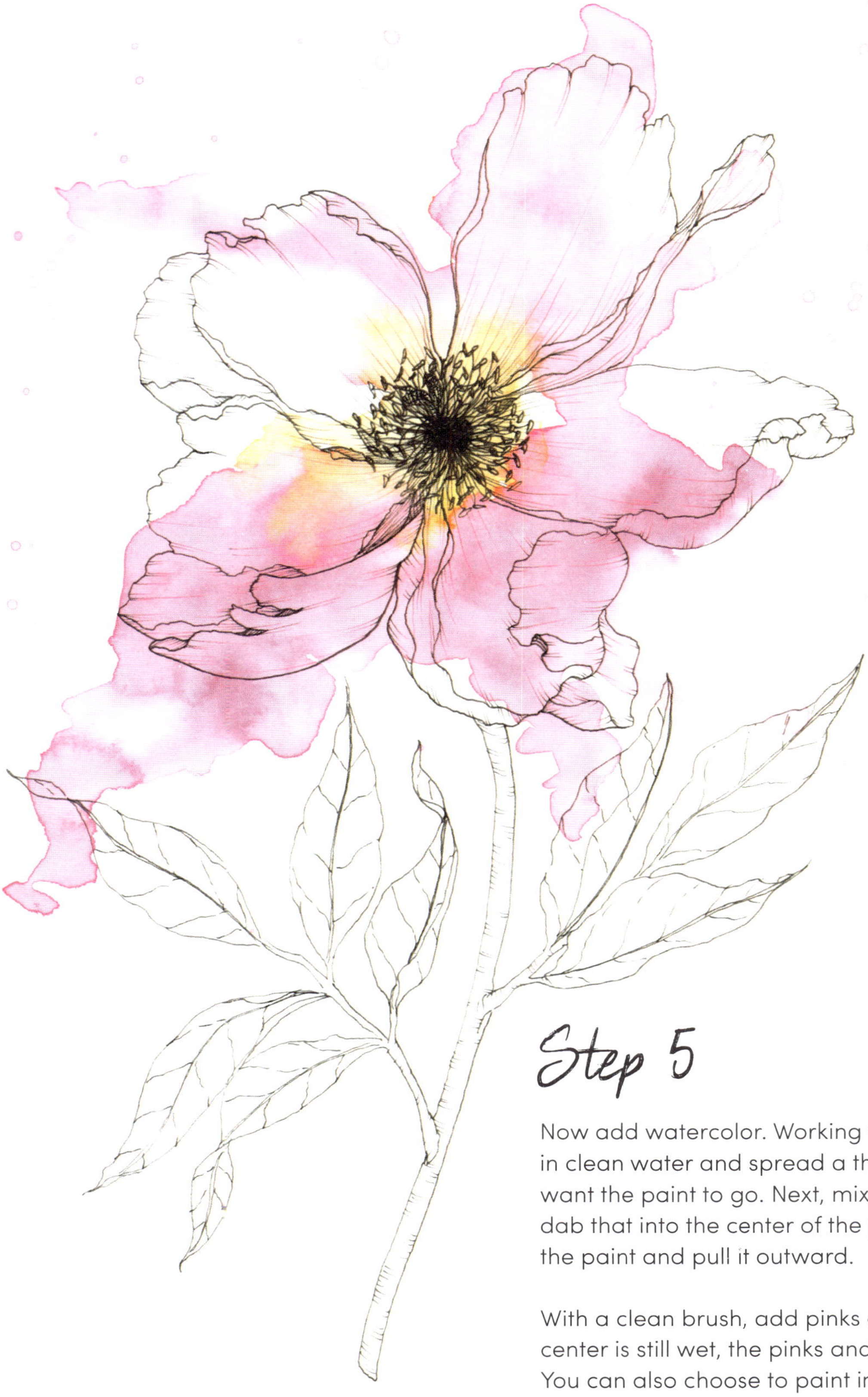

Step 5

Now add watercolor. Working wet-into-wet, dip a round brush in clean water and spread a thin layer over the page where you want the paint to go. Next, mix lemon-yellow with ochre and dab that into the center of the peony, letting the water pick up the paint and pull it outward.

With a clean brush, add pinks outside the yellow center. If the center is still wet, the pinks and yellows should blend beautifully. You can also choose to paint inside the lines using the wet-on-dry technique to create a more realistic-looking peony.

Drench a round brush in water and pink pigment and tap the brush gently about 10 inches above the page to let the spatter land whimsically.

Lupine

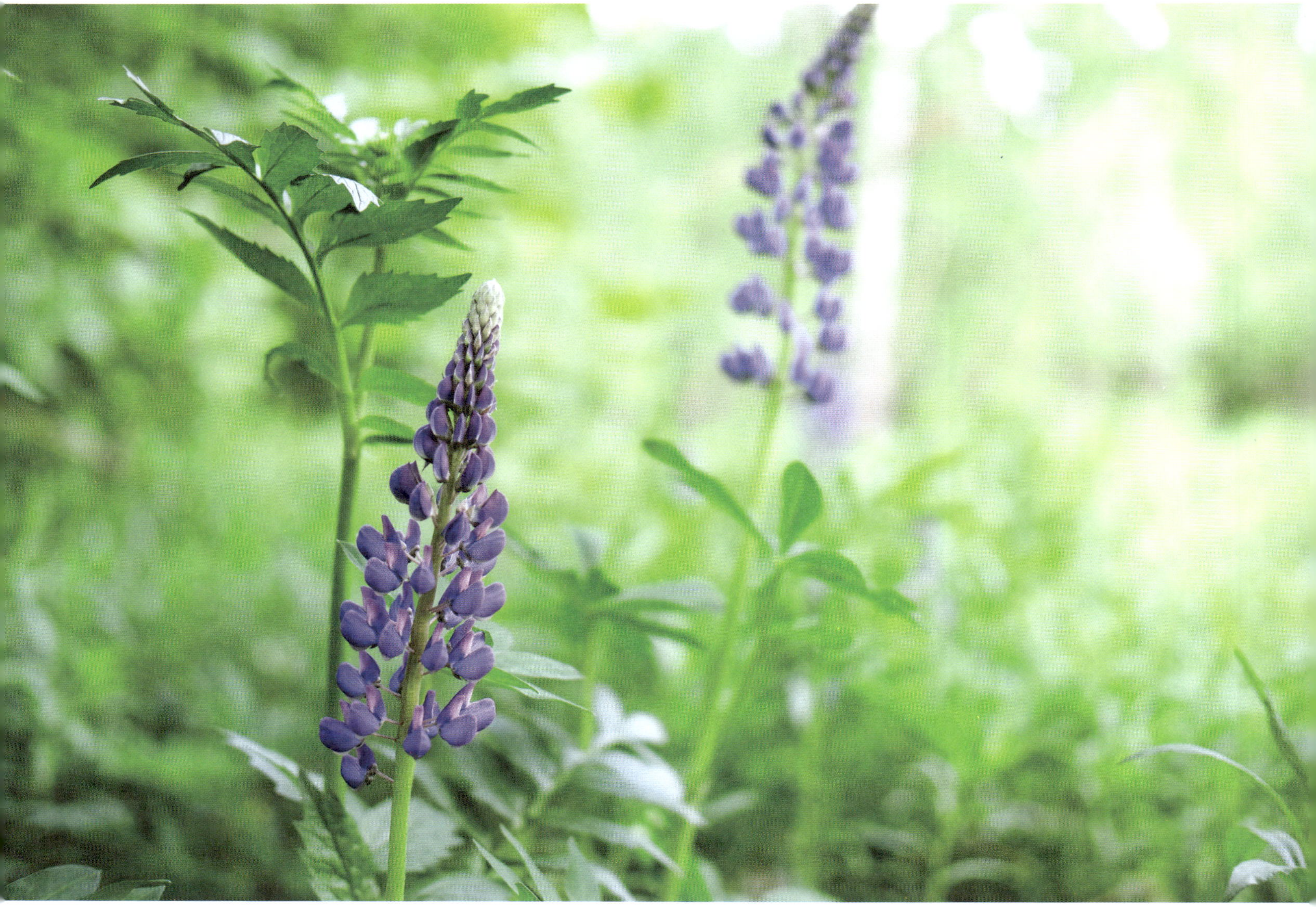

This is another flower that really builds upon itself and can be made as simple or complex as you like, depending on how intricately you layer the flowers along the stalk. Lupines feature a complexity that's different than the flowers we've drawn so far, and each flower may seem a bit daunting at first. However, because the basic components and shapes that make up the entire flower are straightforward and simple, lupines are great practice for building up your skills before moving on to slightly more difficult but similar flowers, like the snapdragon (pages 110–113).

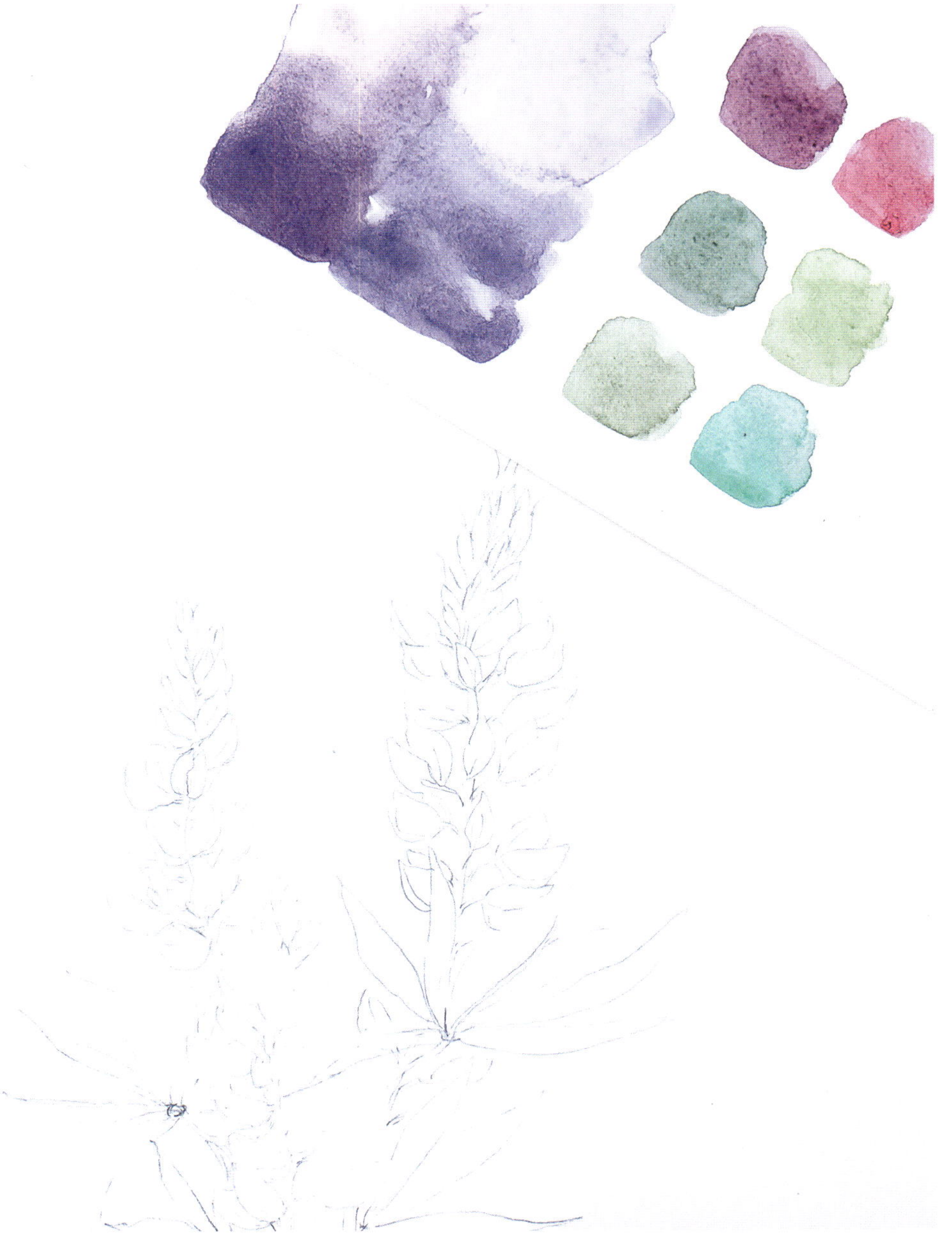

Step 1

Building up these flowers is pretty simple. Keeping in mind the angle from which you are looking at a flower—whether it's directly, at an angle, or from the side—will help you correctly draw the elements of each flower. Lupines have a rather conical shape, so make sure to give the impression that they are filled in all the way around.

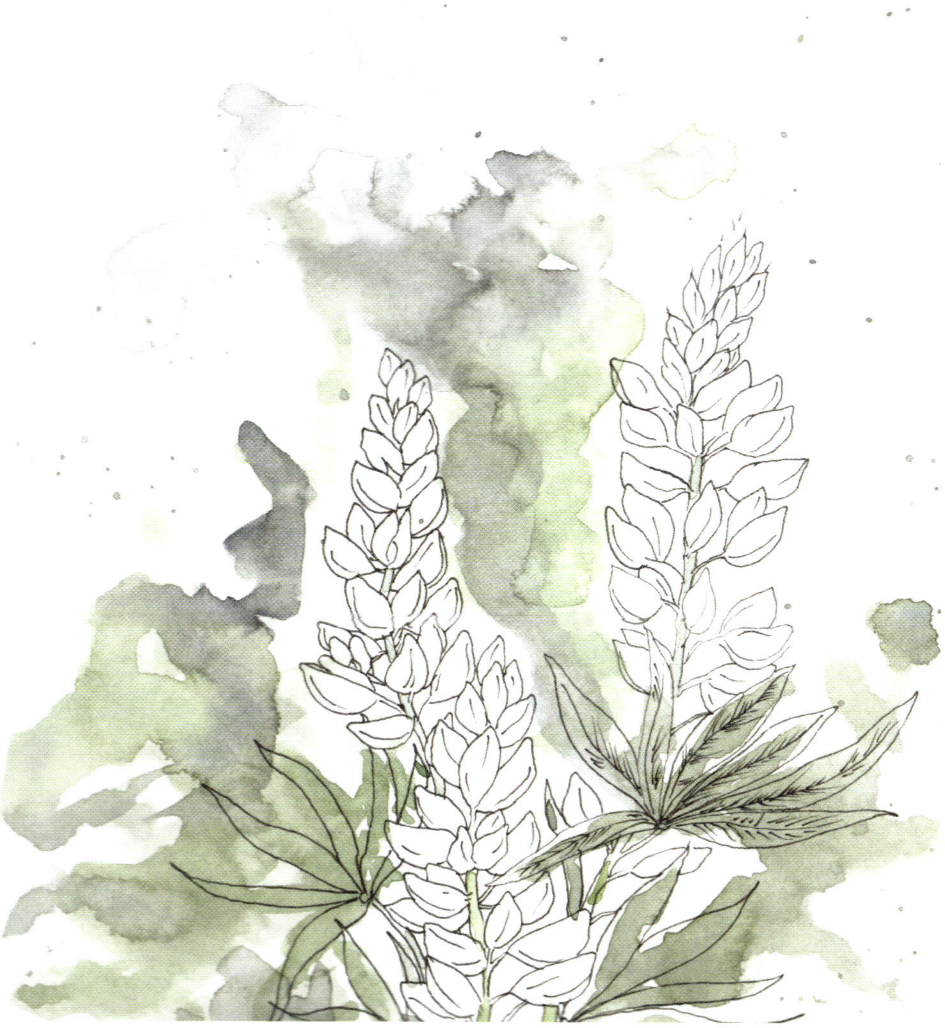

Step 2

For the thicker stalks that hold up the lupines, you can shade with curved horizontal dashes that reach one-third of the way across the stalk to give the impression of roundness and sturdiness.

I particularly love featuring lupines in bouquets, either as the singular flower in the display or as part of a multi-flower bouquet.

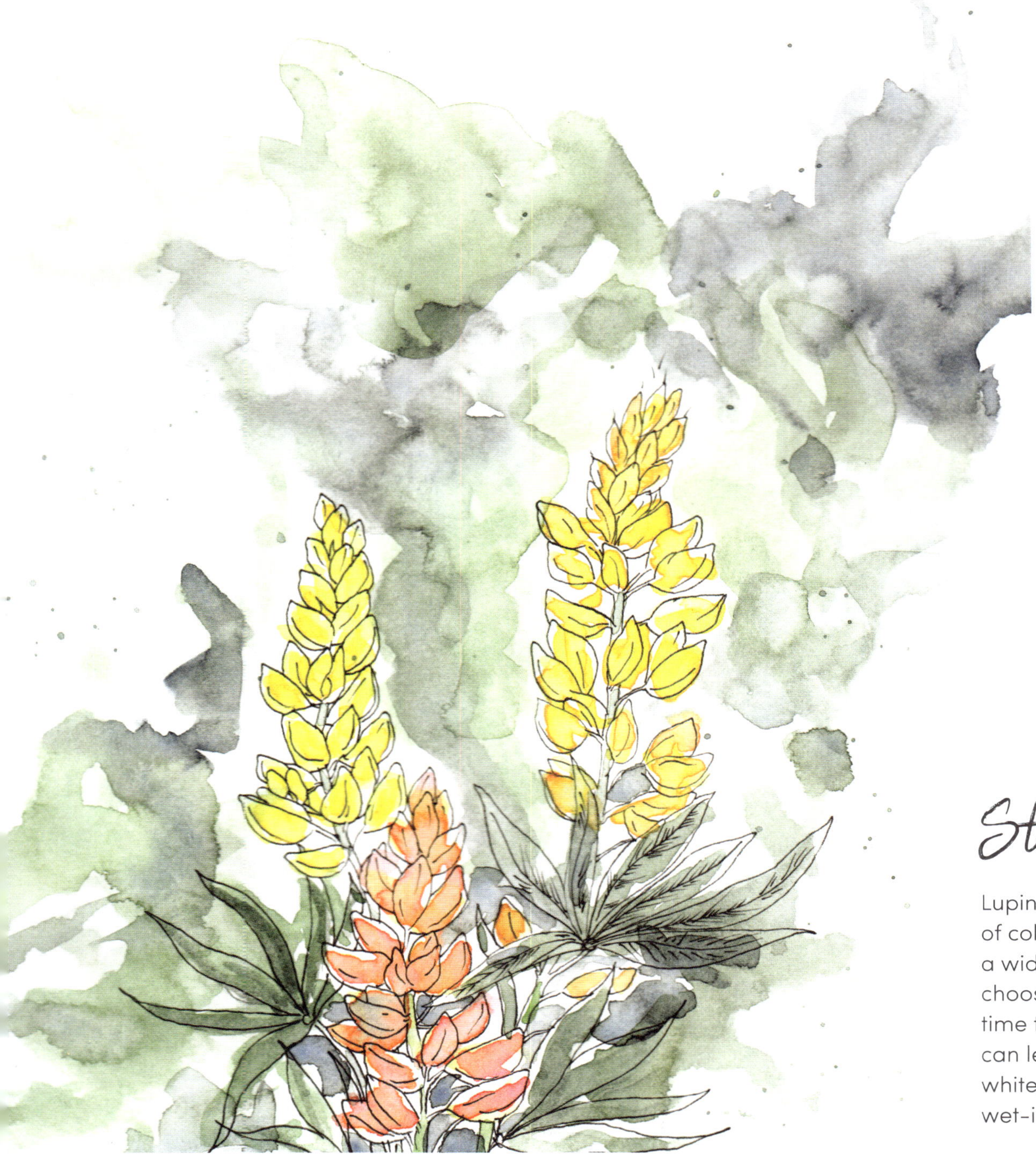

Step 3

Lupines come in all sorts of colors, so you will have a wide array of hues to choose from when it's time to add color. You can leave the flowers white, or add a splash of wet-into-wet color.

Snapdragon

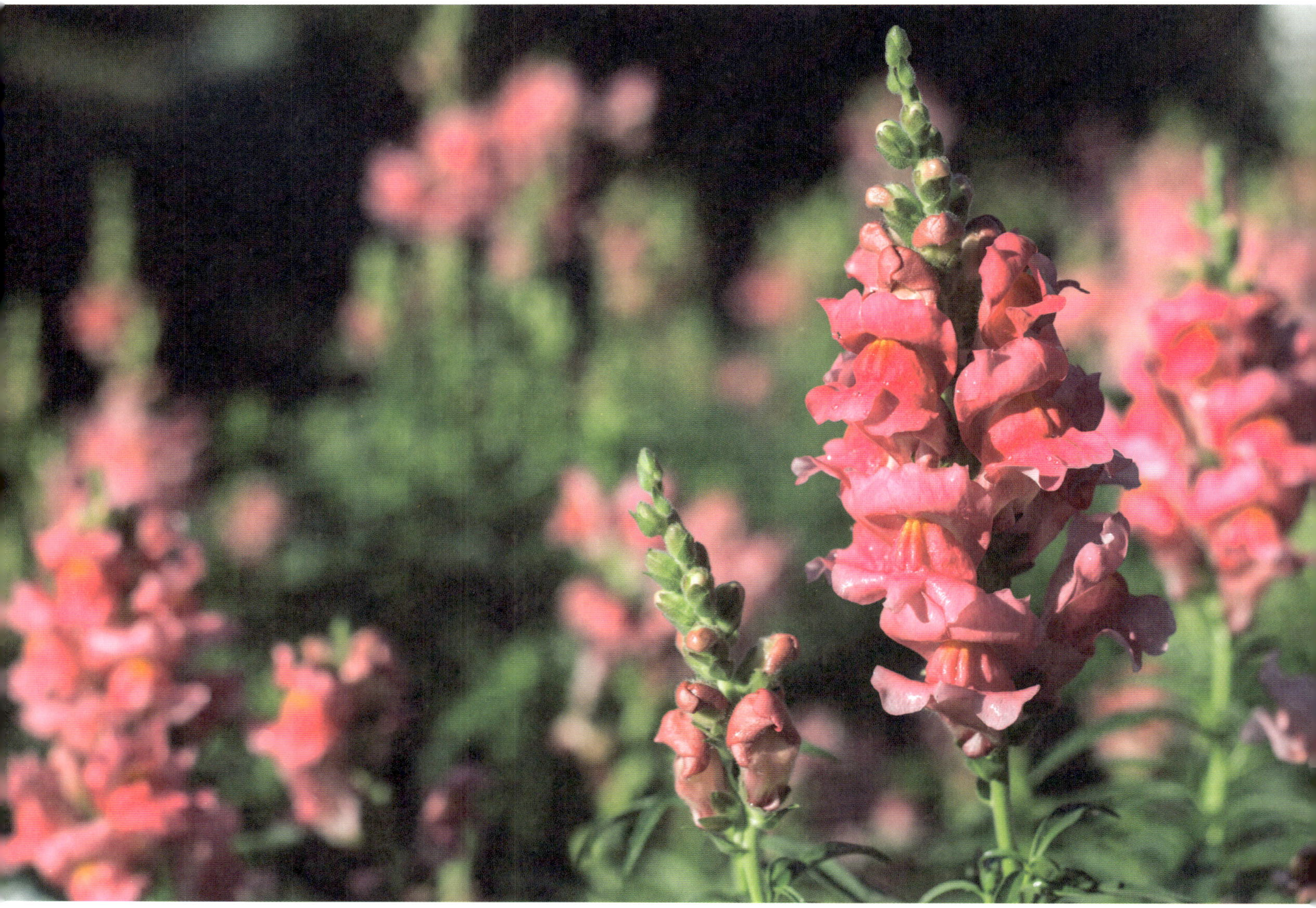

Snapdragons are so much fun to play with. Their name comes from their resemblance to the head of a dragon; by pinching near the base of the flower, you can make the flower's "jaws" open like a snapping dragon!

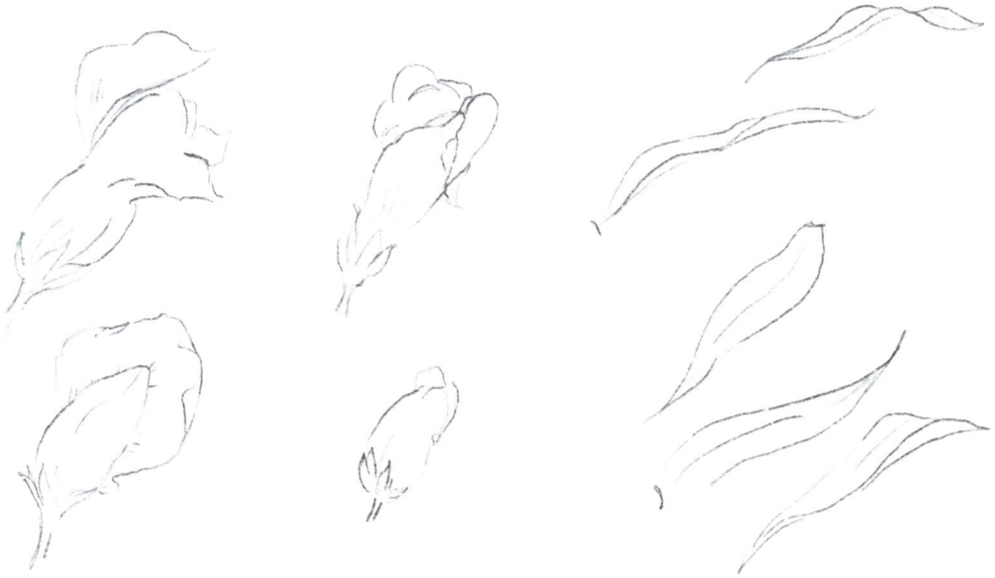

Step 1

Slowly build up the flowers using different angles; then add sparse shading.

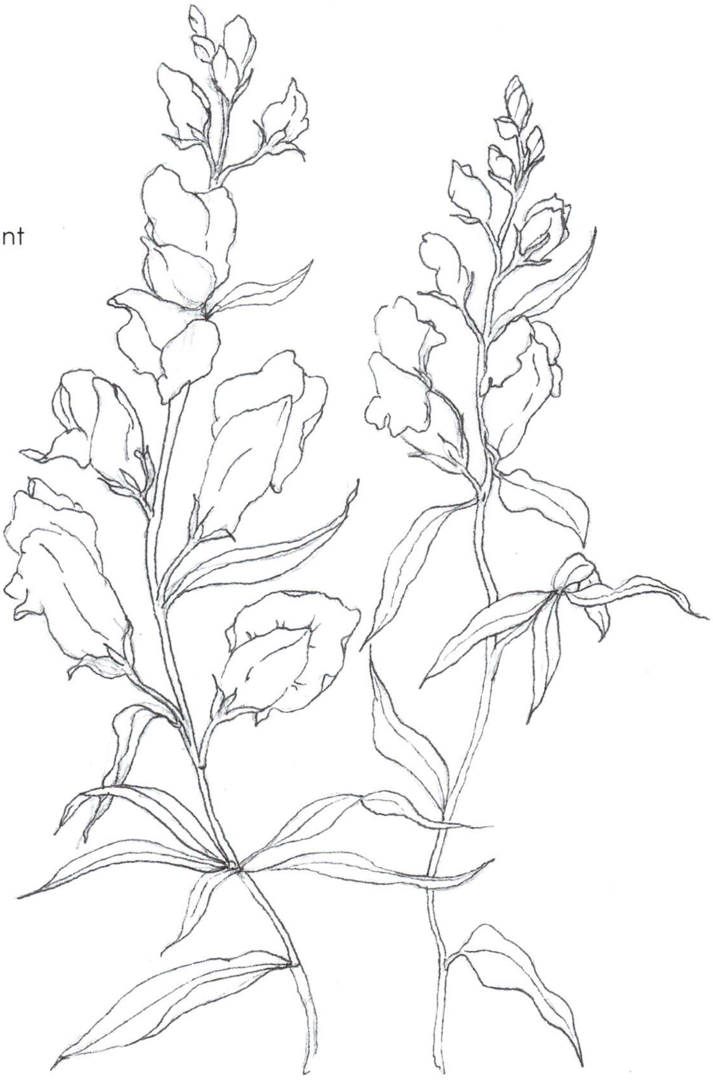

Step 2

I decided to make my snapdragon look almost like a rainbow. In order to give snapdragons' rainbowlike state the best showing possible, keep your colors inside the lines. A splashy watercolor might look too muddy and messy, but by keeping the watercolor constrained, you can really showcase the beautiful color and whimsical ink lines.

Begin with the palest of pinks and fill the flowers by painting wet-on-dry. While this paint layer is still wet, you can come in with darker pinks, yellows, and oranges to create the rainbow effect with a wet-into-wet technique. This allows the paint colors to blend beautifully and seamlessly.

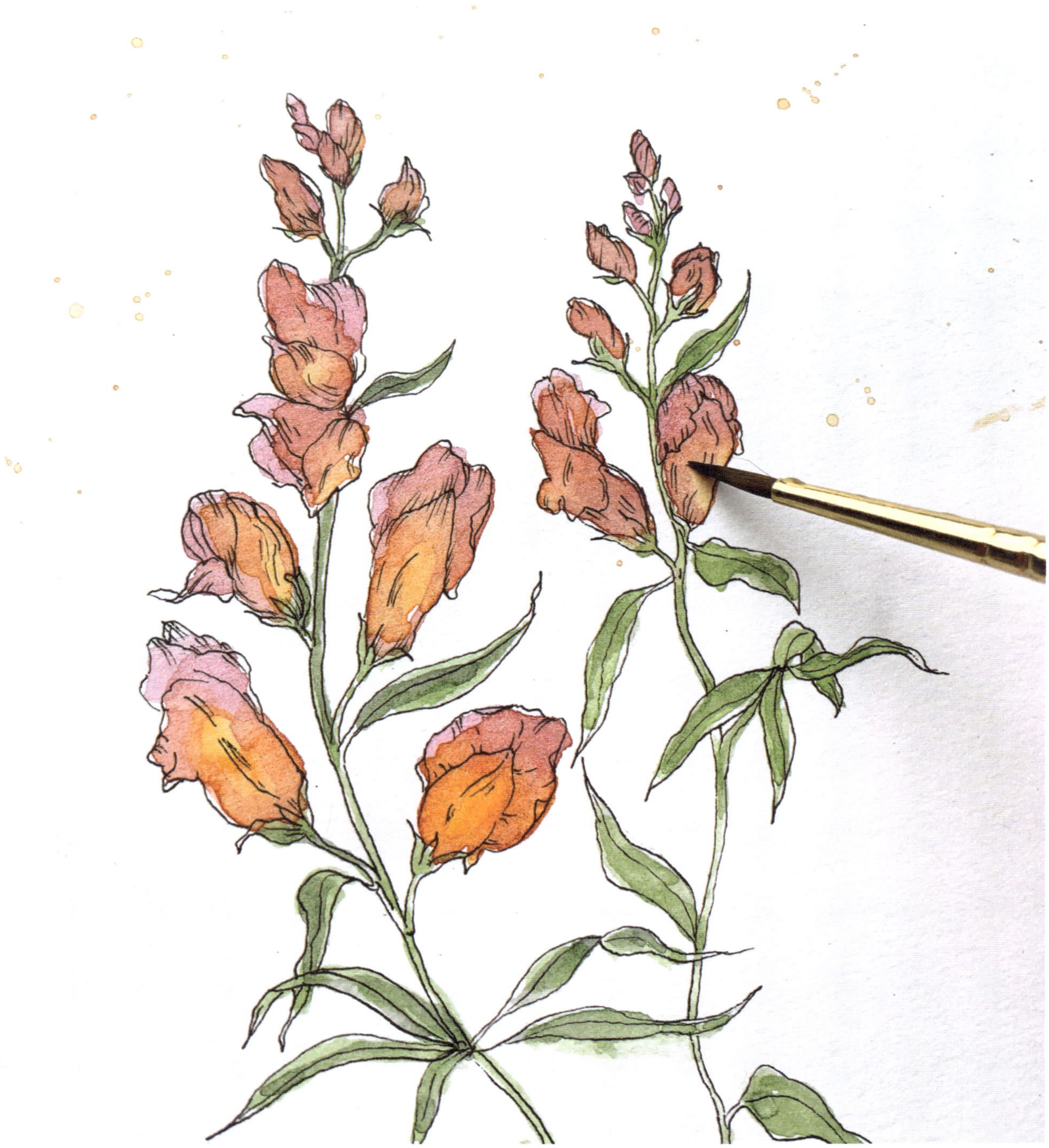

Step 3

For the leaves, begin with a pale green, and add darker green while the paint is still wet, as well as a few spots of gray and green for darker effects. Leaving some parts of the leaves pale green allows you to show highlights and remain consistent with your whimsical, loose watercolor vibe.

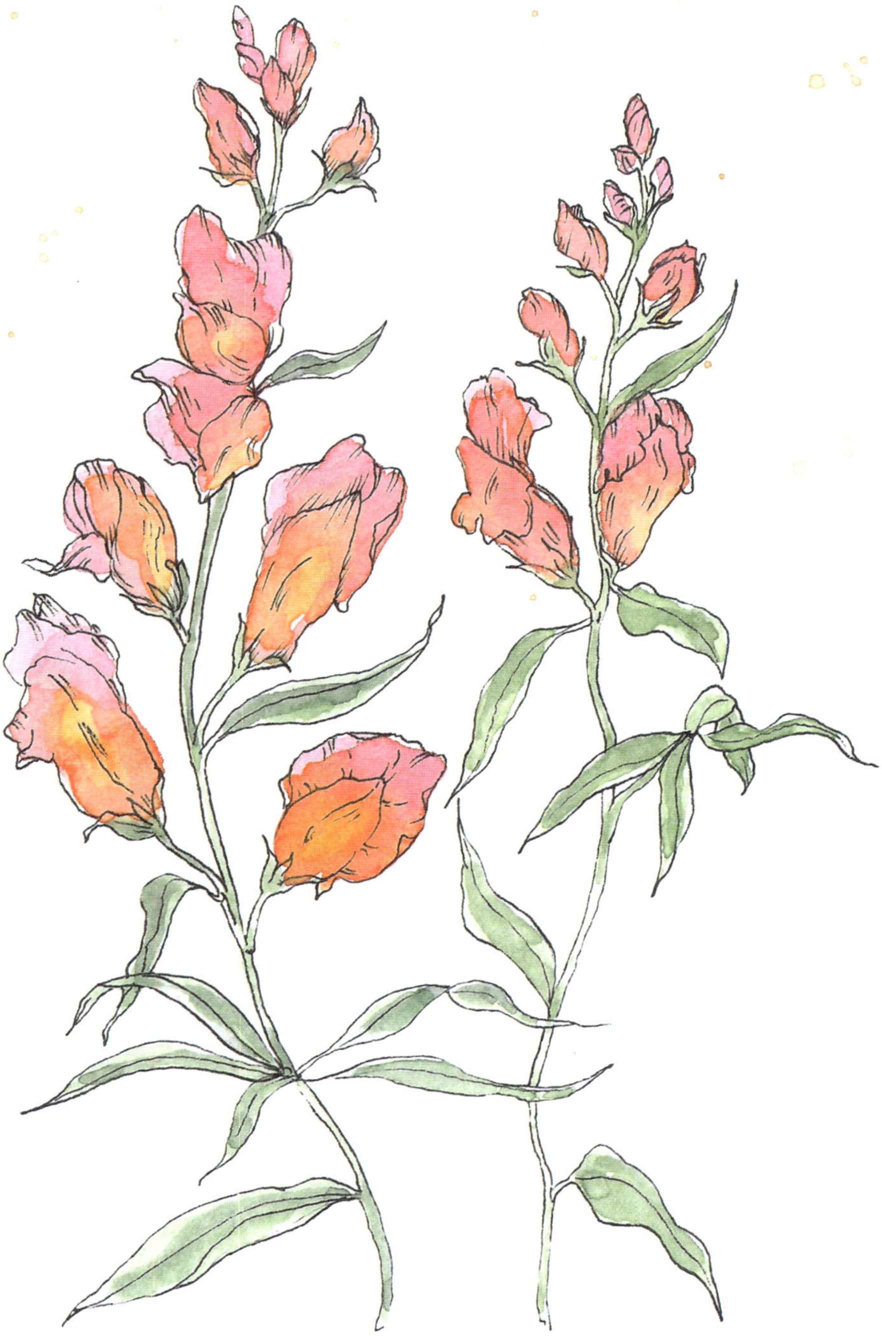

Chrysanthemum

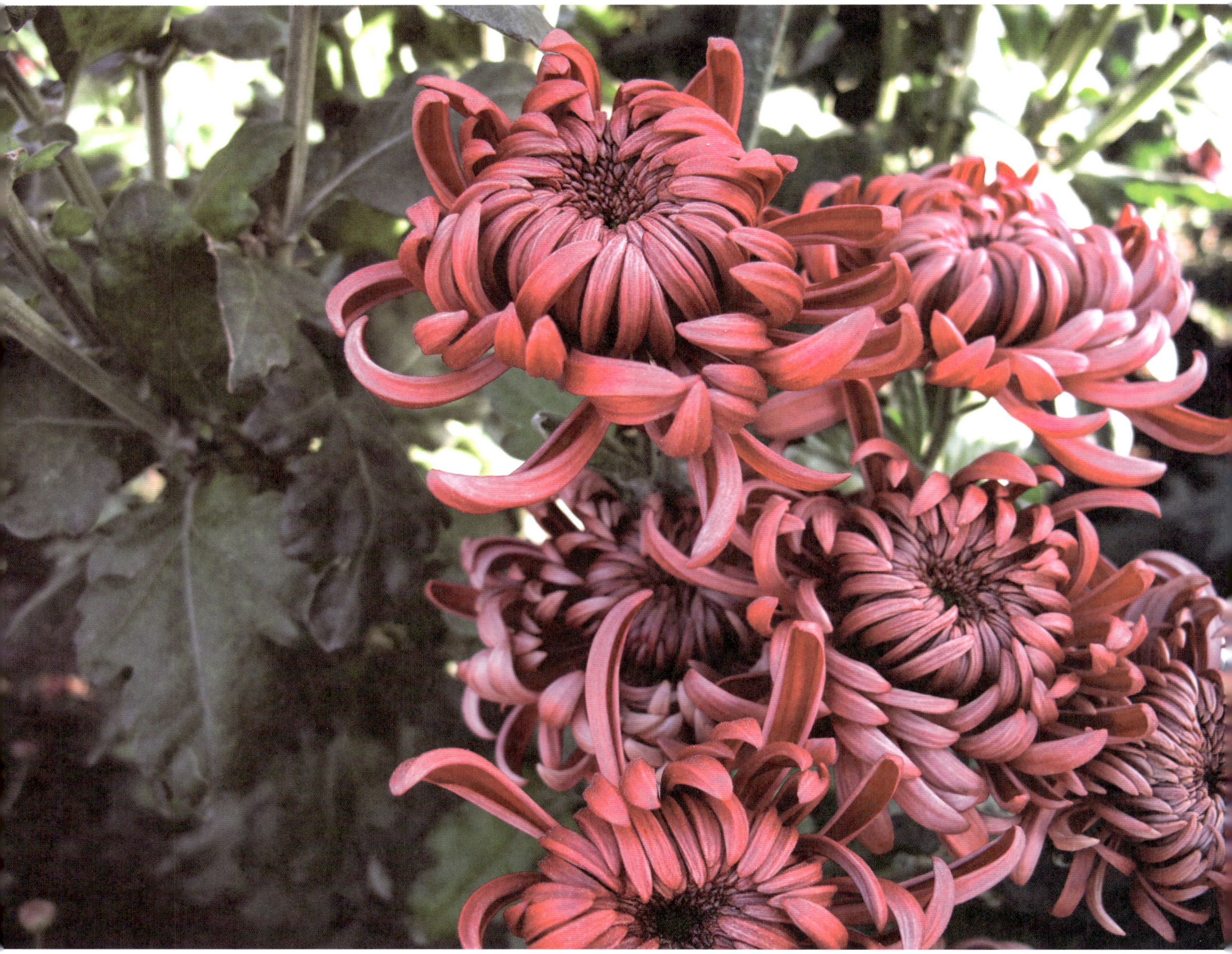

There are many chrysanthemum classifications—13 to be exact! For the purpose of this tutorial, we will look at one with a very simple petal that's layered in a way that creates a complex appearance. The general principle of building the petals over each other applies to all types of chrysanthemums. Once you learn how to break chrysanthemums down into simple steps, you can draw all of the different types.

Step 1

Determine the shapes of the individual petals; then practice drawing them from different angles. This chrysanthemum has a very uniform way of building petals onto each other. Knowing which angles to use in each section of the image will help you greatly.

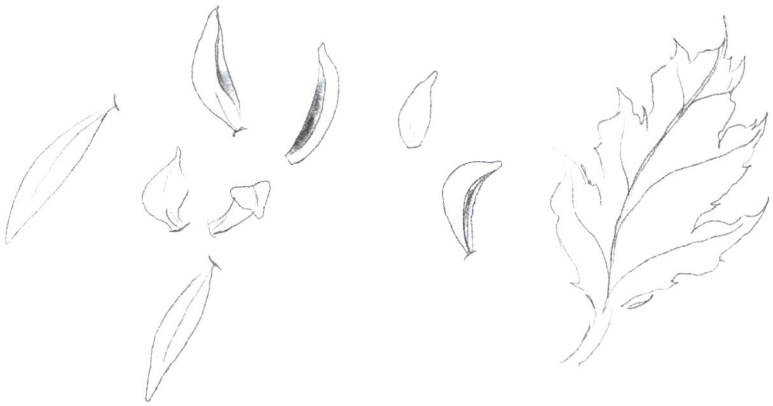

For this flower, start at the center and move outward in a circular motion. Notice how I drew this circular pattern, using numbers to order the rows of petals.

The petals are relatively uniform, even in their chaos, so you can add some more character to the leaves to help the flower "pop" on the page.

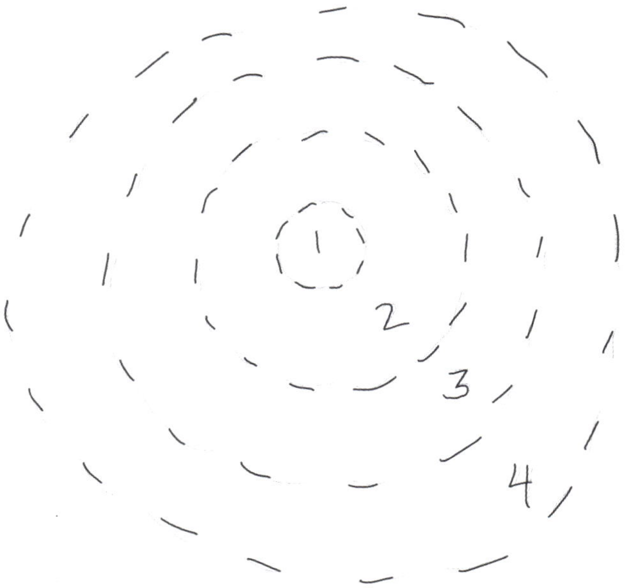

For more complex flowers, I like to have a reference photo on my phone. This way, I can zoom in exactly where I am working, and slowly start zooming out as I add layers.

You can also print out your reference photo on cheap printer paper and cross out the petals as you work your way through them.

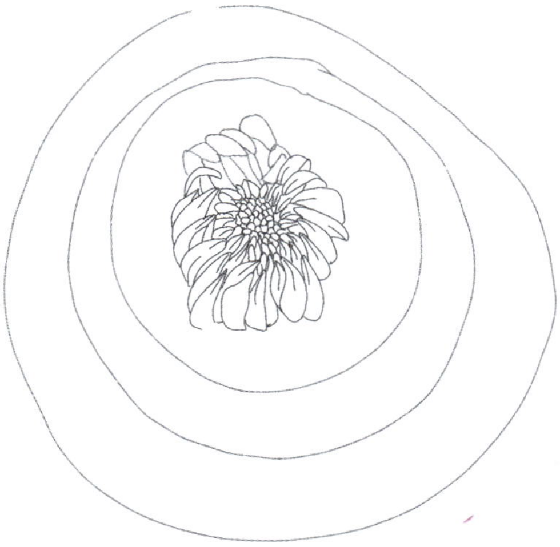

Step 2

Start with a pale purple base using the wet-on-dry technique. Then begin layering, ensuring that the darkest parts are in the center of each petal, where the shadows fall. As you add layers, you will create the appearance of a wet-into-wet technique, which allows for a looser-feeling paint that still falls within the constrained lines.

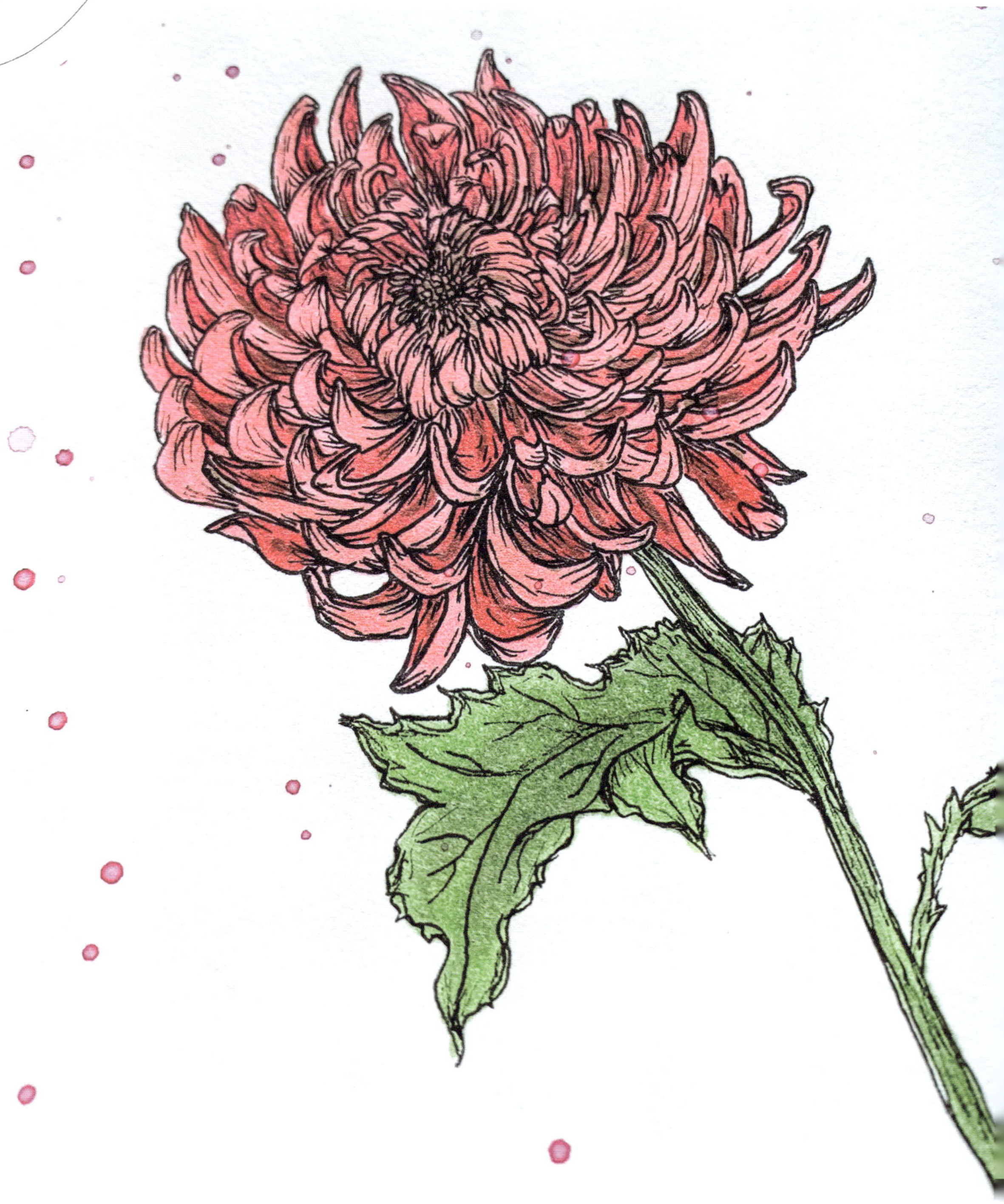

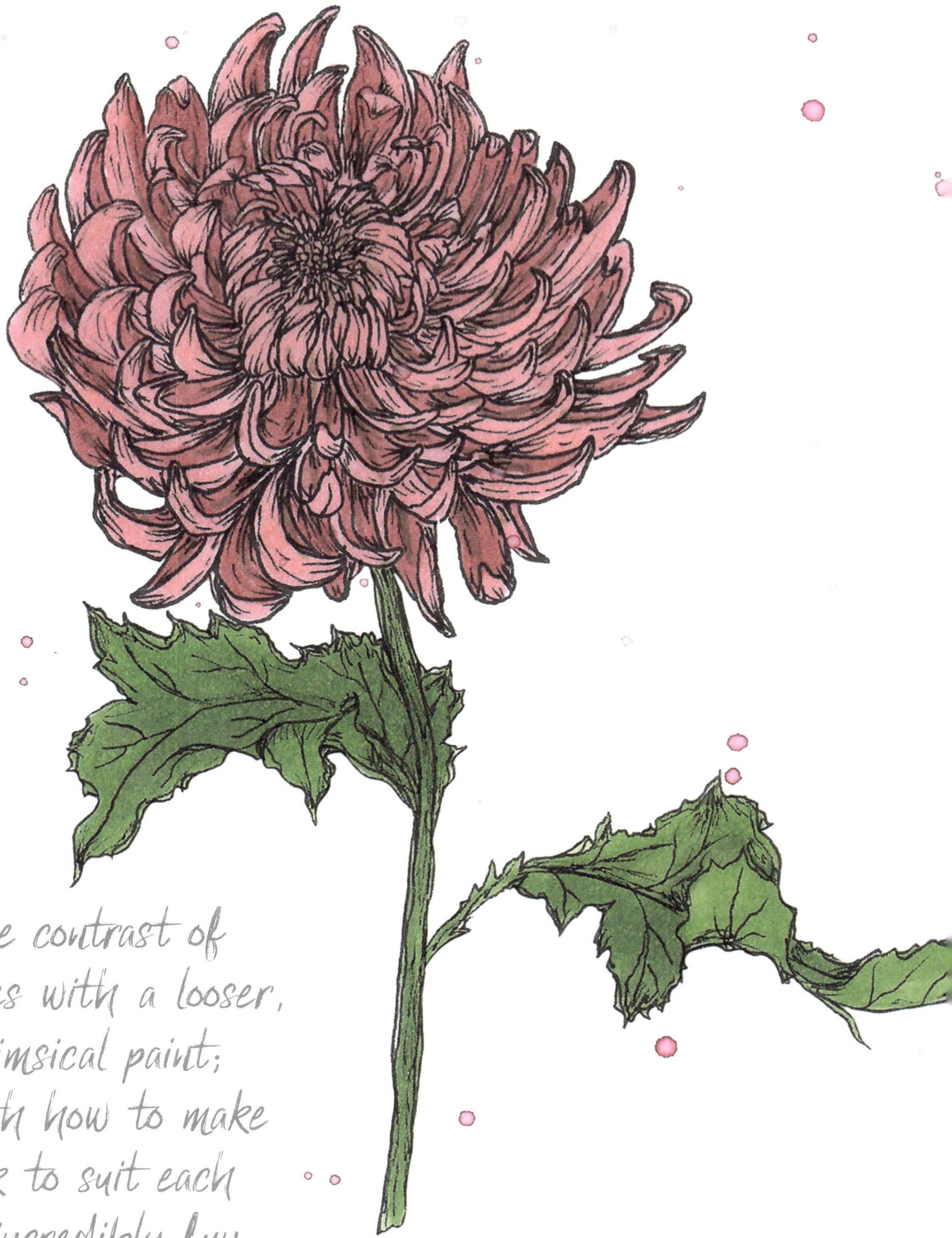

I love the contrast of
straight lines with a looser,
more whimsical paint;
playing with how to make
this work to suit each
flower is incredibly fun.

Filler Foliage

Filler foliage is versatile and incredibly easy to create. If you know the basic structure of a plant and a handful of leaf shapes, you can create any number of filler greens for wreaths, bouquets, gardens, and more. They're lovely for filling space, adding contrast, and creating lines that draw the viewer's eyes to your central piece: your florals.

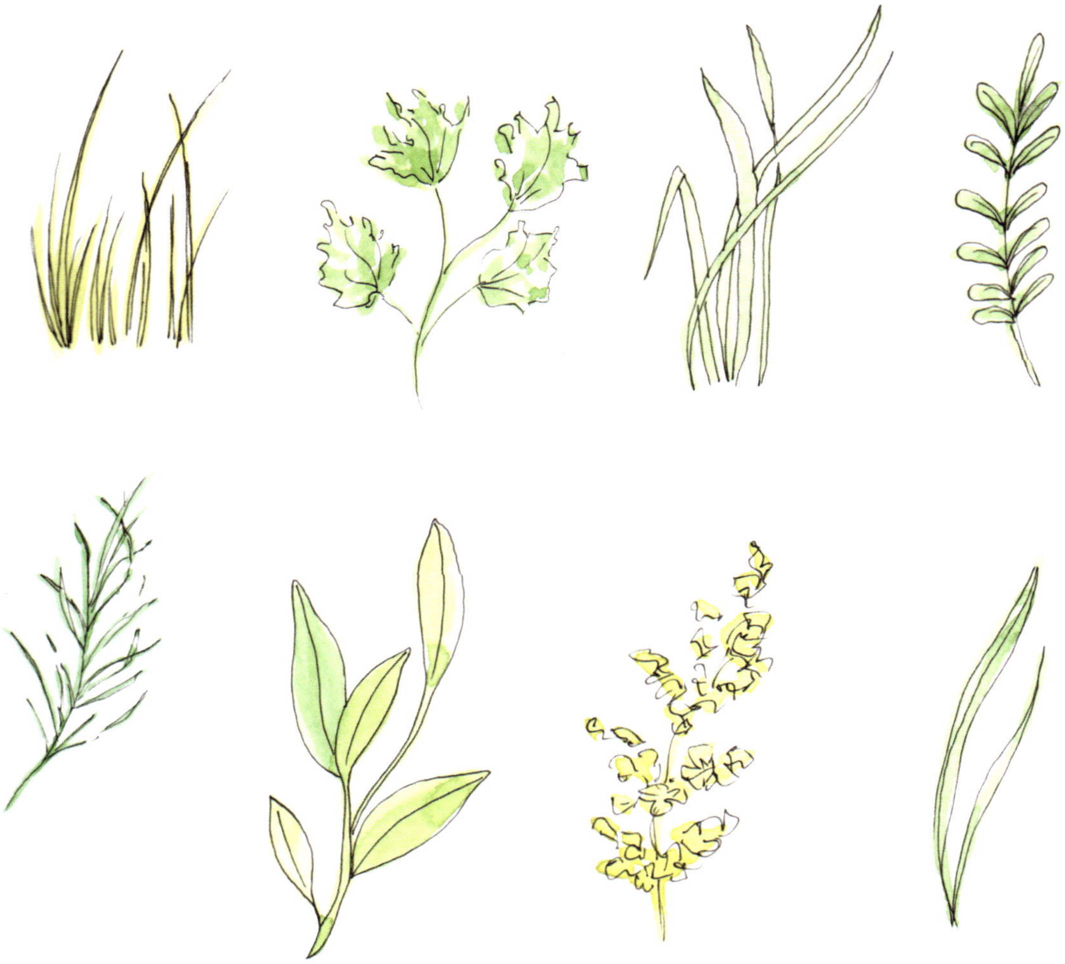

Here, we will look at several simple ways to use similar shapes to create different looks and styles of filler foliage. For variety, I used different colors for the leaves and incorporated plain branches and pine boughs for a contrasting effect against the soft florals.

Once we get into the next section, which features bouquets, you will learn how to use this filler foliage in simple, elegant, and eye-catching ways. Filler greenery can be used to create a denser bouquet or wreath, as well as to add whimsy and lightness to a piece.

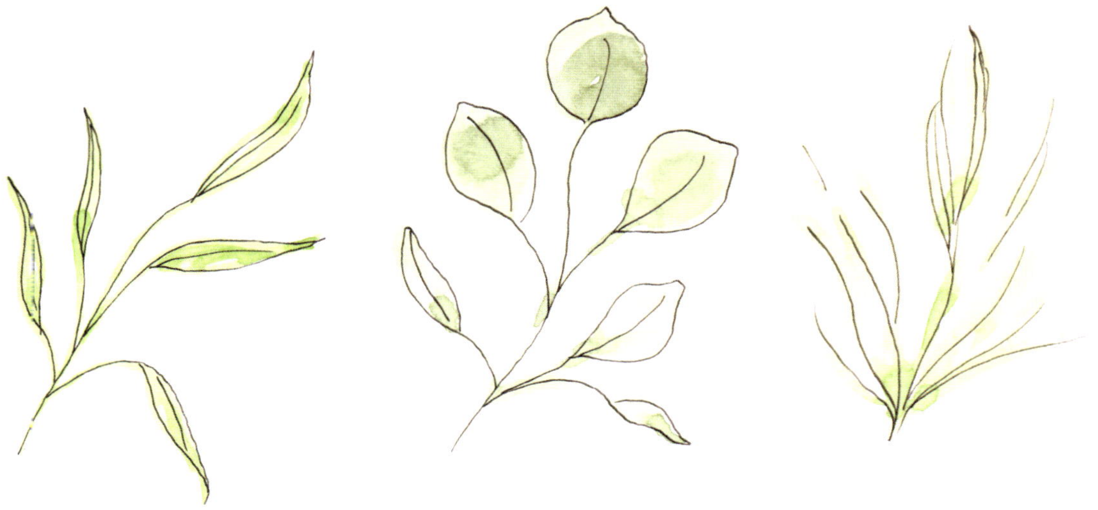

As you can see, it's possible to use a simple leaf shape to create various types of foliage and greenery. Depending on the season you wish to portray, you can fill foliage and greenery with different colors to make your scene flow beautifully. For instance, for springtime filler, you could draw a leafy branch featuring buds with bright green splashes or even blossoms. In a summertime bouquet, this same leafy branch might have dense, full leaves. For autumn? You guessed it: Add a beautiful yellow or red display to the same branch. For winter, use just a sparse branch as filler. This can be beautiful too!

I also love to incorporate coniferous branches and trees into my work. These can beautifully accent a winter scene and create a strong contrast with soft, curvy florals.

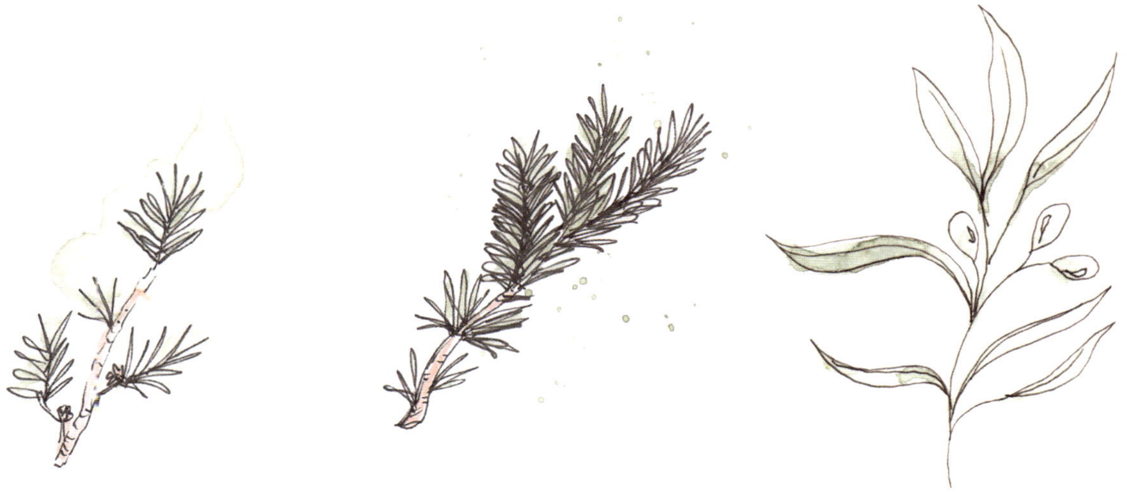

Putting It All Together

My art style is pretty simple and straightforward: a little bit of detailed or loose ink, plus some loose watercolor. However, this style can also evolve and become more complex over time, depending on what you're looking to do.

Take a look at the cover of this book, as well as its full image on page 4. It's complex, intricate, and simple, all at the same time. Do with this style what you will! Here are a few examples of ways that you can use this art style to create different scenes and moods.

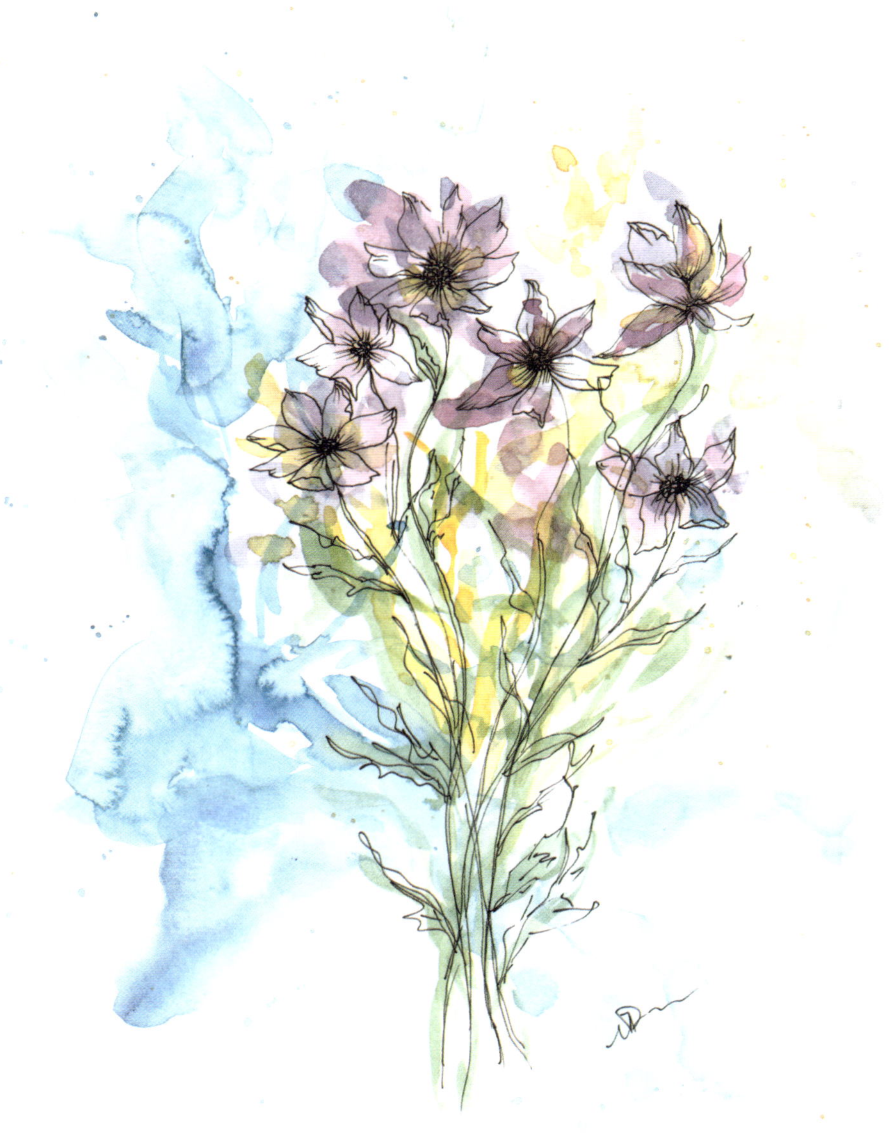

Bouquets

Bouquets can be complex and dense or loose and whimsical. Here, I very loosely laid the watercolor paints, keeping a general idea in my head of where I might want to add ink flowers.

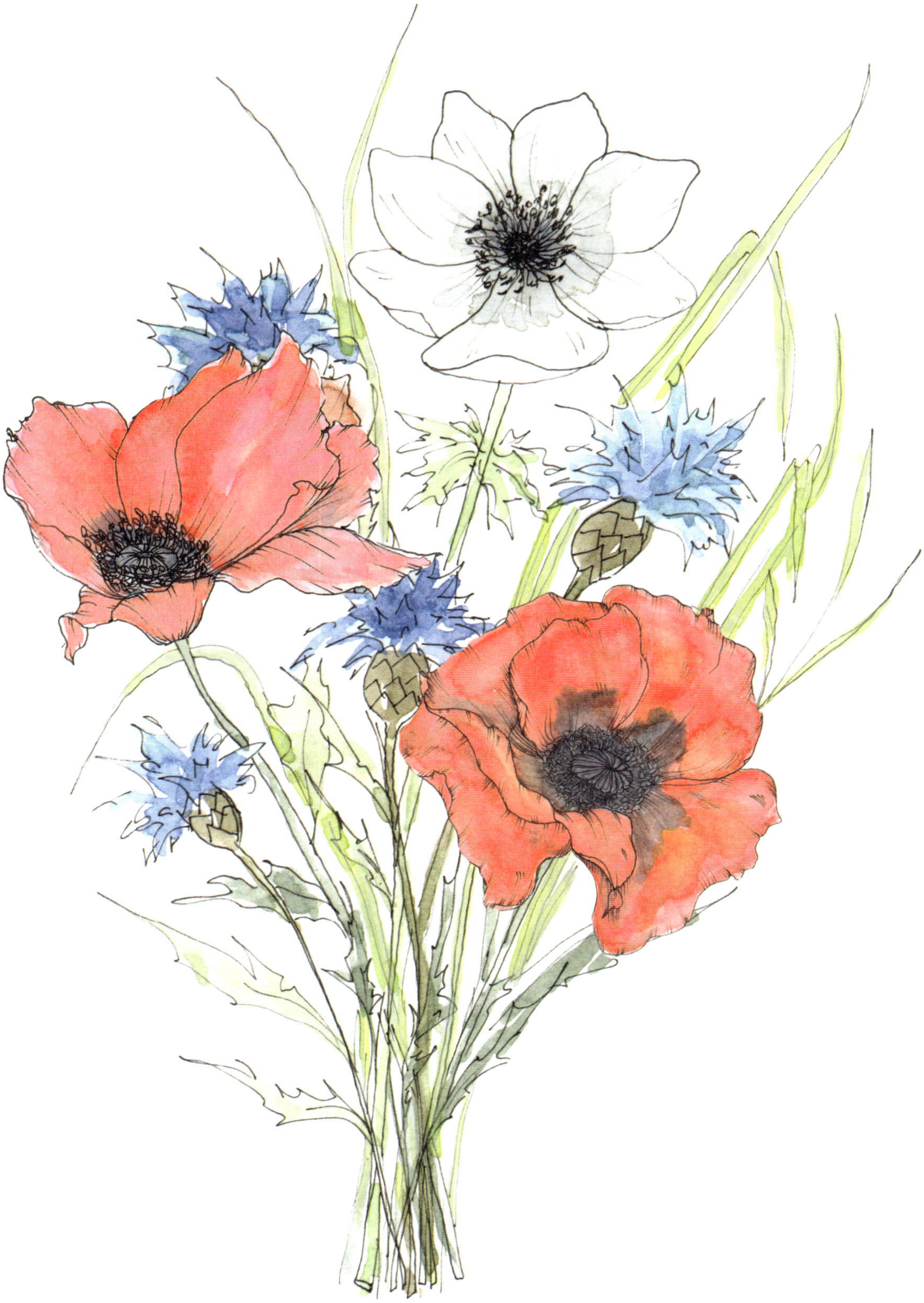

You can also build on your ink skills, creating a wholly black-ink bouquet and going more in-depth with your ink shading; then create a loose watercolor overlay behind your finished bouquet.

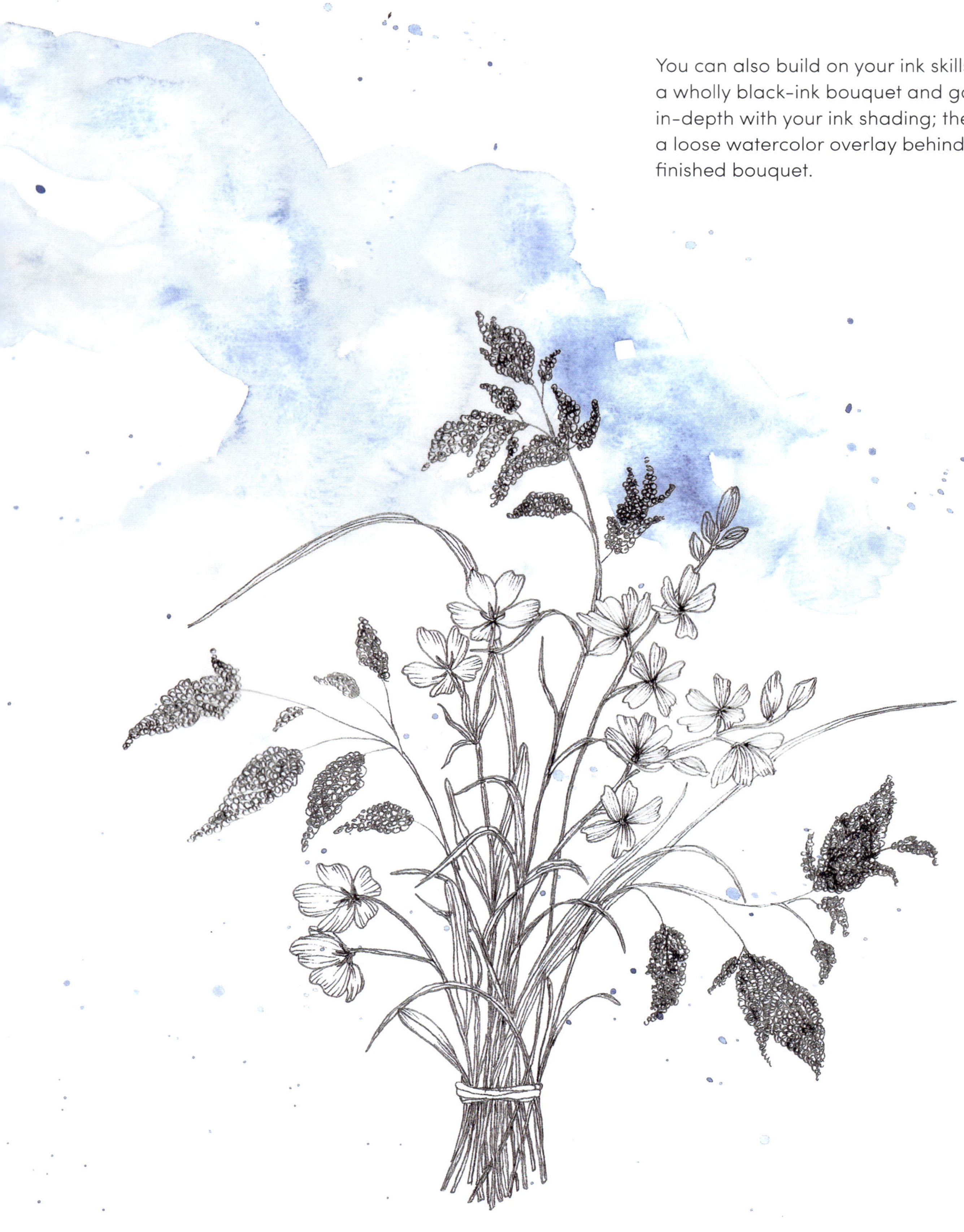

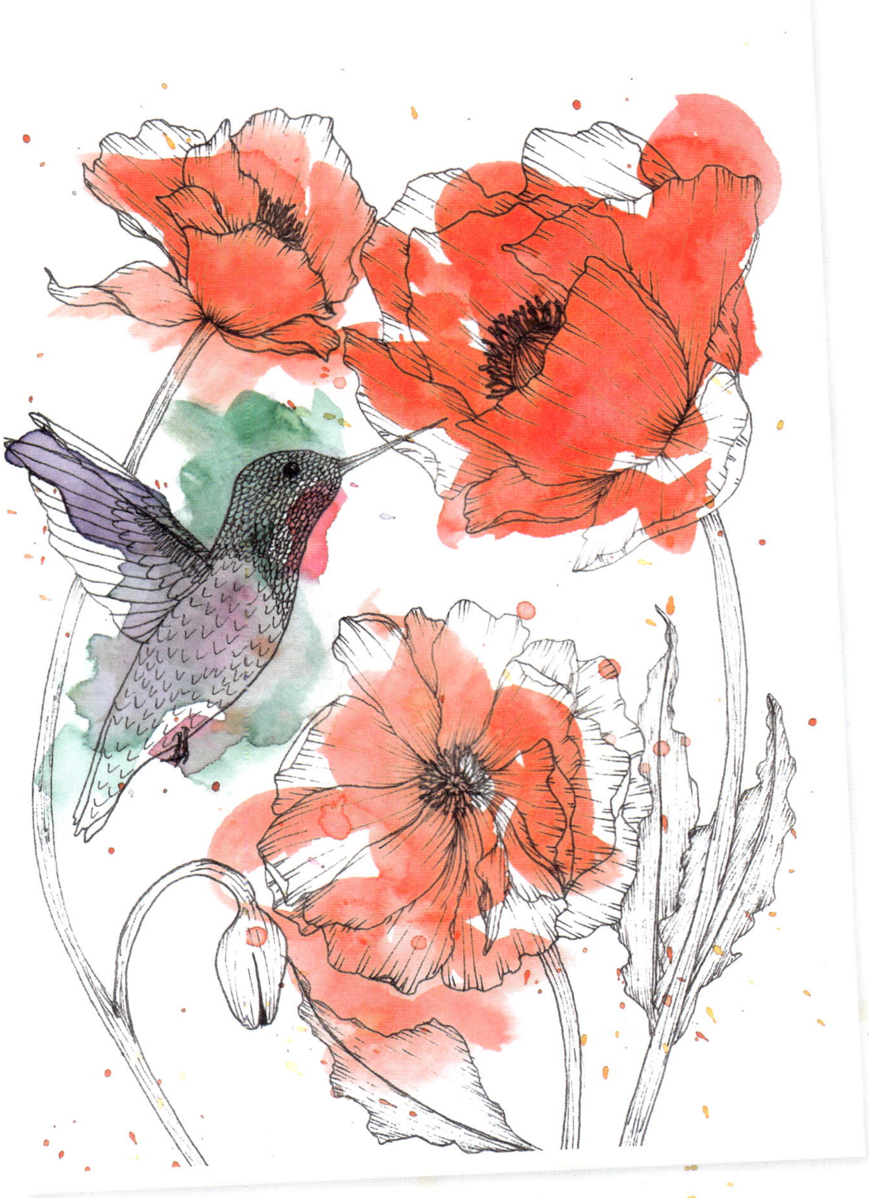

Animals

When creating floral and nature pieces, I love to add animals, as they are so integral to the proper function of nature. The two go seamlessly hand in hand!

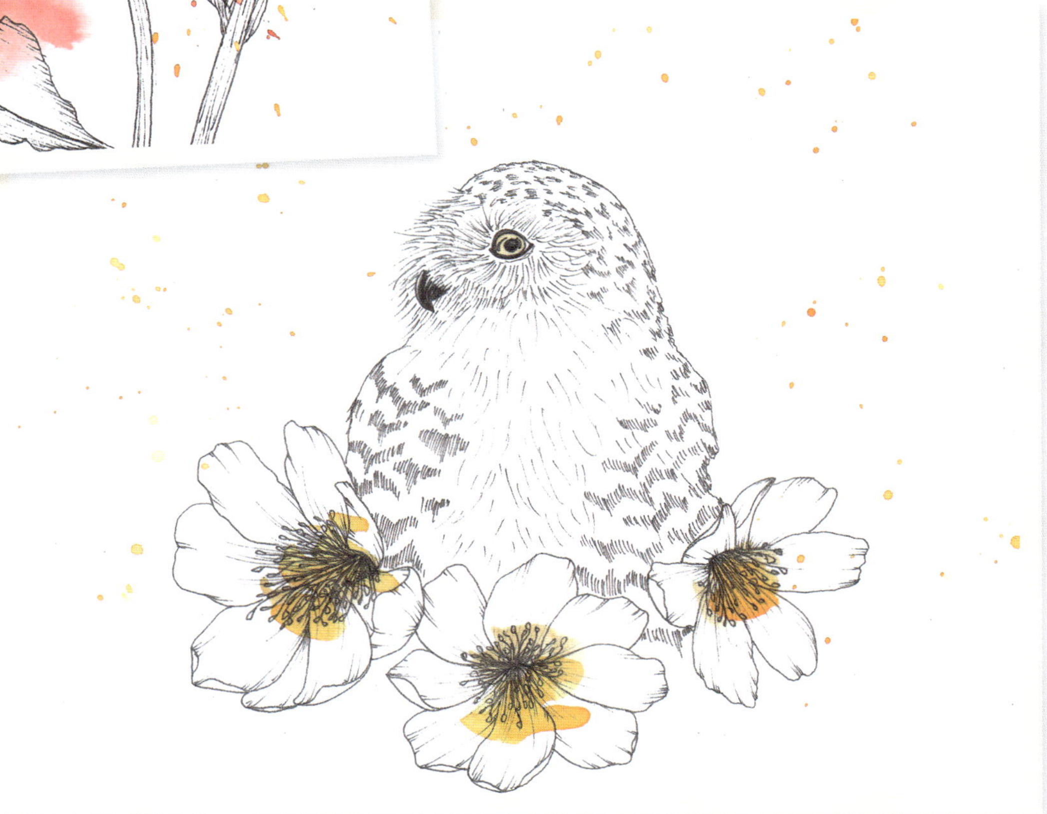

More Ideas

There are so many more ways that you can use the techniques and styles presented in this book to create unique and beautiful artwork. Here are some ideas.

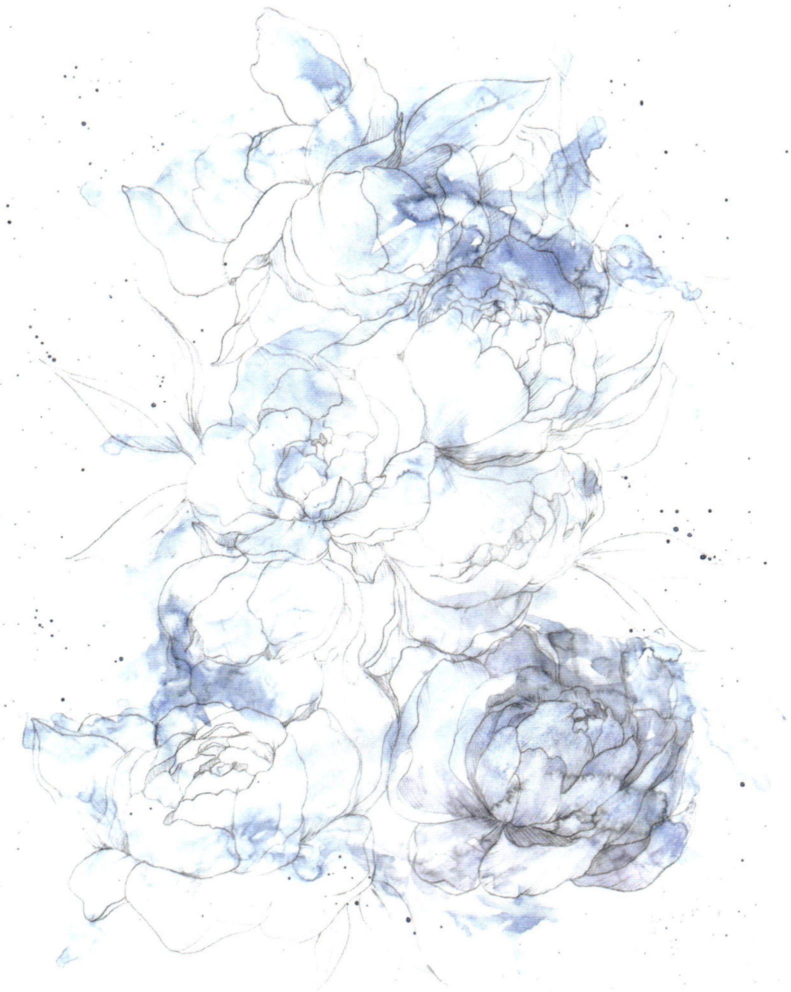

Create a graphite and watercolor piece.

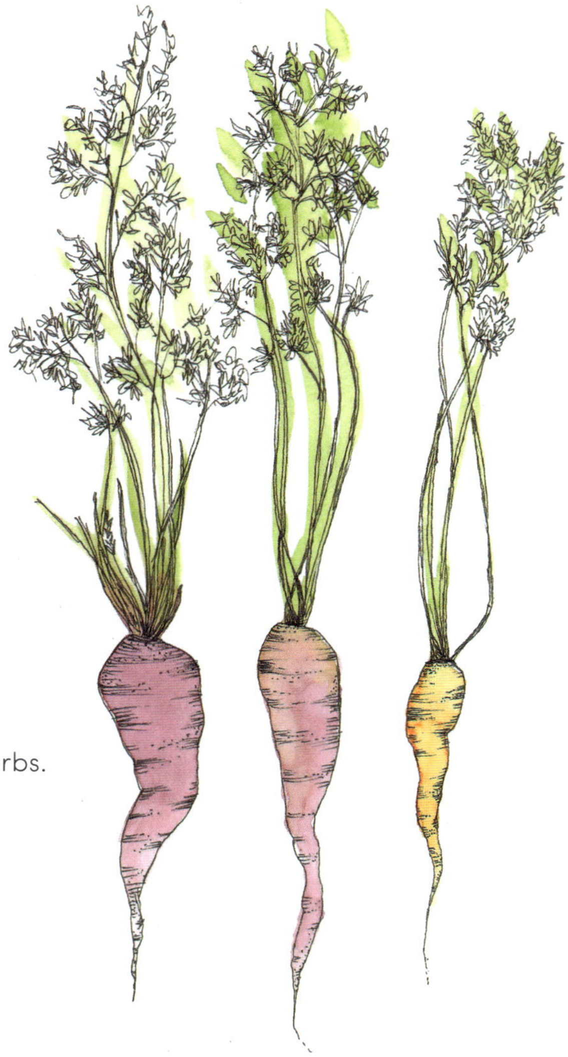

Explore vegetables or herbs.

Create a slew of minis, like I did here when I challenged myself to one month of miniature loose florals.

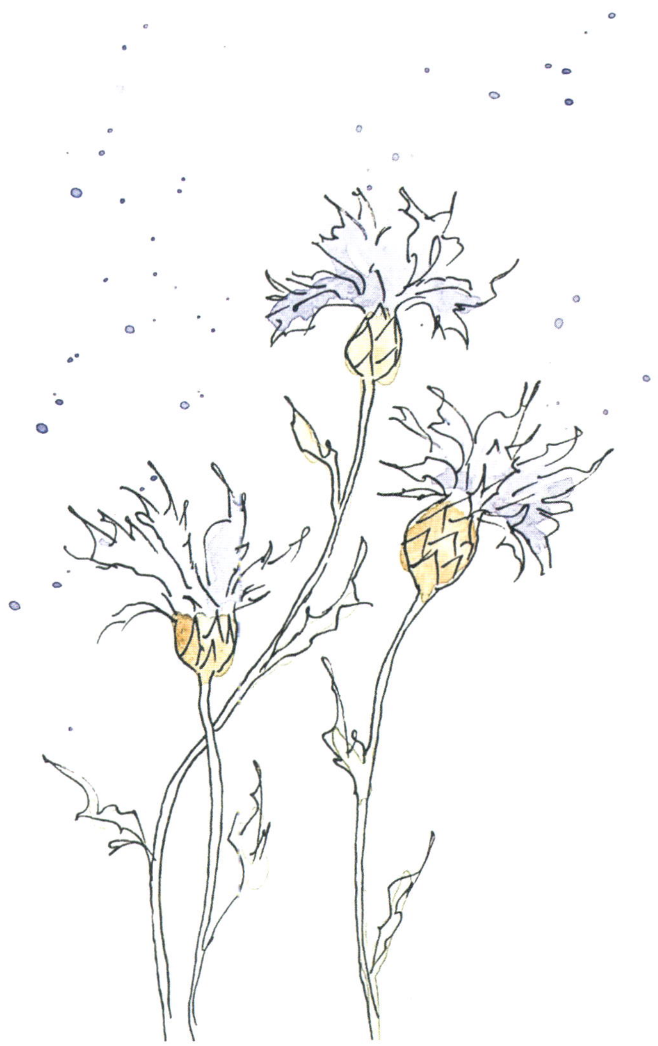

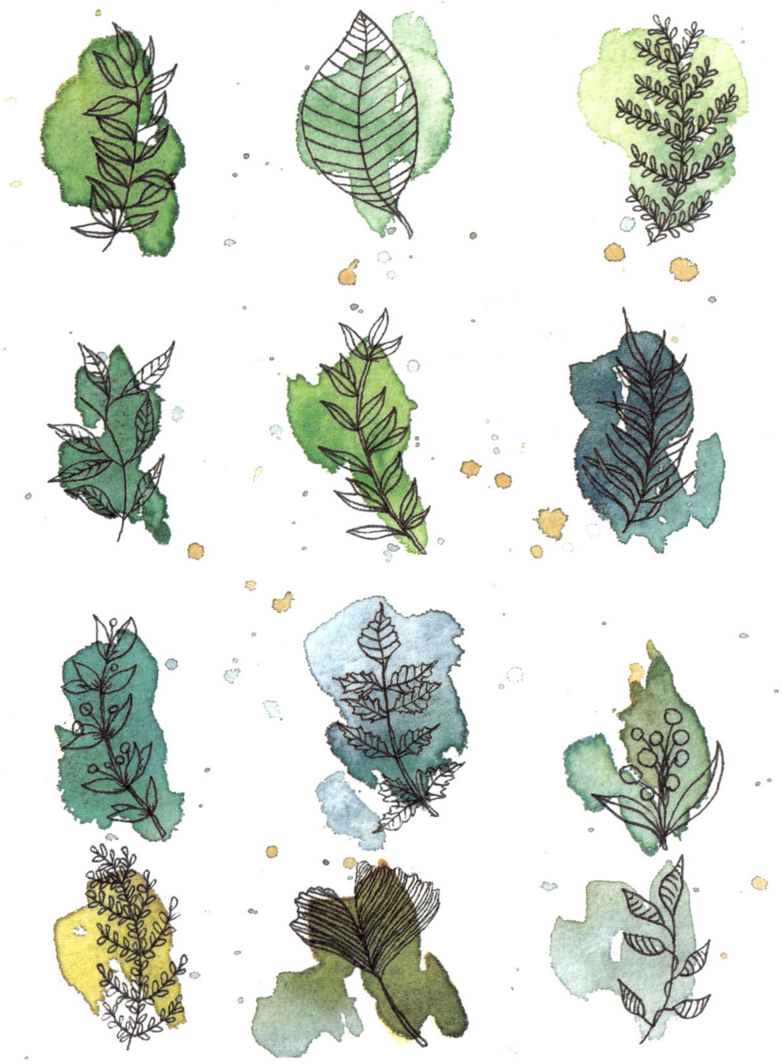

Or create a modern display via a color-and-leaf study.

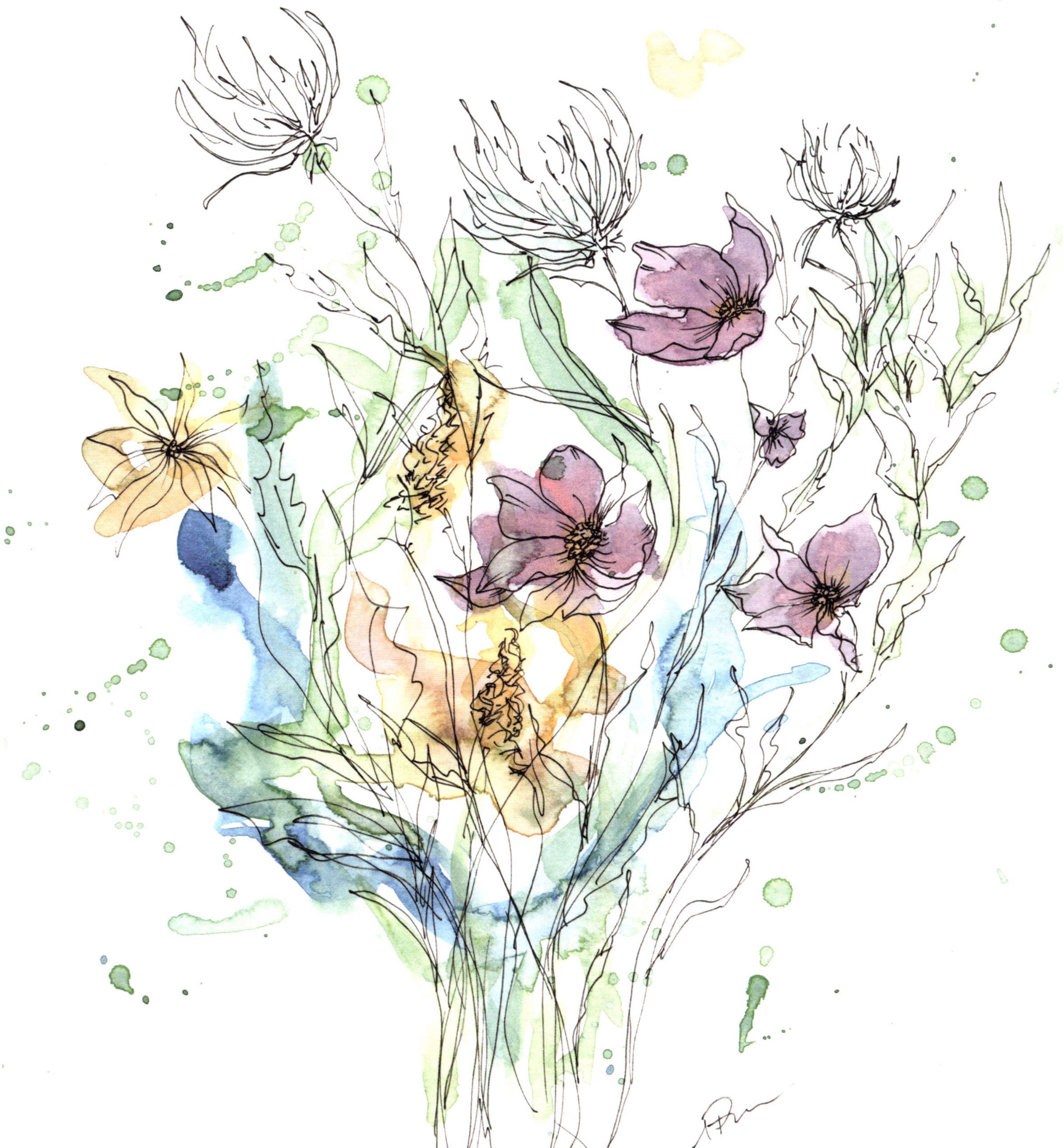

Conclusion

The joy of this style of ink and watercolor art is that it is limitless—you can create whatever type of scene you want, from cityscapes to animals. The formula is simple, but the inner heart and belief in yourself to sit down to the page and create can often be complex. I implore you not to waver. Believe in yourself. Embrace the imperfections, learn to adapt them to create beauty, and let your inner artist out. There is room for you, as there is for me.

You've read my story.

Now it's time to go and create your own.

Acknowledgments

This book is dedicated to my son, Wilder, whose birth welcomed an abundance of creativity in my life. He is the catalyst for this creative life I lead, and for that I am forever grateful.

I also want to thank those who have supported me along the way: my parents for providing the foundation for my creative and entrepreneurial tendencies; my mother for childcare duties; my editor, Annika, for her guidance along the way; my friends who have forfeited seeing me in favor of letting me meet deadlines late into the evenings; my dear N. for an unwavering belief in me and my ability to create something beautiful and worthwhile; and my very best Fran for absolutely everything (and then some).

And last but certainly not least, I want to thank you, my reader. Without the support of my phenomenal creative friends, followers, and readers alike, I would not be where I am today.

There is room for all of us creatives here, and I am so grateful to be in this place with you.

About the Artist

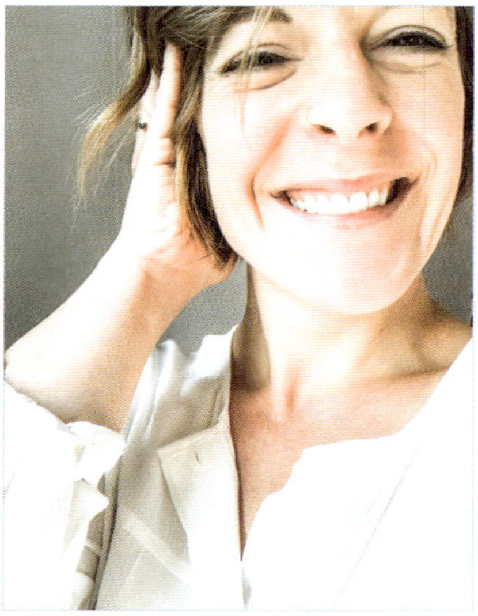

Isa Down is an artist, an educator, and a writer. Always a creative, she began her artistic career when she picked up a pen and drew a flower. This beginning has created the foundation for her passion: to show anyone that they have an inner artist and that they are capable of creating art. Isa gains inspiration from the natural world, her imagination, and a true sense of connection with others. She is a creator of beauty, a cultivator of joy, and a conjurer of abundance, striving to create true connection and community.

Isa teaches both online and in-person workshops and offers one-on-one creativity and business coaching. She is endlessly inspired by flowers, mixing medias, and finding the perfect balance between fine details and whimsical abstract marks on the page.

To learn more, visit www.poppyandgrayco.com, follow her podcast on Instagram @gatherhomecreatives, and find her artwork @poppyandgrayco on Instagram.